1240   86/6

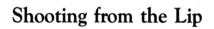

Shooting from the Lip

Shooting from the Lip

Essays, columns, quips, and gripes in the grand tradition of dyspeptic sports writing

Mike Lupica

Bonus Books, Chicago

92   91   90   89   88   5   4   3   2   1

Library of Congress Catalog Card Number: 87-73447

International Standard Book Number: 0-933893-60-4

Bonus Books, Inc.
160 East Illinois Street
Chicago, Illinois 60611

Printed in the United States of America

For these special four, God bless them:
First, Susan Lupica, who always shoots from the heart.
And then our remarkable aunts—Mary, Theresa, Peggy—
who helped teach her how.

Contents

Part 8 **QUARTERBACKS, AND SO FORTH...** / 191

Part 9 **A FEW FROM MAGAZINES** / 219

SHOOTING FROM THE LIP III / 269

Part 10 **GOODBYES** / 271

Foreword

The great columnists are the soloists of the American newspaper business. Although most are possessed of quite sturdy egos and each works alone, they do not believe they are the band; they could not exist without that splendid orchestra of craftsmen who send newspapers roaring off presses every day of the year. But it is impossible to think of most newspapers without merging their identities with those of the star columnists. Through the force of style and talent, such columnists often establish the moral tone of the newspaper, generally infuriating the anonymous scribes who write editorials, periodically inspiring apoplexy among the businessmen who own the newspapers and must apologize for the columnists to their social friends. That, of course, is the way it should be. If *someone* isn't angry with him (or her), the columnist is not doing the job. Contention, as the Irish say, is better than loneliness.

Here, at last, we have an album of work by one of the most gifted soloists to walk into a newspaper office in many years. Mike Lupica is a fine and accurate reporter, but that is not the essence of a gift for the column. Neither is mastery of the writing craft. I've known many splendid newspapermen who have longed for a column and failed in its practice. The reason is simple: the columnist must have a voice. This is a natural gift, like being able to punch with the right hand; it can't be taught, cer-

tainly can't be manufactured. And Lupica, like Sinatra or Ben Web-
ster or Billie Holiday, has his own distinct voice. That voice can be
infuriating, it can be the song of the wise guy, it can be celebratory or
charged with pity: it is always his.

It is a fruitless task to try to seek out the roots of a distinct style.
Lupica is from New Hampshire, so he wasn't shaped by the cadences
of Brooklyn or the Lower East Side, nor did he grow up reading Red
Smith and Jimmy Cannon, whose inflections have seeped into so
many other sport columnists. Perhaps it was some mysterious amal-
gam: the astringency of New England, the raffish linguistic inven-
tions of the Boston Irish, some golden trace of the Mediterranean.
I'm sure even Lupica would not risk such a dissection.

What matters is that by the time he was in Boston College (1970-
74), he was writing for three school papers and the weekly *Boston
Phoenix,* and was working nights at the *Boston Globe.* His apprentice-
ship was accelerated by his friendship with columnist George Frazier,
whose own solo turns at the *Globe* and for *Esquire* were built almost
entirely around the possession of a voice. Frazier was a dandy, an ec-
centric, a Menckenesque elitist, whose later years were driven by ob-
scure furies. Still, he saw something in the young man from New
Hampshire. At the *Globe,* he would wait for Lupica to finish his shift,
and then the young man would drive the old man around Boston in a
beat-up Volkswagen, Frazier delivering a seminar on life, love, art and
writing, until they finished the night at a seedy bar called Mary Ann's
in Cleveland Circle near Boston College. There, Frazier would tell
stories about Billie Holiday, which is to say, he would relate caution-
ary tales of far greater use to a newspaperman than any college course.
"He was crazy," Lupica says of his mentor, "but he could write a sentence."

For a year after graduation, Lupica freelanced around Boston. He
turned down an offer to write high school sports at the *Globe,* since
he'd already written more than fifty features for the paper while he
was in college. He kept working for the *Phoenix,* for *Boston* magazine.
Jimmy Breslin heard the voice, and put him in touch with Jim Bel-
lows at the *Washington Star,* where he wrote some pieces. And down in
New York, two others were reading him in the *Phoenix:* Larry Merchant and Joe Valerio of the *New York Post.* They brought his name to
the attention of Ike Gellis, the sports editor, who in turn mentioned
the Lupica kid to Paul Sann, the *Post's* executive editor. Gellis and
Sann were shaped by the 30s; Gellis often played Edward G. Robinson

to Sann's Bogart. They were tough guys, gamblers, sports freaks, Celtic fans. And Sann was an extraordinary judge of talent. He made columnists of Murray Kempton and Jimmy Cannon. He hired Don Forst (now the editor of *New York Newsday*), Ed Kosner (now editor of *New York* magazine), Vic Ziegel (now sports editor of the *New York Daily News*), Nora Ephron, Leonard Shecter, Larry Merchant and dozens of other men and women who went on to grander careers. He even gave a column to me.

Lupica was covering the United States Open in 1975, when Gellis called him. They set up a meeting. Lupica brought his clips. And at first it did not go well. Gellis never let a discussion of journalism get in the way of his gambling. "He was giving me a hard time, as if I'd walked in off the street, begging for a job," Lupica remembers. "I finally said, 'Ike, *you* called *me*. Read the clips. You'll like them and offer me a job—or you won't.' "

Two weeks later, Lupica started working for the *Post*. He was 23 years old. Ike told him later that he liked his "moxie" (ah, the old school, ah, the blessed Thirties. . .). During his first week, Lupica wrote four features and then Gellis told him he was covering the Knicks. Just like that. For fourteen months, the young man wrote game stories and sidebars (along with occasional columns) almost every night. He got into a feud with Walt Frazier. He took no guff. He was working on a New York paper and nothing else mattered. To attentive readers, he seemed to be having a hell of a good time. And we began to hear a voice.

The next call was from the *New York Daily News*, the largest circulation newspaper in the United States. This was the equivalent of being offered a gig with the Basie band. At the time, the *News* was looking for a sports columnist whose viewpoint might balance the increasingly cranky conservatism of their veteran columnist, Dick Young. Lupica agreed and started his solo act on January 1, 1977. He has been there ever since. This has not always been easy. Young resented or felt threatened by the younger man, sneered at his skills, often took vicious shots at him in print (which Lupica answered, if only in a kind of code). Young did not give a performance with a high content of grace. Eventually Young shocked the New York newspaper world by departing for the *Post*, in the worst example of organizational betrayal since Leo Durocher left the Dodgers for the Giants. He continued firing mortar rounds at Lupica until the day he died.

If any of this intramural nastiness bothered Lupica, he didn't show it. In the decade that followed, Lupica's work deepened and matured and he learned more about the range of his voice. Some of the work, of course, was the immediate reaction to a day's events, written at high speed, with a consequent perishability; some of it (I believe) is still marred by his just but brutal fury at the likes of George Steinbrenner and Billy Martin. Lupica is still not old enough to have learned all the lessons of pity and terror.

This is another way of saying that not every Lupica column over the past decade has been perfect. If they had been, Lupica would have long since retired, having accomplished what no columnist in history has ever managed. By definition, the form is imperfect and the reasons have to do with the limitations of time and space. There is never enough time to make it perfect, never enough space in the daily newspaper for a single piece to be complete. Narrative, for example, is often beyond the limits of the column space, because it depends so much upon the accretion of detail and adherence to sequence. Most columnists learn the trick of focusing on a fragment that can stand for the whole; they become more aphoristic; at worst, they fall upon lazy shortcuts and mannerisms. And in the hasty scramble to make the edition, they often suspend thinking and are thus prey to glib judgments. Every columnist I know has made impetuous assertions in print that he later regretted; I've done it myself. Sometimes the columnist *knowingly* sends in the copy understanding that another hour, another day might lead to the fact or quote that will grant the piece a blinding lucidity, but the clock has made such a goal impossible. He knows, in short, that he has failed. And that simple admission should keep him human. He is not, after all, alone: the great hitter fails seven out of ten times at bat. The soloist in a band often discovers on Thursday the true direction of his performance the previous Tuesday.

That is why so few newspaper columns deserve preservation between the covers of a book. They are, in a way, an extended work in progress. If the columnist is good enough, if he maintains his sensitivity and capacity for wonder or horror, then he will finish these first drafts in a more solid form: history, memoir, the novel. What is astonishing is how many columns *do* deserve to be collected and preserved. That is, to be remembered. I have books by Kempton and Cannon and Red Smith on my shelves, along with Pegler, Mencken and Liebling, the Lardners (John and Ring) and Runyon, Royko and Breslin. Some are still in the prime of their careers; others exist for us now only in those books. But the very existence of the books means that kids fresh to the craft can still search them out, and be moved by them and exhilarated by them and taught by them. If the apprentice has no voice, reading will not help; nothing will. But of this I'm sure: if the young wish to be soloists they must know who rose before them to essay 16 bars. Here, upon that shelf, goes Lupica.

Pete Hamill
March, 1988

Preface

There is this joke around the Lupica house.

When our son was an infant, and would decide that crying and fussing were more enjoyable than sleep, my wife would say to me, "Tell him the story of your career again, honey."

She meant, give him a tranquilizer.

So I would tell about how the first story I ever wrote for the Boston *Globe*, when I was still in college, was run on the front page.

That would stop the crying.

And I would tell about covering the Knicks for the *New York Post* when I was 23 years old.

Eyes getting heavy now.

By the time I would get to the part about the *Daily News* the year after I showed up in New York, my kid would be out like I'd hit him in the head with a sap.

Point? Writing about sports has always worked a lot better for me than *talking* about writing about sports.

I've never been able to describe properly what it is like to see a great sports event, run down to the locker room or clubhouse, talk to the people I need to talk to on the dead run, get back up to the press box, and write about 1000 words in about an hour and jump out of the way of another deadline the way I would another New York City taxi.

But I will tell you this: I was a sucker for the life

when I was in college, and as I write this, I am a sucker still. A few years ago, a terrific New York newspaperman named Sid Zion gave me a copy of Ben Hecht's autobiography, *Child of the Century.* Hecht, of course, defined the romance of a newspaperman's life, with Charles MacArthur, in *The Front Page,* from the first time somebody yelled "Baby, get me rewrite" to "The sonofabitch stole my watch!" at the end. In front of the book, Sid just scrawled, "For Mike Lupica, Whose life was born out of the pages of this book, Sid."

It was probably the nicest compliment I've ever received. Because being one of those Front Page guys was all I've ever wanted to be. When I was working for nothing at *The Heights* at Boston College, I thought I had the best job in the world. When I sit down today to write my column at the *New York Daily News* or my "Sporting Life" column at *Esquire* magazine, I feel the same way.

They do pay me now, of course. I have always heeded the advice of Jimmy Breslin. Not long after I joined the *Daily News* in 1977, I became delirious one day and told Breslin I sometimes felt like I would do the job for free. Breslin snorted.

"This isn't the Lawn Tennis Association," he said. "Around here we don't play for the love of the f------ game."

How do you forget good, sound vocational guidance like that?

What I have been able to accomplish in my professional life, I owe to my newspaper column. I have written two novels now. I have written the autobiographies of Reggie Jackson and New York Giants coach Bill Parcells. I write for *Esquire,* and I have done some television, from ESPN to *The CBS Morning News* to *The Coors Sports Page* on Ted Turner's super station to my role as sports essayist on *The Mac-Neil Lehrer Newshour.* I have a wonderful time trading funny lines (we hope) and insults (constantly) on the *Imus in the Morning* radio program in New York City.

But it always goes back to the column. Goes back to the job: I go to sports events, and tell people what it was like to be there, what I saw, what it felt like, what it sounded like. Sometimes, there is no event, just someone I have to get after, from George Steinbrenner or Billy Martin to NFL owners, from a palooka like Gerry Cooney (I once suggested that if he ever retired he would have to come out of retirement to do it) to figure skating judges at the Olympics, who frequently have the value system of oldtime Chicago ward healers.

Hockey fans, I like to write about them too.

And every Sunday, in what I hope is the tradition started by the likes of George Frazier, the great old Boston columnist, and Jimmy Cannon, I write one-liners in a column called "Shooting From the Lip":

*If I could get by this one question, I would understand Macho Camacho a lot better. Here is the question: Is he in drag or not?

*An incoming Notre Dame freshman football player was declared ineligible the other day because of low SAT scores. In the Southwest Conference, not only do you get to play with scores like this kid's, they give you a Trans Am.

*(After a gun was found during an airport check of bags belonging to Gerry Cooney's manager, Dennis Rappaport): I myself can never decide what to take on the road with me, a loaded .38 or my toothbrush.

*Ron Luciano has written three books about his life, and I'm not sure there was enough life for one.

*(After the Giants Lawrence Taylor said he cured himself of cocaine addiction by playing golf): The next step for Lawrence Taylor is a chain of "LT Pitch and Putt Rehab Centers." Get the ball through the windmill on No. 18 and pronounce yourself cured of drug addiction and alcoholism. And get a free round.

*Billy Martin broadcasts baseball like he's cutting a hostage tape.

It is all part of the job. Get a laugh, if you can. Make them mad. Sport is not always serious for me, never has been. It is a lot of the time. Just not all the time. There are more columns in this collection about losers than winners, I think; it is the wrong side of the score that has always appealed to me. The columns I like the best come at the end, when the subject is goodbyes. There are pieces in there about the deaths of old friends like Bill Veeck and Dick Howser, about Dennis McLain being sent to prison; and there is one, maybe my favorite, about a blind Mets fan named Victoria Crawford, who died not long after I listened to a Mets game with her one Friday night in a long ago summer.

If Breslin, one of my newspaper heroes, taught me anything, it was this: You want people to keep coming back, you better be able to change speeds. There are plenty of one-note singers out there.

I have always tried to do a little more. With 200 or so columns a year, it's not like I don't get my chance.

Roy Campanella used to say you have to have a lot of little boy in you to play baseball. Same deal in sportswriting. You better like what you are watching, because if you don't, you're just another slug punching a clock.

Every time I walk into a ballpark, or an arena, I'm still thinking I might see something that day or night I've never seen before. There is plenty of garbage in sports. There are too many agents, too many strikes, too many busts. There is too much artificial turf and too many commentators who remind me of Buffalo Bob. There are too many owners and bosses like Steinbrenner, who don't care anything about the athletes or the fans or the game, just seeing their name in the paper.

They rarely play the World Series in the afternoon anymore.

But the games. The games are still fine. For nine innings, or 60 minutes of football, or 40 minutes of college basketball in the Final Four, or the three or four hours of a Wimbledon final, there is rarely anything wrong with sports.

The games make the job easy. The games make you pick up your own game. I remember sitting in the press room in Lake Placid, New York, on a February night in 1980, after the United States Olympic Hockey Team had beaten the Soviet team, the greatest sports event I have ever witnessed, or expect to witness. It was late in the night and time to write, and a friend of mine came over and said, "How can I write this?"

And I thought, How *can't* you?

I thought, This is why we all got into the racket in the first place. See something like this. Tell people what it was like.

I saw that game. I saw Reggie hit three home runs in the Series and I saw at least a part of Bjorn Borg's 42 straight wins at Wimbledon, and I saw Borg and John McEnroe play that unforgettable tiebreaker match in the 1980 final. Good and bad. Triumph and tragedy. Saw McLain stand in front of the judge, heard the judge tell him he was going away for a long time. Saw Joe Theismann's career end because of a hit from Lawrence Taylor.

I have seen all the great college basketball finals of the last 10 years, from Al McGuire to Keith Smart. I saw the Mets come back in Game Six of the 1986 World Series against the Red Sox.

I saw Mary Lou Retton get her 10.

Saw a Canadian skier named Ken Read get 15 seconds of Olympics one time.

I have seen Jimmy Connors win some and lose some. Same with Chris Evert. I saw Dwight Gooden when he was Dr. K, and when he was just another guy gone off to get clean from drugs.

I remember what Dick Howser's face looked like the night the Royals won the 1985 Series, and it was important later on to remember that, because he would be dead within two years from brain cancer.

John McEnroe once interrupted a semifinal match at the U.S. Open to yell about something I'd written. Walt Frazier told the *New York Times* once that I'd run him out of New York. My columns send Steinbrenner into such a tailspin his public relations men have to keep a file on them; maybe he plans to do a collection of my work, too.

Someday, I firmly believe I will see a good Super Bowl game.

There are many people to thank. Ernie Roberts was the sports editor of the *Globe* who gave me my chance; if he had stayed sports editor of the *Globe*, I might have started my career there after college, and the career might have been a lot different. And I will always remember George Frazier, impeccably turned out at two in the morning, the last true Boston newspaper legend, getting into my Volkswagen after I finished my night shift.

There is Bob Ryan of the *Globe*, best pro basketball writer of them all. There is Larry Merchant, a genius at writing a sports column, who helped get me to New York. There is Dave Anderson of the *New York Times*, who keeps trying to show me how gentlemen are supposed to act in this business. And Red Smith, who died before I ever got a chance to tell him I used to watch every move he made.

And there is Ike Gellis, who gave me my shot to be a New York newspaperman with the *Post* back in 1975. He looked like a Runyon character, bet like one, and ran the best sports section in New York for 25 years.

I wish I could thank the late Michael Burke, one of the true gentlemen of sports, for telling *Daily News* editor Mike O'Neill to give me a chance at the column in '77. So I will thank O'Neill instead, and managing editor Bill Brink, who always backed me up. Never told me to back off. I have had a lot of sports editors at the *Daily News*—we go through them the way the Yankees go through managers—but just about every one has been good to me: Buddy Martin, Gene Williams, Bob Decker, Vic Ziegel; Decker taught me hard work, Ziegel taught me style. And all of us have always been helped mightily on the desk by Chuck Slater, who loves newspapers the way I do, and goes all the way back to the *New York Post* with me. And by Delores Thompson, boss of us all.

Lee Eisenberg and David Hirshey, an old newspaper friend, gave me my space in Esquire; it is only one of the most stylish addresses in print.

And I would be remiss to not thank George Kimball, who took me in at the *Boston Phoenix*; Ron Bookman and Susan Baker Adams, now *World Tennis* alumni like me; and Jim Willse, my current managing editor at the *Daily News*, who just always seems to get it.

Finally, after my incredible parents, there are five people in particular to whom I must give special thanks:

Bud Collins, tennis savant, *Globe* columnist, as close a friend as I will ever have; Dan Jenkins, friend also, a man who used wit and skill to revolutionize sportswriting in his years at *Sports Illustrated*; Gil Spencer, *Daily News* editor and the best newspaperman I ever expect to know; and Pete Hamill, who not only showed me the possibilities of a newspaper column, but told me something more important: that all newspapermen didn't have to drink.

And to Taylor McKelvy Lupica, the most special thanks of all. I think I've been a better writer since she came into my life. I know I've been a better person.

Mike Lupica
New Canaan, Connecticut
March, 1988

BABY, GET ME REWRITE!

The column about Al McGuire is the first I ever wrote for the *Daily News* in 1977. The one about the Twins is one I wrote just the other day. The events change. The names change. The years change. The job doesn't change.

•

Part 1

McGuire comes uptown
...in McGuire style

ATLANTA

e had always been the hard guy, the one from Rockaway
with the fast mouth and the funny lines, and the special
style that maybe you can only bring with you from the
streets. But now here was Al McGuire sitting on the Marquette bench for the last time, and there were 10 seconds
left before his team would be national champion, and
McGuire put his head into his hands and began to cry.
He had come all the way uptown at last.

"I'm not ashamed to cry," he would say later. "I'm
not afraid to show my emotions." No, Al McGuire has
never been afraid to show his emotions. In these last 20
years, he has shown us all of them.

The last 10 seconds were long gone by now and the
scoreboard above the court in the Omni still said Marquette 67, North Carolina 59. When it had ended,
McGuire had not moved a muscle in his seat. His assistant, Hank Raymonds, slammed him joyously on the
back, and his team surrounded him. Bo Ellis, so brilliant
all night long, made one last quick move to the basket,
was hoisted up, and began cutting down the net. While
all this was happening, McGuire made as great a move as
he has ever made as a coach; he hid himself in the crowd
and made his way to the dressing room.

Some reporters saw him go, and followed him.
McGuire began an impromptu press conference. His toe
hurt him from when he had kicked the scorer's table early

in the game, and his eyes were red. But Al could still talk. Al has always been able to talk.

"Are you happy?" someone asked.

"Yes," he said, "Yes, I am very happy. For Bo and the guys. I am happy for my family and everyone."

"Does the toe hurt?"

"It may screw up my golf game," Al McGuire said. There had been emotion, yes, but there were still the funny lines.

A press aide pushed through the crowd and told him he should be on the court. "Yes," Al said. "I should." He looked at the man. "Should I put on my jacket? I guess I better put on my jacket." He put on the jacket that is part of a lucky suit that had not been cleaned in the two weeks of the NCAA tournament. He calmly walked out to receive the plaque that meant he had come uptown at last.

Security men pushed their way through the crowd to make way for him, but still his people began to get to him, to shake his hand, to touch him, to say, "Great one coach." McGuire thanked them all. Finally he got near the awards stand. Bo Ellis came over with the net he had just cut down. "Hey, man," said Ellis. "This belongs to you." He stuck the net in McGuire's hand, and the two of them embraced.

McGuire looked up into the Marquette cheering section, all madness and celebration now, looking for his wife, Patty, and his three children. He leaned over to a security man. "I want my family," he said. "Can you get my family down here for me?" The man nodded, and McGuire waved his family down to share the greatest moment—and the last—that he will ever have as a coach.

His family was around him. There was Patty, and his son Allie who once played for him. "Where's my daughter?" he said. "I want my daughter." And then she was with him, too. And then they were all with him, and he was raising the plaque, and the Marquette fans were showering a little more love on a man the likes of which we will never see again in the business of college coaching.

"My type of style is over," he would say in the official press conference a few moments later. "All the street fighting and the alleys and so forth." And he is so right. No one will ever bring the streets and the alleys to the game in the McGuire way ever again. He takes that with him now.

Even before his last game last night, McGuire was still going out like McGuire. His team was already on the court, and McGuire was pacing the floor of his locker room. Father Leonard Piotrowski, a longtime friend, was with him, as was another friend named Bill Hughes from Milwaukee. McGuire looked like a condemned man, biting his fingernails, taking the six steps to the wall, turning around and walking back.

"I'm like the guy in that movie," he said. "Papillon. The butterfly guy. He spent all those years in prison, and he could walk his cell without even looking. I'm like that. I guess the only difference in this business is that the size of the locker rooms is different."

Just then it was time for him to go. He put on the lucky jacket and turned to Father Piotrowski. "Let's go play the number," he said.

• 1977

Twins took roar to victory

T hey would not let go of the night.

The Minnesota Twins, champions of the world, would not leave the field. And the Metrodome crowd would not leave the Metrodome. There have been other October romances between cities and teams, but never one as loud as this one, or improbable. Never have a city and a team ever felt quite like this, like they were really in it together.

"What do you want to feel as a fan? You want to feel like you can make a difference," Twins' general manager Andy MacPhail said in the runway outside the Twins clubhouse. He is 34 years old, young as a general manager the way his team is young. He is the son of a fine baseball gentleman named Leland MacPhail, who celebrated his 70th birthday last night at the Metrodome.

Andy MacPhail said, "Well, as this month built, these people could see that they had an impact on their team. They could see the proof. They saw on television the way we played in St. Louis. And they saw the way we played at home."

The Twins won the World Series, four games to three. They became the first team in the history of the World Series to win all four of its home games. They beat the Cardinals last night, 4-2, because a St. John's kid named Frankie (Sweet Music) Viola pitched his lungs off for eight innings in the biggest game of his life, and then turned the ball over to Jeff Reardon for three ninth-inning outs.

The last was a ground ball to Gary Gaetti. He threw the ball across the diamond to a Minneapolis kid named Kent Hrbek. Then the Twins were hugging each other, and jumping into a pile near first base that had Jeff Reardon somewhere at the bottom, and Frankie Viola was standing near second base, tall Long Island kid wearing No. 16, waving his cap at all the noise and Homer Hankies and music in the Metrodome.

They were all in it together. A team and a town. And isn't that the way sports is supposed to feel like, at least once in a while? In an age of strikes and holdouts and mean-spirited NFL owners and scab games and court cases, can you understand why they didn't want to let go of the night or the baseball season in Minneapolis?

Somebody joked Saturday that they had turned the World Series into a musical, and maybe they had, one of those 30's college things. Now, on the field at the Metrodome, they were having the big finish, the pep rally number after the team had won the big game. And the World Series looked fine.

The scoreboard thanked the Minnesota Twins for "the ride of a lifetime." The theme from "Star Wars" played over the sound system. Now the message board flashed "World Champions." More noise, a kind of noise baseball has never known, exploded again. Then the organist began to play "Take Me Out to the Ballgame." The 55,000 in the Metrodome began to sing. Corny. You bet. The World Series had gone indoors and gone crazy. It looked and sounded fine.

"We love these people," manager Tom Kelly said.

The Twins stopped hugging and got out of the pile near first base, and suddenly there was this wonderful sight at the Hubert H. Humphrey Metrodome. The ballplayers stood and applauded the fans.

Roy Smalley, who turned 35 yesterday, was near third base. He kept the sixth inning going by working Todd Worrell for a walk; later on Greg Gagne got what turned out to be the winning run home with an infield single. Three walks and an infield hit produced the third Twins' run. Funny, huh? They had won the World Series finally with a Cardinal run. Wimp run. Ball never got out of the infield.

"Beyond description," Smalley had described the Metrodome noise Saturday. "Beyond imagination." Now he applauded. He started to leave the field. Then he looked for his wife and son behind home plate. He found his wife. He made a gesture for her to hold up his seven-year-old son, Jeffery Smalley, who wore a No. 5 uniform like his father's.

The players went inside finally, but only for a few minutes. The World Series trophy was presented. Frankie Viola was presented as the Series MVP for winning Game 1 and Game 7. He is a tough left-hander out of East Meadow with hard stuff and soft stuff and a ton of heart. He had trouble in the second inning, gave up four hits and the two Cardinal runs.

After the inning, Kelly and pitching coach Dick Such told him he was getting the ball up.

"No, I'm not," Viola said.

"Well," Kelly said, "we sort of think you are, and we'd like you to get it down."

"Okay," said the East Meadow kid. "But I still don't think I've been up."

He went out and gave the Cardinals two hits after that, retiring 11 in a row at one point. After a double to Tony Peña with one out in the seventh, Viola was masterful. He got ahead of the last five batters he faced, got them all. Strikeout. Fly to center. Ground ball to Gaetti. Fly to right. Ground ball to second. Reardon finished up.

Somebody joked to Andy MacPhail that, sure, that's why he got Reardon from Montreal, to get the last three outs in the seventh game of the 1987 Word Series.

"I wish I could say that," Andy MacPhail said. "What I can say is that this is the nicest present I ever could have given my father."

The rest of the night was about the present the improbable Twins had given the cities of Minneapolis and St. Paul, and the whole state of Minnesota, which had known only losing in big games for so long. The Twins lost the big games when they had good teams in the 60s. The Vikings lost four Super Bowls in the 70s. And now it was all different. It was all good, and so loud.

Thirty minutes after the World Series was over, the Twins' wives came out on the field at the Metrodome, to huge cheers. The Twins theme song was played. And now here came the world champions, in various states of undress, to a cheer to match any from the weekend. One by one they came to the microphone, and toasted themselves, and the fans. Al Newman hugged his wife in the outfield.

Newman and Dan Gladden unfurled a banner that contained a message that had become the rallying cry of the Twins, and their Metrodome fans: "Feel Our Thunder." The noise built a little more. The music was "Star Wars" again.

Finally, the Twins and their wives began a victory lap at the Metrodome, meandering up the third baseline and across the outfield, and the people waved their Homer Hankies, and the organist played "Take Me Out to the Ballgame" and the P.A. announcer said the next game was April 8 against the Blue Jays.

Moments to remember. In a lousy sports October, the Metrodome looked, sounded, just fine. So did the game of baseball. No one wanted the night to end.

• *1987*

THE OLYMPICS

The Olympics, for a journalist, are not Club Med. You are somewhere for three weeks. The hours are bad, the venues are never close. But there is no pageant quite like it in sports, at least not in my experience. Every four years, the athletes get one shot at doing something great. Some of them are still around in another four years. Most of them aren't. There is no other drama like this. For them, the moments in the arena are a lifetime.

●

Part 2

She'll always be a 10

LOS ANGELES

I
•

n memory, of course, she will be 14 years old forever. It will always be Montreal, always 1976, always The Forum, and the little wraith from Romania will be reaching into the air and taking her Olympic moment and fashioning it into perfection. She will strut and prance and throw back her head, laughing without laughter. She will twist and fly and land like a whisper and throw her arms out wide to the world. The music will stop. The cheers will wash over her. Then the scores will come one after another. The 10s. Seven of them. For Nadia. Just the first name, then and always. Nadia.

In memory, she will be Peter Pan, the perpetual child, wreathed by the song. She will be fixed there in The Forum, the announcers screaming and the crowd on its feet and a television audience all over the world offering this collective gasp.

But that is for memory. Yesterday was for the present, for the 1984 Summer Games in Los Angeles. Nadia Comaneci, 22 now, retired now from gymnastics competition, is here as a special guest of the Los Angeles Olympic Organizing Committee, and yesterday she came out of the past to conjoin with the assembled Olympic press corps. She received a scarf from Peter V. Ueberroth, president of the LAOOC. She denied, as did Ueberroth, that she will light the Olympic Torch tomorrow during the Opening Ceremonies at the L.A. Coliseum, a rumor that got out of control early yesterday morning. And Nadia Comaneci answered questions.

The most obvious question came early and went something like this: "Nadia, do you think anyone here can duplicate your performance in Montreal?"

Nadia Comaneci smiled a win smile and shrugged and said this through a translator: "We'll see who follows in my steps."

It is difficult to believe anyone ever will. She froze Montreal, and the '76 Summer Games, with that first perfect 10, then she got six more. It was a glorious performance by an extraordinary child, and the only problem with any of this is that she then had to go out and live the rest of her life. It was one heck of a first novel, and there was no living way that anything could again match up. She was treated shabbily by a Russian judge and a Polish judge at the '80 Summer Games, and did not win gold. She finally retired this year, after there was some talk about a comeback in Los Angeles. She may be the only athlete ever to have her life story told in a movie (an absolutely unwatchable mess called "Nadia") at the age of 22. She was asked about the movie yesterday.

"I haven't seen the film," she said through translator Agnes Mura. "But many people have commented that they wasted their time in front of the television watching it."

The little girl grew up: it is a rule they passed a while back. Peter Pan had to get on with it. And there was something sad and fragile about Nadia Comaneci in the Press Center, like a flower that has been absent too long from the sun. You see it with the girl gymnasts, who trade their youth for the chance at the 10s, then see their careers ended before they can drive a car, then say "What now?" You see it with girl figure skaters. You see it with all those toy tennis players on the women's tennis tour. Even in their early 20s, there is the air of the aging movie queen about them. There is something used up about them. It was the same way with Olga Korbut in Montreal. It seems they have gone from 14 to 40. There is something quite joyless about it all.

But Nadia is in Los Angeles, an honorary member of a gallant Romanian delegation that ignored the Russian boycott, became the only Eastern-bloc country to join these Summer Games.

"We have come to show the world that Romanians are the best sportsmen," said Nadia Comaneci, voice as tiny as always, through Agnes Mura.

The best Romanian sports person of all was this girl, Nadia. Seven tens in Montreal, when it must have seemed like a perfect world, and she would be a perfect girl forever.

• *1984*

The faces unfold like the flag

hat you end up with are these great faces. You take the faces away with you from any Olympiad. The flag and the National Anthem make wonderful television, at least as far as Roone Arledge and his ABC army and America are concerned. The Soviets aren't here and the East Germans aren't here and the Cubans aren't here, and so when the XXIII Olympiad is over, America will have seen the all-time highlight film for Stars and Stripes. Forever.

Already, everyone watching on television is sprinkling Stars and Stripes on cereal, papering the walls with them, washing the dishes with them, brushing teeth with them. America goes to bed with its athletes on the medal stand and the Anthem playing, and wakes up that way. It has become a two-week Francis Scott Key retrospective.

But it is the faces that count, on the medal stand or on the mat in gymnastics or climbing out of the pool or trying to lift barbells. It is Bart Conner, in his third and last Olympiad, crying when they finally put the gold medal around his neck. It is even Rick Carey, the swimmer, putting on a full pout because he did not break a world record in the 200-meter backstroke. The faces give you elation and disappointment and everything in between. The faces are the real stars in L.A.

The best ones of all are in women's gymnastics, because women is inaccurate really, because they are just girls. The sport is like a lot of others, and assassinates childhood, but when the competition is on, and all those

16

Mary Lou Rettons and Julianne McNamaras and Tracee Talaveras are trying to do something fine in the vault or on the floor, when they are slipping on the balance beam and hanging on for dear life, they are just kids. The faces hide nothing, and give you everything.

The U.S. girls did not win the team gold medal in gymnastics Wednesday night at Pauley Pavilion. Romania, best in the world coming in, did that. Romania ended up with a score of 392.20. The U.S. had a score of 391.20. A grinning, slippery, 16-foot, five-inch monster called the balance beam beat the U.S. girls, made them look as if they were in a log-rolling contest. The girls tried to come back. McNamara, who just about fell off the balance beam and could earn just a 9.2 score, picked herself up and dusted herself off and produced a 10 (second of the night) in her floor exercise. Retton got a 10 on the vault. These were the first 10s ever produced by American females.

But they came up one point short as a team. Yet even in this Olympiad of American Gold Frenzy, it didn't matter. Women's gymnastics has become the marvelous theater of the XXIII Olympiad. With the exception of 24-year-old Kathy Johnson, they are all just kids.

NcNamara, freckled and round-shouldered and frail looking until the music starts, is pale and scared as she waits nearly 10 minutes for a judges' conference about Johnson's balance beam scores. Then she nearly falls off the beam, smack on her Stars and Stripes. Coach Don Peters puts an arm around her shoulders, takes her off to the side, consoles her, like a father telling a daughter there will be other proms. McNamara, tough kid, turns around and lights up Pauley with her floor, and gets her 10. Freckles explode into a smile. It all happened in the space of 15 minutes.

Michelle Dusserre, 15 years old, nearly bursts into tears after her slip-slidin' away performance on the beam. Johnson glares angrily at the judges after her 9.6 on the beam. Retton, all bounding joy, throws out her arms to crowd, and world, after her 10 in the vault. Retton says to Peters when it is over, "Theirs (medals) are shinier than ours." All moments to remember at Pauley. Romanian Ecaterina Szabo goes right on her nose coming off the uneven bars, comes back with a 10 of her own on the vault. Another Romanian, an elf named Simona Pauca, does some lighting up of her own after a 10 on the beam.

Young girls at the XXIII Olympiad. Forget flags and anthems. Remember the faces.

• *1984*

Figure 8s will never replace home runs

SARAJEVO

I
•

f there is one significant conclusion to be drawn at the
end of another Winter Olympics, it is this one: I feel very
strongly that figure skating will never replace baseball as
the national pastime.

I say this knowing full well that there are obvious
comparisons between the two sports. Designer footwear,
for example. Baseball players often wear red spikes now.
Figure skaters wear purple skates. Then there is the termi-
nology. It would have been perfectly logical Thursday
night to begin a story by writing, "Scott Hamilton had a
single, double and triple as he won the gold medal at the
XIV Winter Olympics." A guy would have had to go on
and explain that the single was a single flip, the double a
double axel and the triple a triple salchow, but at least
we're in the same ballpark.

But there are just fundamental differences and problems that will not go away. I hate to be cynical, but at this
time I just do not see figure skating cutting into baseball's
popularity. Here are just a few reasons:

Uniforms: There are a lot of baseball uniforms very
much worth hating. The Houston Astros look like a
bowling team. The Montreal Expos have ugly uniforms
and ugly caps. I have never liked the uniforms of the
Oakland A's. The Mets should throw away their blue jerseys and burn them.

But in men's and women's figure skating, the uniforms are even worse. Katarina Witt of East Germany, who is a total joy to watch once she begins skating, often looks as if she has been dressed by the Plasmatics. I also think the sport is a little over-sequined.

In baseball, if you fall down and hurt yourself, everyone says, "Rub some dirt on it." If you fall down in figure skating and rub some ice on it, your sequins fall off.

I think the average sports fan would embrace figure skating more heartily if everyone wore pinstripes. Healey, the greatest of all living Yankee fans, suggested this before I left for Sarajevo. I now concur.

Music: Baseball has "Take Me Out to the Ballgame." Baseball p.a. systems frequently play rock 'n' roll between innings. At Yankee Stadium, they play "New York, New York" when a game is over.

In figure skating, they really wear you out with a lot of "Flight of the Bumblebee" and "Swan Lake" and "Limpid Brook." I just happen to think that the free program on both the men's and women's side would be livelier if the skaters would go with '50s and '60s tunes.

I still have great anxiety attacks when it comes time to distinguish between the triple salchow (pronounced SAL-cow), double toe-loop and triple lutz, but I think everybody would enjoy them more if they were performed to, say, the soundtrack from "The Big Chill."

A little Temptations, please. A little Three Dog Night. Back them up with "Peggy Sue" and "Rockin' Robin" and maybe some Elvis. And some Fats Domino.

Turn the boys and girls loose to "I found my thrill. . ."

Umpiring: There have historically been major problems between baseball players and umpires. Hitters are never happy with umpires' grand vision of the strike zone. Neither are pitchers. Then there is always that messiness with a close call at home plate.

Well, figure skating judges make baseball umpires seem perfect.

All you have to know about figure skating judges is that they sit where the penalty boxes are at hockey games. The penalty box is where they belong. Most judges come to the Olympics with their minds made up about who should win and who should lose. Scott Hamilton is a terrific young man and a worthy champion, but he would have had to suffer an extreme reaction to Sarajevo meat pies if he wanted to lose his gold.

Then there is the scoring system. It's pretty straightforward in baseball, where if you score three runs and the other team scores two, they let you move up in the standings. Doesn't work that way in figure skating.

Brian Orser of Canada won the short program and the long program in the men's figure skating competition here. Hamilton only won the compulsory program. Hamilton got gold. Orser won 70 percent of the competition and got silver.

Figure skating, I figure, has to come up with a scoring system where it is possible to win in the bottom of the ninth. That way, people won't keep walking out during "Flight of the Bumblebee" and "Limpid Brook."

Batting cage chatter vs. rink chatter: Ballplayers stand around during batting practice and gossip about baseball. Figure skaters, especially the girls, talk to you about their clinical psychologists and their favorite foods and such.

Elaine Zayak of Paramus, New Jersey, informed us the other day that her favorite ice cream was Haagen-Dazs Cookies 'N Cream, which narrowly beat out pistachio. When asked what her plans were for after the XIV Winter Olympics, Elaine said—and I quote exactly —"I want to make a lot of money and be famous and make movies about figure skating."

I have a solution: All figure skaters should chew tobacco. Men and women; the whole tone of interviews would change. The whole personality of the sport. Once you get them on Red Man Chew, I think the days for sequins will be numbered.

After that, it would be short work to get Phil Rizzuto into the broadcast booth. Can't you just hear him yelling. "Holy Salchow!"?

• *1984*

Moses soars with his 13 strides

F
•

or seven years he has taken the 13 strides between the hurdles and then taken the hurdles with a most striking grace, and run ahead of the world, and eased himself into a special club, into the company of streaks and legends. The man's name is Edwin Moses. The event is the 400-meter hurdles. The streak is 102 races, 89 of them finals. The last loss was August 26, 1977 to West Germany's Harald Schmid. Since then Edwin Moses has run against himself and the clock, run with the powerful wind of history at his back. Edwin Moses loses as often as the Harlem Globetrotters do.

In this one event, the 400-meter hurdles, Moses has been DiMaggio's hitting streak, Lou Gehrig's extraordinary legacy of playing one baseball game after another. He is Bjorn Borg's five Wimbledons, and 41 consecutive Wimbledon victories. He is all the years when Chris Evert did not lose a match on a clay court. He has stood head and shoulders above a sport, an event, the way so few athletes ever have; owned the sport; redefined it. In the 70s and 80s, in the hurdles, he has been Babe Ruth. Edwin Moses, age 28, going for gold in Los Angeles, is perhaps the greatest athlete in the history of track and field. There has never been anything quite like this.

Seven years. One hundred and two races. Truly, since Moses won the gold medal in Montreal in 1976, the only man to beat Edwin Moses decisively was someone named

Jimmy Carter. Carter kept Edwin Moses from going to the Moscow Olympics, or Moses would be going for his third Olympic gold medal here, instead of his second. Over the coming days, you will hear about Carl Lewis and Mary Decker, about swimmer Rick Carey, about basketball players like Chris Mullin and Michael Jordan and Wayman Tisdale. Moses is better than all of them. The best we have.

"I don't think that much about the streak," Moses was saying here the other day. "Whenever it ends, I'm willing to accept it. I can't think about the streak here. I'm not going into the races feeling as though I'm guaranteed a gold medal somehow. I'm going in like any other competitor."

He is not like any other competitor. He is Moses, moving across the stage in a Press Center interview hall with a familiar elegance, a self-assurance that is second nature, his beautiful wife Myrella at his side. He is wearing a tailored brown suit and red silk tie, and as he takes his seat behind the battery of microphones, this thought occurs: Doesn't Edwin Moses take the hurdles in that same suit?

"I feel I'm psychologically more adept than I ever was, physically stronger." Moses said in his rich bass voice. "I've run in so many different types of conditions, so many different meets. My body still thinks it's 18 years old. And as long as this 28-year-old body keeps beating 18-year olds, it's going to keep thinking it's 18."

Moses talked about being his own coach in the Press Center. He talked about "the dynamics of motion." He talked about taking 1982 off to rejuvenate himself, beginning a two-year plan that will find its last chapter here in the Los Angeles Coliseum. He talked about how the crucial 13 strides (they insure he never has to change his lead leg going over the hurdles) come naturally to him, while all the others in the race have to fret over the strides, have to take 14 or 15, have to trail Edwin Moses.

"It's not like I draw up an equation or anything like that," said Edwin Moses. "It's just the way I run."

He is of Dayton, Ohio, and Morehouse College and the world now, and no one has ever run in such a breathtaking way. Edwin Moses. The very best we have. Jimmy Carter can't beat him in Los Angeles. No one can.

• *1984*

A special lady's special trip

O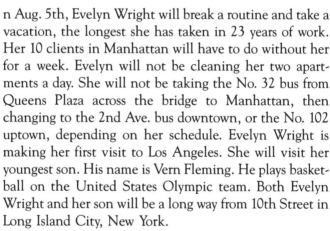n Aug. 5th, Evelyn Wright will break a routine and take a vacation, the longest she has taken in 23 years of work. Her 10 clients in Manhattan will have to do without her for a week. Evelyn will not be cleaning her two apartments a day. She will not be taking the No. 32 bus from Queens Plaza across the bridge to Manhattan, then changing to the 2nd Ave. bus downtown, or the No. 102 uptown, depending on her schedule. Evelyn Wright is making her first visit to Los Angeles. She will visit her youngest son. His name is Vern Fleming. He plays basketball on the United States Olympic team. Both Evelyn Wright and her son will be a long way from 10th Street in Long Island City, New York.

"I have an exciting feeling." said Evelyn Wright. "My heart beats fast all the time. I always told the boys to dream. But I never knew the dream could get as big as the Olympics. I wanted them to be playing basketball when they were growing up because it would keep them out of trouble, and help them be better people. And now, I'm going to Los Angeles."

A long way from 10th Street. A long way from the Queensbridge Houses, where Evelyn raised her two youngest, Vern and his twin brother Victor. A long way for a dream to travel. From Mater Christi High School, Vern went to the University of Georgia, became one of the most poised and solid college guards in the country, played in a Final Four once, got himself drafted by the Indiana Pacers, then made all the cuts on Bobby Knight's Olympic team. Victor went to Xavier University in Cincinnati, got himself drafted by the Portland Trailblazers and is playing in a San Diego summer basketball league. Victor will be in Los Angeles, too. There are a lot of lovely stories about families in any Olympics. This one just happens to be for New York.

Evelyn Wright was not a basketball fan when the story began on 10th Street. She is a basketball fan now. She is a part of the Olympics. Talk about proud sponsors.

"My mom," Vern Fleming was saying yesterday, as he and his mates met the world press, "is having the time of her life. And she ought to, because without her strength, I probably wouldn't be here."

Vern Fleming was talking about his sophomore year at Georgia, when the dream began to get away from him. He was already married. He already had a child. Vern Jr. Student. Basketball player. Husband. Father. Dreamer. It became too much. Vern Fleming picked up the phone one night and called Evelyn Wright and told her he was coming back to 10th Street.

I'm homesick," was his thesis.

"Welcome to the world," was Evelyn Wright's basic rebuttal.

She talked by telephone yesterday about a long distance call that was a turning point for a boy becoming a man; when she reached out and touched someone but good.

"He just couldn't make the whole thing work with a wife and a child," she said. "I told him he had to make it work. I told him that basketball was his dream, what he wanted to make his life. I told him he would be foolish to throw it away because if he did, he would never know what he might have done."

"My mom just told me to get on with it," said Vern Fleming. He got on with it. As a junior, he was on the Georgia team that upset North Carolina in the East Regionals before losing to eventual champion North Carolina State. Now he is in Los Angeles.

It is another basketball trip for Evelyn Wright that is not just another basketball trip. When her two sons were still in college, she would collect a gang of Vern and Victor's stepbrothers and sisters (from her first marriage) and they would pile into a car and drive to Athens, Georgia, to watch Vern. Or she would do the same thing with Victor in Cincinnati. Then she would drive back, get back on the No. 32 bus, get back to work. She started doing maid work just about the time the twins were born. Evelyn Wright did not know about basketball scholarships then. But she knew about college. Her dream was to get the boys away from 10th Street.

"It was only later that I saw all the good things that basketball could bring." she said.

And so it came this summer that there were different sorts of phone calls from Vern Fleming to his mother. He called when Knight cut the team from 72 players to 32, and he was one of the 32. Then when he made the cut from 32 to 20. Then 20 to 16. Then the last cut, from 16 to 12. Obviously, when the phone rings on 10th Street, there is always something big happening for Evelyn Wright.

"He called and said, 'Mom, I made it,' " Evelyn Wright said. "I told him it was old news. Victor had already called me. He's as proud as I am."

The sons learned pride from the mother. And they dreamed big dreams on 10th Street. Now Vern Fleming plays for his country. And Evelyn Wright is going to Los Angeles, and that is a fine thing indeed.

• *1984*

Psychologists could win gold for U.S.

SARAJEVO

osalyn Sumners is an American figure skater from the state of Washington. She could very well win a medal in Sarajevo—it's a dirty job, but some American has to do it sooner or later—if the canned tuna fish from the state of Washington gets here on time, if she doesn't fall down too much and if the sessions with her own clinical psychologist over the weekend work better than the phone system in Bosnia-Herzegovina.

The other afternoon, all the national champions on the U.S. figure skating team had a little press conference at a meeting hall in Skenderija. The 19-year-old Sumners was there. Scott Hamilton was there, as was the Ice Dancing team of Michael Seibert and Judy Blumberg, and the Pairs Team of Peter and Kitty Carruthers. And there was a lot of heady talk about double axels and quadruple jumps and the condition of Kitty Carruthers' ankle and Miss Sumners' diet before Miss Sumners mentioned her clinical psychologist, Dr. David Koppel, who is on the scene in Sarajevo.

Miss Sumners' dissertation on Yugoslavian food and her need, indeed craving, for tuna had pretty much put everyone into snooze control until she double-axeled Dr. Koppel into the press conference.

Question from the floor: "You have your own psychologist?"

Sumners: "Oh yes. A lot of the skaters do."

(Hamilton doesn't, by the way, which is another reason to root for him.)

Question from the floor: "What sort of things does he do for you?"

Sumners: "He's a stress expert. We do a lot of visual therapy. Like I'll lie down in my room and close my eyes and put on the music from my program, and I'll be able to visualize the whole program."

It turns out that Seibert and Blumberg have a stress therapist named Gary Jennings. A lot of the U.S. speed skaters have therapists and psychologists.

The hockey team doesn't, though it could probably use one right now. Lugers definitely do not have therapists and psychologists; if they did, they wouldn't be crazy, and they wouldn't be lugers.

Question from the floor: "How often do you meet with Dr. Koppel?" Sumners: "Three times a week, one hour per session."

As soon as I heard this news from Rosalyn Sumners, my mind began to race with possibilities concerning Dr. David Koppel. If he could just set up shop in the Press Village when he is not doing visual therapy with Sumners, Dr. Koppel could have himself a bonanza by clinical psychologists' standards. See, everyone in Press Village is getting a little grumpy and cranky (not to mention sneezy and dopey) because they are still in Yugoslavia, the hockey team is 0-2, no Americans are winning medals right now, and this is the home office for snow. Everyone is majoring in stress.

Dr. Koppel could start in my modest suite, 11 e, in the fashionable AB building. The two of us would have a lot to talk about:

"Mike, when did you know you were grumpy and cranky?"

"I'm pretty sure it was Friday morning, Doc."

"What happened Friday morning?"

"I was in the press center, and someone came in and told me Bill Koch had finished 21st in cross-country skiing, instead of winning a medal."

"And what was your response?"

"I think I said, 'Good.'"

"Anything else?"

"Well, yes. After that I went up to the speed skating oval at Zewtra and rooted for Communists to fall down."

"So you're not happy to be here, Mike?"

"Go eat a lamb's head, bozo."

"Hmmmm."

(They serve whole lamb's heads here, incidentally. Teeth, jaw, eyes, everything.)

"Mike, have you tried visual therapy?"

"You betcha, doc."

"And what do you see?"

"I see my hands around the necks of my editors."

"Do you see anything else in visual therapy?"

"Judy Blumberg's legs. She's an ice dancer from Manhattan. No big deal. Sarajevo fantasy."

"I've seen the legs. So you don't like winter sports?"

"Doc, I'm gonna level here: It's not that important for my cheeks to be rosy."

"One last question: Are you the most depressed person in Sarajevo?"

"Second. Roone Arledge, president of ABC sports, is first. He's putting these Olympics on back home, and nobody's going to come."

• *1984*

Nine-year dream ends in tears for Randy, Tai

LAKE PLACID

e finally took the injection at 8:45 p.m., 15 minutes before the Short Pairs Program was scheduled to begin, about 30 minutes before a nine-year-old dream of his would officially die. Tony Daly, doctor for the U.S. Olympic team, came into Locker Room No. 4 at the U.S. Olympic Fieldhouse and shot three cc's of Xylocaine into Randy Gardner's upper left thigh. Daly knew the shot would not help Gardner, would not repair the pulled muscle there. John Nicks, Gardner's coach, knew. But Gardner wanted the shot, wanted to soften the pain somewhat. Maybe he wanted to simply hang onto the dream about an Olympic gold in Pairs Skating for one half-hour more in Lake Placid.

The road to Lake Placid had begun in 1971, in a little ice-skating rink in Culver City, Calif., when a coach named Mabel Ferguson suggested that Randy Gardner, age 11, and Tai Babilonia, age 9, join hands and skate a little bit, together. Along the road, they would startle the figure-skating world with a fifth-place finish in the 1976 Olympics at Innsbruck. They would win national titles. They would win the 1979 World Pairs Championship, ending years and years of Soviet domination. And they missed out on a lot.

"There was a world we never lived," Randy Gardner said Saturday. The world included "proms we missed, going to the movies in the middle of the week." And now this final act at the Olympics was being played out in a locker room with an injection that would not keep the dream of a gold medal alive for even one more night.

"I'm really not in favor of this," said Dr. Tony Daly to Gardner in the locker room Friday night. "I want the shot, Dr. Daly," said Gardner. "I want to at least try."

Later, Daly would talk about treating Bill Walton. He would point out that Walton took a painkiller once, took so much of it that he went out and ruined a foot, and almost a career. Daly was explaining why Gardner was given such a small (and legal) dose of Xylocaine, "My heart really wasn't in shooting up Randy," said Daly.

Daly could do nothing for the abdominal tear Gardner had added to the muscle pull Wednesday evening. Gardner suffered the original injury two weeks ago. Then late Wednesday, at practice with Babilonia, he aggravated the injury in his groin area, and tore the abdominal muscle. At that moment, whether Gardner wanted to admit it to himself or not, it was really over for him and Babilonia. They would not challenge the Russians, Irina Rodnina and Aleksandr Zaitsev, for the gold medal. They would not exchange the years of practice for anything at all in these Olympics. Gardner got hurt. One shot would numb his leg; it would not make him well.

"But I've never seen an athlete try harder to get well," Daly said.

At a little after nine, Gardner and Babilonia skated out to a great cheer from the crowd at the Olympic Fieldhouse. But Gardner was obviously not right, skating stiff-legged, stopping every so often to test his left leg. The most simple movements, movements Gardner had not thought about in years, were forced and awkward. He tried a simple flip, and drew a harsh, audible gasp by falling. "He hasn't fallen making that move in years," said Nicks. Before the warmup was over, Gardner fell twice more. Something had gone wrong with what was supposed to be a glamorous evening at the Olympics. There had been a serious accident with a dream carried from California.

The Short Pairs Program is the first half of the Pairs Skating competition; the longer program is Sunday night. Gardner and Babilonia were hoping they could somehow get through Friday night, get Gardner nearly two days of rest, then deal with Sunday night's challenge. The warmup, however, settled the matter, though Gardner would take the ice once more. There would be no gold. There would be no shot at the Russians.

After the warmup, Gardner and Babilonia stood in a hallway near the rink. Gardner tried a couple of lifts with Babilonia. Then

Gardner leaned against a door that said First Aid, and did not move. Dressed in his maroon outfit, he looked like a store-window manne- quin. Babilonia mechanically did knee bends, one after another. They were supposed to be the fourth pair in the evening program. Still Gardner would not give up. After Susan Garland and Rob Daw finished their routine, Gardner went onto the ice with Tai Babilonia.

Gardner tried another spin. He fell again. The arena fell dead si- lent. Gardner looked over at Nicks, leaning over the hockey boards and wearing a white cap. Nicks waved him off the ice. Gardner did not move for one long moment, then nodded to his coach, under whom he and Babilonia had found greatness. Gardner skated slowly behind Babilonia, and off the ice.

Tai Babilonia began to cry. She said she had let everyone down. Somehow, in this moment, in her mind, it had become her fault, not the injury's.

"She didn't understand that she hadn't let anybody down," said Nicks. "It was very moving."

"It was like a nightmare," Tai Babilonia said at a press conference late Saturday afternoon.

It all happened very quickly after that. Nicks, Gardner, Babilonia and Claire Ferguson, the women's team leader for the U.S. figure skaters, left the rink four abreast, arms linked. Babilonia was sobbing quietly now, mascara streaking the dark, lovely face. Gardner stared straight ahead and saw nothing. They walked down a long corridor, trailed by the press. Mrs. Babilonia trailed the parade by about 20 yards. When they all got to the door for Locker Room No. 4, they waited while someone found a key. Mrs. Babilonia touched her daughter briefly on the shoulder. Gardner leaned forward heavily, head down.

"I felt nothing," Gardner said yesterday. "I didn't know whether to cry, to laugh it off, to feel sorry for Tai, myself, the others. I couldn't believe it was happening."

At about 10 o'clock, Tai and her mother had come out of a side door at the Fieldhouse, been helped into a blue Mercedes with Rhode Island license plates, and driven away by a chaffeur. Tai Babilonia, wearing a white mink, looked stunning as she approached the car, un- til the lights from the speed-skating rink highlighted her face. She had not cleared away the mascara.

Not long after that, maybe 20 minutes later, the Mercedes came back for Randy Gardner. He still seemed to feel nothing. He hopes to be ready for the World Pairs Championships in West Germany in 25 days. He talks about going back to school. He talks about that world he never lived. But as he got into the rented car, his face told you everything. When the blue Mercedes pulled away, he left a big part of nine years behind, years stretching all the way back to Culver City.

• *1980*

The wild and wonderful adventure over for this bunch of 'Big Doolies'

LAKE PLACID

T
•

hey come from hockey rinks in Boston and Madison and Duluth, from Charlestown, Mass., and Grand Rapids, Minn., from all those places where even American kids can now climb up on skates and shoot a puck and dream. They came together six months ago with this vague, sketchy dream about some kind of Olympic medal, and had no idea they were destined to be heroes, because heroes never really know, do they?

And over two weeks in February, in a little place called Lake Placid, they wrapped themselves in an American flag, beat the odds in a most remarkable way, and won a medal and a country. They touched us all. They kept hearing the National Anthem after they finished with their hockey games. They had themselves an adventure.

Some will go on from here to play professional hockey, and some might coach, and Buzzy Schneider of Babbitt, Minn., who played in two Olympics, says he is going to Florida before he does anything. The coach, Herb Brooks, will get some big job in the National Hockey League, maybe with the New York Rangers. Bill Baker wants to be a dentist. David Christian might end up selling his father's hockey sticks. But this special club will endure. It is almost as if they went to war, these U.S. Olympic hockey players. They fought together for six months, then they took Lake Placid, and heard the

cheers. Someday, it will be important to them that they marched together.

Someday, we will remember this crazy army and wonder if they
only won hockey games. It will seem to us that the XIII Winter
Olympics must have lasted much longer than two weeks.

"You know what the saddest thing is?" asked Michael Eruzione,
the captain, yesterday afternoon. "The saddest thing is that after we
see the President tomorrow (at the White House, 11 a.m.), we just go.
We just go different ways. I don't know when I'll see guys like John
Harrington and David Christian again. It will be over."

In their own language, the salty language of the rink and the
locker room, they are just a bunch of "Big Doolies." Phil Verchota, of
Duluth, said a Doolie is a big wheel, and Eruzione, from Winthrop,
Mass., said he thought that "big deal" might be a better description.
Maybe, in the locker room, Doolie means something else altogether.
Who cares? If it is good enough for the U.S. hockey team, it is good
enough for the rest of us. Put it in the language. From now on, a
Doolie is a hero, a little guy who beat the odds. Our hockey players
said so.

They are hockey players who had a country rooting for them, and
singing for them, and waving flags for them, as the country had not in
a long time. And when was there a story in sports quite like this one,
backdropped as it was by the Olympics and world events? When was
there a group of plucky underdogs who won an upset victory this stunning? What is the proper analogy? A small college football team beating the Steelers? Iona beating the Los Angeles Lakers? A minor
league team beating up on the Yankees? Over two weeks in February, a
bunch of American kids went after the best hockey teams in the
world and beat the pants off them.

They tied Sweden, and they slammed Czechoslovakia. And suddenly, they realized that this might be their very own moment, that
they might be able to write the last chapter to their adventure. Let
people talk about silly dreams. They were going to win. They kept
waiting for someone to tell them why they could not have the gold
medal. No one has yet.

"These are 20 guys who are just unbelievable," said Jim Craig, the
goalie, the big man, with true emotion yesterday afternoon. "It is a
team. I love them all."

"They have," said Brooks, the coach, "startled the athletic world.
Not just the hockey world. The athletic world."

On Friday night, Brooks' team beat the Russians, 4-3, and sent a shock current across America on an evening that had only a little to do with sports. So Finland was the last team with a chance to beat them, in a game that began at 11 o'clock in the morning. Finland got ahead twice. The Americans laughed at that. They laugh at everything, most of all themselves, and their unlikely saga. For two weeks, they have been spitting at the leads of other teams. They would end up outscoring the opposition 16-3 in the third periods of their games. They outscored the Finns 3-0 in the third period yesterday, and won the game, 4-2, and won the first hockey gold medal for the U.S. in 20 years.

"These guys," said Jim Craig, "you gotta spot 'em a couple of goals to get 'em going."

Rob McClanahan scored the game-winner six minutes gone in the third period, then the brilliant Mark Johnson scored the insurance goal a couple of minutes later. Over the last 10 minutes, Craig—who allowed no goals in the third period over his last three games—slammed the door. Suddenly, loudly, with a splash of color and all those flags waving, it was over. The sellout crowd in the Olympic Fieldhouse went a little bit crazy, and so did the Doolies.

They threw sticks into the crowd. They threw gloves into the crowd. They hugged each other, and some of the fans coming over the boards. Neal Broten embraced John Harrington. Someone handed McClanahan a flag, someone wrapped another around Craig, along with Johnson the team's most valuable player. David Christian, whose father was one of the heroes of 1960, wiped tears away with his right glove. The celebration lasted a long time. Craig was the last player off the ice. He stuck his right arm in the air. The crowd erupted again. Then, in a corner of the Fieldhouse, between Sections 13 and 9, the people stood and sang the Anthem again.

There was only a brief stay in the locker room. Vice-President Walter Mondale shook some hands. Jimmy Carter called and talked to Herb Brooks, then asked to talk to Mike Eruzione. Eruzione laughed. He was talking to the President. Him. Mike Eruzione, from Winthrop. When Carter finished talking, Eruzione grinned and said, "Good luck."

The entire team, all 20 of the Doolies went over to the interview auditorium after that, entering to tremendous applause from the media, which has been cheering for them for two weeks. This was another of their moments. Harrington made jokes about Brooks' slogans, known to the team as "Brooksisms." Verchota tried to explain about the Doolies. Jack O'Callahan, from Charlestown, Mass., entered late, carrying a beer, and climbed up on the table. Someone asked O'Callahan if this was the first gold medal for Charlestown, a tough section of Boston. O'Callahan thought about that one.

"Charlestown's in the shadow of the Bunker Hill," he said. "We won Bunker Hill, and we won at Lake Placid."

Someone pointed out that we had, uh, lost at Bunker Hill. O'Callahan looked very grave. "I don't want to hear that," he said finally. A pause. "Why'd you think they built that big monument?"

The press conference lasted a long time, and the laughter continued. Finally, the U.S. team hockey stood up and filed off the stage, in ragged formation. There was more applause. Later, around 5 o'clock, they returned to the Fieldhouse for their gold medals. One more flag went up. The Anthem was played one last time. Then all 20 of them crowded onto the victory stand, and each thrust their right index finger into the air. One more storm of noise washed over them. The band played "Stars and Stripes Forever" now. The adventure was over.

• *1980*

Ken Read's Olympics
ended in 15 seconds

O
•

ff to his left, fifty yards from the finish line, the Austrians were still singing. The race had been over for thirty minutes by now but the Austrians, most of them dressed in red and white, were still singing and waving their flags. Some of them chanted the name "Stock." Leonhard Stock, an alternate on the Austrian ski team as recently as two weeks ago, had just won a gold medal in the men's downhill. His teammate Peter Wirnsberger had finished second. Another teammate, Peter Mueller, was fourth. Their fans had been singing for a long time. No one seemed to notice that it had begun to snow harder.

Every so often, Ken Read would look over to the place where the Austrians stood, and smile. Read, who is from Calgary, Alberta, speaks three languages: English, French and German. He is able to say "irony" in all three of them. Ken Read was supposed to take the gold medal away from the Austrians on Whiteface Mountain Thursday morning; he may be the best downhill skier in the world right now. But his Olympics lasted 15 seconds on Whiteface Mountain, and Read was still talking about that while the p.a. announcer gave the order of finish.

"Am I disappointed?" Read asked quietly. "Of course I'm disappointed. But these things happen in the Olympics. That's the sport of skiing."

And that is the downhill. It is the one-shot glamor event of the entire two weeks. They take a skier to the top of a mountain like Whiteface. Then it is the skier's best against that mountain. There is no second chance. Just one run, one crack at a medal. Some have trained all their lives for this one great run; others have been waiting four years since the last Olympiad. They have about two minutes to find excellence and speed. Ken Read had 15 seconds, until a ski fell off and the XIII Olympiad ended for him, on a part of Whiteface Mountain called Hurricane Alley.

Read, who came out of nowhere to finish fifth in the downhill at Innsbruck, is not entered in the slalom or giant slalom. He said there is no chance he will compete in the 1984 Olympics in Sarajevo. And so his last day had gone away from him with brutal speed. The day, and the songs, belonged to Stock and Wirnsberger and Read's own teammate, Steve Podborski, who won a bronze.

"The problem of the Olympic downhill was beautifully illustrated today," he said. "You come down, you're at the third gate, your ski comes off, you go down. It's over. There is just this one race. A beautiful illustration, right? Unfortunately, it was illustrated by me."

Over the loudspeaker, the theme song from "Rocky" blared across the finish area. Behind Read, spectators made their way down Whiteface Mountain with Great care; lifts moved the rest of the people down to where the top finishers would be presented World Cup medals (the race is part of the World Cup competition; the Olympic medals would be presented in an evening ceremony). The staff photographers, who had been stationed at various points along the run, rushed by Read on their skis, and sprayed him lightly with snow. Read smiled again. The entire ritual of the downhill had taken 65 minutes. Read seemed to want to stretch the day out a bit. Next to the finish line, someone shut off the scoreboard lights.

If Read wins the World Cup race at Lake Louise, Alberta, in March, he will win the World Cup. In the four years since Innsbruck, he has become one of the premier downhill racers in the world. He came into Thursday's race thinking, feeling, he was the man to beat. The Olympics gave him 15 seconds. He leaned hard as he approached the third gate, a Salomon safety binding on his Fischer ski released accidentally. His boot came out of the ski. Read went down. Then he skidded off the course. Outside the ropes, he made his way down to the finish line, as someone named Mikio Katagiri of Japan sped past the clock at the end of his run.

"So much goes into one race, so many years," he said. "You take a guy like Stock. He hasn't beaten me in any World Cup race this year. To count him as champion is...not...quite...right."

All along, Read has said that it is more significant for a world-class skier to win the World Cup competition than the Olympic gold. As he stood at the finish area early Thursday afternoon, he had not changed his mind. The fifteen seconds he had at the Olympics seemed to make him quite certain of his opinions.

"In the World Cup," he said, "you've got an entire season, eight races. That way, you eliminate bad luck."

Read had as much bad luck as you can have. By the time he picked himself out of the snow, the race was over. Stock had already finished his stunning run in a time of 1:45.50. Wirnsberger had done 1:46.12. Podborski was about to save a small portion of Canada's dreams with a bronze. The numbers would continue to flash by on the big scoreboard at the bottom of the hill. All of the Americans had yet to make their runs. But it was over.

Someone asked him another question about the '84 Olympics. Read, who was shivering noticeably by now, shook his head vigorously from side to side.

"I don't want to stay too long," he said. "There are other things I want to do in life. I carried the flag for Canada in the opening ceremony. I came into this race the favorite. So I had some bad luck today. There's nothing you can do about a binding."

Most of the spectators were gone by now. Someone came walking up to Read, tapped him on the shoulder, and showed him that he had collected Read's skis. Read looked over his shoulder one last time at Whiteface Mountain, then headed toward the parking lot, where a bus waited to take him back to the Olympic village. The downhill had started at 11:30 in the morning. It was 1:30 in the afternoon. It had not been much of a day for Ken Read, a favorite for 15 seconds. Even with carrying the flag, it had not been much of an Olympics.

• *1980*

THE ONLY REAL GAME

"The only real game" is what Babe Ruth called baseball in his farewell speech at Yankee Stadium. It is probably the most eloquent thing The Babe ever said, apart from, "Another Scotch, please." My three favorite sports are baseball, baseball, and baseball. My favorite column writing days are at the ballpark. I get there about four in the afternoon for a night game, sometimes with a plan, sometimes without one. Then I commence to work the room. As work goes, it is not heavy lifting. A baseball clubhouse has always lent itself to the kind of writing I like to do best.

•

Part 3

Time stands still at witching hour

I

•

t was half past midnight. It should have been half past the baseball season for the New York Mets. Dave Henderson had hit that home run. Marty Barrett had singled home another run. Red Sox 5, Mets 3, bottom of the 10th. Bottom of the 10th. Top of the winter. In a little while, you could turn back the clock an hour, but you couldn't turn it back far enough, past Henderson's home run and Barrett's RBI, past Red Sox three games to two up and 5-3 up and three outs to go in the 1986 World Series.

And then there was one out to go. One strike to go on Ray Knight. Bottom of the 10th and top of the winter.

And then all sorts of strange and wondrous things—Halloween things, early—started to shock Shea and rock Shea and be-devil the Boston Red Sox. Then all the magic of the summer stole into the beginning of an October Sunday and held off the baseball winter, for one more marvelous New York baseball night.

It is why at half-past midnight the people would not leave Shea. The scoreboard said Mets 6, Red Sox 5. The people would not leave the ballpark, because the Mets would not leave the season. Gary Carter singled when the Mets were an out away. Kevin Mitchell singled Carter to second. Ray Knight, with the count 0-2—Mets a strike away, one—singled Carter home, Mitchell to third.

Keith Hernandez watched from Davey Johnson's office. Hernandez had made the second out, long fly to center. Let him tell:

"I went right to the clubhouse after I made the second out, grabbed a beer, went into Davey's office to watch the end of the game on television. Then we got the three hits. I started to go grab my glove and cap, in case we tied it, and I had to go back out there for the top of the 11th. But then I thought, nope, and sat right back down in the chair. Davey's got this director's chair in there. I sat back down and thought to myself, This chair has got hits in it."

It didn't. But maybe it set hobgoblins and demons loose on the Boston Red Sox. Two weeks ago, they had come away from the end of the season against the California Angels. Two weeks ago, when Gene Mauch was one out away from the pennant, he came out to the mound and replaced Mike Witt with Donnie Moore.

Hernandez sat. And here came John McNamara out to the mound, signaling to the bullpen, replacing Calvin Schiraldi with Bob Stanley. Shea was rocking now. Knight on first, Mitchell on third. The people would not let go of the season. The Mets would not let go of the season. The 1986 World Series was going crazy, 'bout half past midnight.

"You go ask Davey," said Lee Mazzilli, who'd singled and scored the tying run, third run, for the Mets in the eighth. "I looked over at their dugout, watched them all, you know, Oil Can Boyd and the rest of them starting to celebrate before we got the hits. And I just said, 'We aren't out of this thing yet.' "

Stanley got to 2-2 on Mookie Wilson.

One strike away. Again.

Mookie just fouled off a Stanley pitch at the plate.

Still one strike away. But the Shea crowd, deadened by Henderson's home run, defeated by Barrett, was now a LaGuardia flight pattern.

Mookie fouled off one into the third-base stands.

One strike.

Stanley threw a wild pitch and here came Kevin Mitchell to the plate.

It was 5-5.

"When I got to third," Kevin Mitchell said in the clubhouse, "Buddy Harrelson (third base coach, someone who knows a little bit about baseball miracles) told me to be alert. He said, 'This guy's gonna throw a wild pitch.' "

Halloween coming early at Shea. Hobgoblin stuff. Magic. And Mets 5, Bosox 5.

"I was hoping to put my foot in the right spot that we could get a win," said Davey Johnson. He moved his foot around. Kevin Hernandez stayed in the manager's chair in the manager's office. Mookie Wilson fouled another one off.

And another.

Still 2-2.

Then Mookie Wilson threw a snake of a grounder down the first base line. Here came Bill Buckner, the Red Sox first baseman—Buckner with the ruined legs—hobbling over behind the bag to field it. In Boston today, they want to know why Buckner was not pinch-hit for in the eighth inning when the bases were loaded and Jesse Orosco was in to pitch for the Mets (Buckner flied to center on the only pitch Orosco threw). They want to know why Baylor didn't hit and why Dave Stapleton didn't come into play first base.

McNamara said in the interview room: "Normally with Buckner, we pinch run for him. And he has very good hands."

But for this one moment at the end of this good and bad and extraordinary and ultimately unforgettable baseball game, Buckner had bad hands. The World Series had begun with a ball going through Tim Teufel's wickets and the Red Sox winning. The World Series was now extended—the baseball season was extended and so was a 68-year Red Sox drought without a World Championship—because Mookie Wilson's grounder slithered through the ruined legs of Buckner and toward Game 7 as Ray Knight came home with the winning run.

Mets 6, Red Sox 5. There will be one last loud roar in the baseball season, tonight at Shea. The Mets would not let go. For this one night and into the bizarre morning, the past would not let go of the Boston Red Sox. The Mets had come back against Roger Clemens, but then they failed to win the game in the bottom of the ninth.

It seemed then that Met fans would learn what it is like to be Red Sox fans, to live with a winter of ifs and might-have-beens and shoulda's. All winter Met fans would say, "If only Hojo coulda got the bunt down." The Mets had first and second, nobody out in the bottom of the ninth. But Howard Johnson couldn't get a bunt down on strike one, then struck out.

If Johnson gets the bunt down, Lee Mazzilli's deep fly wins the game. But Johnson doesn't and Mazzilli doesn't. Then Henderson, who saved the Red Sox when they were one strike away in Anaheim tries to shoulder aside all those Thomsons and Dents and Mazeroskis with a shot into the night, couple of minutes before midnight, minute before midnight when he reaches the Red Sox dugout. It was 4-3, then 5-3.

It was that way for 20 minutes or so. Until about half past midnight, halfway into what had become the witching hour for the Red Sox at Shea.

One strike away once. One strike away twice. Wild pitch. Then through the wickets of Bill Buckner.

We wanted some excitement in this World Series, some drama, something to remember. We got it, early Sunday morning. We got Halloween. Tonight, we get the whole season.

• *1986*

Can't say it ain't snow

T he signs were all there, and we kept ignoring them, because he was the Doc, Doctor K. He gave us this magical summer once, winning 24 and striking out the world. He was 20 that summer. He had one of those arms.

The arm was so strong it held us off for a whole year, right up until it was announced yesterday that Dwight Gooden had consented to enter a treatment program for a drug problem.

And so the story no one wanted to believe turns out to be true.

"I don't know who that person was last season," Dwight Gooden said to me a month ago in Florida. "But it sure wasn't me."

But it was him, after all. It was a young man with a problem. He gets help now. Last year it was Lawrence Taylor. This year it is Dwight Gooden. Lots of years. Big names, little names, dope doesn't care. Just walks in and tries to steal your life.

Now it steals from Gooden, who gave us that summer in 1985, and who still had enough last season to go 17-6 and have a 2.84 ERA and hide a problem with drugs. We figured he was still the Doc, and we liked him so much we started to believe our eyes were liars, even as things kept happening to him.

There was the ankle injury after the '85 season, never explained. There was the car accident during spring training of '86. Was he driving? A passenger? He missed a game anyway. Davey Johnson fined him, but the incident disappeared. It happens with 24-4 pitchers. There was the incident at the Hertz counter at LaGuardia with his sister and his then-fiancé Carlene Pearson. A drink was thrown by one of the women. Gooden's party ended up talking about it with the Port Authority police.

It turned out he had fathered a child, not with Pearson. He skipped the Mets victory parade. He broke up with Pearson. She later was arrested for carrying a handgun in her purse as she went through the X-ray machine at LaGuardia. Whole string of pearls, trying to be a necklace.

Finally, Dwight Gooden was pulled over by the Tampa police in December, beaten as he allegedly resisted arrest; was arrested. A deal was cut; he was put on probation. He showed up at spring training thinner than he had been during the '86 season, promising his troubles were behind him.

Now he comes forward with his drug problem.

The story no one wanted to believe is true. If Gooden had been someone with a drug history, there would have been no question in anybody's mind that he was a user last season. He got by, his numbers still put him near the head of the class, but he was not the same. His fastball was not the same. He struggled. He looked fat. He seemed to be sweating all the time on the mound. The summer before, when did he sweat? When did he need to?

I asked him last July about drugs, told him every sports editor in town had become a narc. He said he didn't use drugs. I asked his teammates, people on the team I trusted to tell the truth, and they said no. He's a good kid, they said. He's just had some bad luck. He's only 22. So on he went. When he had another bad performance, we talked about faulty mechanics. Everybody was helping carry Gooden. Recovering addicts and alcoholics have a word for this. It is enabling. We were seeing, and not seeing, ignoring the signs.

John Lucas knows the procedure. He is a recovering cocaine addict who plays guard for the Milwaukee Bucks. He is most recently clean for 12 months. He was playing for the Houston Rockets when he had his last slip, missed practice, got tested, tested positive, got released, ended up at the NBA rehab center in Van Nuys, Calif.

"At first I wanted to blame Coach (Bill) Fitch," Lucas said when he was in town last to play the Knicks. "Now I look back and see he might have saved my life."

Lucas is 33 now. He has been beaten up by drugs more than once. He knows there are no small drug problems. There are just addicts. Yesterday, Gooden's agent, Jim Neader, made it should like Gooden was getting a hangnail fixed up, and that attitude will be of no use to his client whatsoever.

John Lucas said in New York: "I'm as confident in my individual ability as I've ever been—except when it comes to drugs and alcohol. With them I had to surrender before I could win."

Gooden is there now. The Mets tested him, he came up positive, Frank Cashen went to commissioner Peter Ueberroth. Ueberroth said Gooden either got treatment or got suspended. The main thing is, Gooden gets help now. Hopefully, he gets real help, not one of those 28-day miracle cures they seem to love so much in professional sports.

This Gooden business is good, and bad. The good is that he gets the help. The bad is that this keeps happening in professional sports, just as it keeps happening all over the place. It does not matter who they are, how gifted they are, how young, how strong. They apparently think: It won't happen to me. It happened to Len Bias, it happened to Don Rogers. Happened to Michael Ray and John Lucas and the two guys from the Rockets, and rookies like Chris Washburn of Golden State. Washburn was the pick behind Len Bias and he saw Bias get dead, and Washburn ended up in rehab anyway.

Nobody is learning. Education is like shouting at the ocean. I used to think mandatory testing was an invasion of privacy, and now I think that is bunk. I think testing gives a bigger chance to save lives, and careers. I wonder if Gooden would have come forward on his own without being tested. Again: Nobody is learning. Today I am writing about Gooden checking himself into some kind of treatment, and I do not think he will be the last Met this season. I believe there will be another.

The stories and rumors are always around now. You slip, you get fingered as a doper. The calls started coming in last summer when it was obvious that the Doctor K of '85 and the Gooden of '86 were distant relatives. Somebody knew somebody who saw Gooden with somebody who used dope. There was this bar in Queens. It's not just Gooden, it's a couple of his buddies. On and on. But there was nowhere to go without real proof, without catching Gooden in the act.

And there was enough right arm to hold us all off. And we didn't want to believe the story was true anyway.

Here I was with Gooden in the Mets' St. Petersburg clubhouse a month ago, listening to his talk about the upcoming season with optimism. He was, he said, older and wiser. He looked lean. At Mets camp, his fastball looked to have its bite back. Then I saw him give up nine runs in one inning to the Cardinals, and the word "enabling" came back, like it did after Gooden got into it with the Tampa police.

Now comes the word about drug treatment. No one is safe any more. Dope is great. It kills people, it kills careers, it keeps killing the magic in our games. Today it is Gooden. Tomorrow it will be someone else.

- *1987*

Day of future, past

T
•

here will be other days for Kent Hrbek, who hit the grand slam yesterday. He is 27 years old. He is young, the way this Minnesota Twins team is young. There are no guarantees in baseball, but there will probably be another World Series for Hrbek, another loud baseball October in the Metrodome.

Hrbek, a Minneapolis kid, will probably get another chance to be a hometown hero. To feel the things he felt yesterday in the sixth inning when he hit a Ken Dayley fastball over the centerfield wall.

"I wish I could have run around the bases twice." Kent Hrbek said. "I can't tell you how big a thrill it is with your friends and family in the stands."

Don Baylor hit a big home run in Game No. 6 of the World Series yesterday. It came in the fifth inning, with Gary Gaetti on base. It came off John Tudor and made the score 5-5, and officially turned the Metrodome crowd loose on the Cardinals.

Don Baylor had family in the stands just like Hrbek. His mother was there, and his father, and his son. His fiance, named Becky, was there too. And this one meant as much to Baylor as the grand slam did to the hometown kid. Don Baylor is 38 years old. He knows he might not get a chance like yesterday's again in what is left of his baseball life.

Baylor, a true baseball star for his generation and a

true baseball gentleman, did not make the World Series until the age of 37. He did not get his first World Series home run until yesterday afternoon. When this Series is over, Kent Hrbek will still have the future.

Baylor might just have yesterday.

"It was very emotional for me," Don Baylor said in front of his locker in the Twins clubhouse. "And the people who know me pretty well know that I'm not an emotional person, that I try to keep things inside. I think it probably meant as much to my mother and father and son and fiance as it did to me. They know how long I dreamed about just getting an at-bat in the World Series, and they know that I had to wait a little longer to get a home run."

His first World Series, with the Red Sox last October, went wrong for Baylor. He will go through the rest of his career, the rest of his life probably, thinking he could have won the Series for the Sox in the famous sixth game. Baylor was on the bench, because there was no DH in the National League park. The Red Sox were ahead a run in the top of the eighth, and had the bases loaded with two outs.

Jesse Orosco was on the mound. It was Bill Buckner's turn to hit. Buckner bats lefthanded, Orosco is lefthanded. It seemed there was a chance for John McNamara, the Red Sox manager, to put the Mets away, pinch hit Don Baylor, bring in Dave Stapleton to play first in the bottom of the eighth.

Baylor stayed on the bench. He would never get off the bench in that game. Buckner made an out. The rest is unforgettable history for both Mets and Red Sox. When Baylor finally got to pinch hit in the seventh game, the Red Sox were already dead.

"The whole experience left a very bitter taste in my mouth," Baylor said. "It's why I had to get away from Boston—all those sad faces— as soon as the Series was over."

On Aug. 31, Baylor left the Red Sox for good, traded to the Twins an hour before the Sept. 1 deadline. After midnight, Baylor would not have been eligible for the postseason. But he was eligible. He is eligible. Eligible enough to jerk a low Tudor changeup out of the park and get the Twins even.

It was that sixth-game swing he did not get for the Red Sox.

In front of his locker, Baylor smiled and said, "Another time, another clutch hit." His last home run came on Aug. 23. It was against the Twins, against another famous lefthander named Carlton. "I've gotten hits since then," Baylor said. "But I haven't had the stroke."

He has gotten hits. He had the game-winning RBI in the first game of the American League Championship Series against the Tigers. He had an RBI single his first time up yesterday. Then he took Tudor deep in the fifth.

"Whatever happens, the home run makes the overall year worth it," Don Baylor said. "I mean, after the way things went with the Red Sox, I was glad just to find myself in this spot in the World Series. I looked back on what happened on Aug. 31, coming over here the way I did, and I feel like I got a reprieve."

There will probably be another season for Don Baylor after this one. Maybe he guaranteed that with the big swing yesterday. He says the desire to play is still there. He says it will be a loss of such a mental desire, not a deterioration of physical skills, that will most likely drive him out of baseball.

He can still get around on the fastball. He can still take "a good pitch for Tudor" and get it out of the park.

"John Tudor has gotten me plenty of times," Don Baylor said. "Today, I got him."

In his corner of the room, Kent Hrbek was still talking about a hometown boy making good in the World Series.

"I've rooted for the Twins since I was 10," Hrbek said. "I don't remember the playoff games in '69 and '70, but I've been with them a long time."

In '69 and '70, he was with them as a young fan. Now he is with them as a young star. It is all still ahead of Hrbek. It is mostly behind Baylor. But both got a chance to do something big in Game No. 6 yesterday. Both hit home runs. The World Series didn't ask them where they came from, where they were going, how old they were.

The World Series just told them to go ahead, try to be a hero.

• 1987

A good day for 'firsts'

T hey asked Tom Kelly to take them through his day. He stuck the mitt under his right arm. He smiled at the notion that such a log was suddenly important.

After a baseball career in the bushes or in the shadows, Tom Kelly was asked not to leave anything out. After all the years as a baseball grunt, Tom Kelly was asked to go minute by minute.

"I got up around 8," Tom Kelly said. "I had a cup of coffee. I had a piece of toast. Then I read the paper."

Someone started to ask another question. Kelly said, "Wait, I might have folded some clothes."

Deadpan all the way. Like Kelly was thinking: Make fun of the day, it can't eat you up, right?

But the crowd around the Twins' manager was growing, like the day was growing, until the first pitch would be thrown at the Metrodome, and the Twins would really be in the World Series, and so would Tom Kelly. Someone wanted to know when Tom Kelly, the 37-year-old manager of the Twins, had gotten to the ballpark.

"I had to meet some people, give them tickets," he said. "So I was here at 11 o'clock. That's late for me." The World Series had come again to Minneapolis, and it was a big thing for Minneapolis. But the story is always the World Series coming into people's lives.

Like Frank Viola, the lefthander from Long Island and St. John's, who would throw the first pitch to Vince Coleman. Like Tom Kelly, who was born in Graceville,

Minn., but really is of St. Mary's High School in South Amboy, N.J., and Monmouth College in Long Branch.

At 4:30 in the afternoon, with the World Series rolling into the Metrodome and the noise and the day building, someone asked Tom Kelly the question that would bring the best answer on Saturday:

"When did you see your first World Series game in person?"

Tom Kelly, mitt under the arm, tobacco wad between his feet, smiled again, "What time is it? Four-thirty? I'll be seeing my first World Series game in about three hours."

"You're kidding?"

"TV," he said. "I always seemed to be watching it on TV in the Instructional League."

It was the best first yesterday in Minneapolis, Minnesota. It was the first World Series for the Twins in 22 years, since Zoilo Versalles and Mudcat Grant and Harmon Killebrew went after the Dodgers. It was the first World Series gamed played indoors.

And it was the first World Series game Tom Kelly, out of St. Mary's High, had seen in person. It all went into notebooks around Tom Kelly. There were thirty people around him, maybe more.

Kelly said, "What's the matter, Whitey (Herzog) go upstairs or something?"

Kelly said he had a chance to go to the World Series last year, when it was in New York. He had finished the season managing the Twins, going to the dugout from the third-base coaching box. He didn't know whether he would keep the job. He skipped the World Series in New York. But he kept his job. The Twins won the American League West. Here he is.

He worked a lot of minor-league towns as an outfielder. He made it to the big leagues once with the Twins. He coached. Interim manager. Manager with a one-year contract for 1987.

Tom Kelly finally made the big show yesterday. He took an elaborate route from Graceville, Minnesota, to the best seat in the house.

He looked around the Metrodome. At plastic and plexiglass and the blue Hefty bag in right and the lights on the ceiling and all the funny, high-tech indoor things. There were more people on the field. There was some noise now in the stands. Day kept growing. Someone asked Tom Kelly about the Metrodome.

"It is a great place," he said. "It is a beautiful building. It was a great place to be a third-base coach especially. And especially before they put the new lights on the ceiling. Balls would get lost in the ceiling. Balls would bounce one way off the plexiglass and funny when they hit the turf, and you could score a lot of runs, and there was always a lot of action at third."

Someone said, "You don't like to talk too much about yourself, do you?"

Tom Kelly, who has seen enough of the baseball life to understand it, said, "I like talking about players. The players are the game. People come to see the players. They come to see Kirby Puckett and Kent Hrbek and Tom Brunansky and Greg Gagne and the rest. Not me. I don't think anybody ever paid to see a manager manage or a coach coach or an umpire umpire."

Tom Kelly's cover story is that there was nothing to it from his corner of the dugout, that the players did everything. You have to know better. The Twins did more than hit home runs this time. The Twins created runs and 85 wins, and here they are.

"I had two meetings all year," Kelly said. "The last one was at the end of August. I just told them that we were all in the boat together, and if we kept rowing together, we would win the thing. I told the guys that they weren't going to raise their batting average 50 points from then until the end of the season. So I told them to go one at-bat, one game, see what happened. After it was over, I said to my coaches, 'I'm all done, I don't know what else to say.' The players took it from there. Guys like Tim Laudner and Sal Butera and Gagne and Dan Gladden, who'd been a little down, stat-wise, really came on until the end. So maybe my speech helped."

He said there was another meeting last winter, after he found out he was keeping his job. He brought his coaches into Minneapolis. They met for three days. They went over every player on the roster. They drew up an outline, what they needed from each player.

"We knew we had to change the attitude and approach to the game around here," he said.

Attitude changed. Approach changed. The Twins stole a base once in a while. Jeff Reardon became one of the premier stoppers in the American League. Gaetti became one of the best third basemen in baseball. Hrbek was Hrbek, and Puckett was Puckett, and Viola and Blyleven were one of the best 1-2 punches in the league. Eighty-five wins. Four games to one over the Tigers. Now the Cardinals.

The big show came back to Minnesota. And into lives. Like Tom Kelly's.

Thirty-seven years old, and he finally got to come to the Series.

• *1987*

Miller's old, tired but still plugging

H
•

e is smoking more, and all of the smoking has put new
scratch marks all over a baritone rough to begin with. He
is not eating regularly and not sleeping very well, and he
says his backhand is a horror and his tennis game has
gone all to hell. He is a 64-year-old man who has begun
to feel 64 years old. But the fight goes on and the troops
look to him for strength more than they ever have, so
Marvin Miller keeps moving from city to city and preaching his gospel, keeps trying to win a nasty little war.

"But I am feeling my age," Marvin Miller says, "and
for me that is old." He goes from meeting room to press
conference, from New York to Washington to Chicago to
Los Angeles, trying to hold it all together, using his com-
mon sense, an honorable man playing a game where they
keep changing the rules on him. He meets with player
representatives in Chicago one day, then he gets on an
airplane and flies to Los Angeles to brief as many more
striking baseball players as possible, as they all make their
way through a jungle of words and lies being propagated
by the other side. He is Marvin Miller, and he is a hero in
a most unpopular labor battle, but he is tired.

"The game goes on and on," he was saying Tuesday
afternoon in his room at the Los Angeles Marriott, "and
I just don't know where it is going to end."

He was asked what keeps him going.

"I revive from time to time," he said. "Sometimes a

meeting like the one we had last night (in Chicago) will do it, the kind of meeting where I find out just how solid we really are. Sometimes it will be a fan coming up to me in an airport and telling me to stick with it, and not give up. That can be a very energizing sort of thing."

He tells representatives, and he tells the other players, that this is the hard part now, the ugly, unpleasant part of the strike business, that the impatience and confusion sometimes, and the check simply not coming on the first and the 15th. The owners will try to run their end runs on Miller, try to sell plans and solutions that merely disguise free agent compensation, but do not hide it. The owners' public relations men in the media will keep painting the players as villains, despite the fact that the players only fight for what is rightfully their's. In that deep, quiet, weary eloquent voice, Marvin Miller keeps telling them to be patient, because they will win. He just does not know when.

It was mentioned to Miller that some players are getting ornery, and recalcitrant. A Dennis Eckersley here, a Champ Summers there. They make sounds about breaking ranks, giving in.

"You are just dealing," said Miller, "with a few players who haven't caught up with the facts."

He was asked about the so-called "pool" plan—which some of the owners have been trying to sell to the players over the last week.

Miller cleared his throat, and tried to laugh, but the sound was only harsh and grating and sad.

"There is no more resemblance to a pool in that plan than I resemble Mahatma Gandhi," he said wearily. "It is the same format they have been peddling for 18 months."

He must keep explaining this to his union. He must keep preaching the gospel. So here with Marvin Miller in Salon Number Four at the L.A. Marriott Wednesday morning, wearing a gray suit and a dark blue shirt, looking tired, working the room, getting ready for another meeting, this time with about 50 players in the Los Angeles area. Bobby Grich was there and Steve Garvey and Ron Cey and Fred Lynn and Davey Lopes, and they sat at long tables with green tablecloths on them, and there were notebooks and pens set at each place.

At about 11:30 in the morning, the television cameramen and all the reporters began to disperse from Salon Number Four, at the request of Miller, who moved around the room and thanked them for coming.

"We've just got this meeting started," said Marvin Miller. In four hours, he had to be on a plane headed for New York. He has a 2 p.m. meeting with the owners.

- *1981*

Old friend thrills again

And so on the day that he took his proper place in history, in a most proper setting called New York City, Tom Seaver still was something splendid to see on a summer afternoon. It was Yankee Stadium, not Shea, and it was the White Sox for whom he was pitching and not the Mets. He is 40 years old and not the miracle boy from the summer of '69. But for three shining, emotional hours yesterday, Tom Seaver said to a New York crowd, "This is who I am. This is who I have always been."

And the crowd at Yankee Stadium that became his fully by the end, whose cheers built as afternoon became twilight and finally blew across toward the empty ballpark in Flushing that was his once, too, said to Tom Seaver with those cheers, "Hello, old friend." Years do not harm this sort of romance. Years do not damage greatness such as Seaver's. At 6:11 p.m. on the fourth of August in 1985, baseball's 300 Club received a most honored guest.

The ceremony seemed more special because of New York. Again: Hello, old friend. He grabbed the 300th by the throat and he was a Seaver with whom New York was well-acquainted. He gave the Yankees six hits. He struck out seven. He went the distance. The White Sox won, 4-1. Tom Seaver is 300-189 lifetime. Tom Seaver has gone the whole remarkable distance from the April day in 1967 when he beat the Cubs, 6-1, and won the first, and the glory road to yesterday began.

"The emotions today were like the first time I pitched in the big leagues," Seaver said in the interview room afterward. He talked about feeling sick to his stomach all day, carrying a bucket of nerves he thought he'd deposited in the past. Then he laughed. "I'm glad I don't feel this way every time out anymore," Seaver said.

Someone wanted to know when the nerves left him for good.

"When Reid Nichols (left fielder) caught the ball," he said. He was talking about the last out of the game, the one that got him into The Club.

He threw his first pitch at 3:11 in the afternoon, after an interminable ceremony honoring Phil Rizzuto that nearly became a telethon. And for the next three hours, this was a game like so many for Seaver across his career. He was like a plodding club fighter, throwing his punches inning after inning, picking his spots, giving up a run in the third, waiting for his team to get him runs. Remember that Seaver's teams are right there at .500 for his 19 seasons; triumph has never come easy. He has always been better than his teams. There has been a lot of scuffling, a lot of waiting. There have been a lot of days when he was on the wrong side of 1-0.

"I knew we would get some runs somewhere," he said. "My job has always been to keep my team close." Tom Terrific has always been real good at hope. And keeping his team close.

Then the White Sox got four runs in the sixth. The table had been set for history. Seaver could smell the 15th round. Then the whole ceremony became riveting at Yankee Stadium, in New York, as the crowd rose again and again and cheered a familiar and noble efficiency. He ran the table with three fly balls in the seventh, from Ron Hassey and Willie Randolph and Mike Pagliarulo. Six more outs to 300. In the eighth there were runners at first and third and David Winfield came to the plate.

"You're never almost there with two runners on and Dave Winfield at the plate," said Seaver.

He struck out Winfield. Another standing ovation. The Met fans at Yankee Stadium understood the noise. Now they had been united with the enemy. The Stadium rooted for Seaver now. Three outs to go.

"I've got some beautiful memories in New York," Seaver said. "I gave New York some great thrills, and today they reciprocated. They know what I've done over 19 years."

The Stadium said, "Go get three hundred, old friend."

The ninth. A screaming single from Dan Pasqua off the wall in

right. Looked like a home run coming off the bat. Harold Baines held
Pasqua to a single. Seaver got Hassey for the seventh strikeout on a 2-
2 pitch. Randolph sent one deep to right, like something out of an air
rifle. Baines ran and leaped and made a breathtaking catch against
the wall; so Baines had his assist for history. Two outs. The Stadium
sounded like Shea when the planes are taking off, banking over the
old ballpark. And Seaver walked Pagliarulo. Pitching coach (and act-
ing manager; Tony LaRussa had been thrown out of the game) Dave
Duncan came to the mound, along with catcher Carlton Fisk. Pinch-
hitter Don Baylor was getting ready to step into the box.

Duncan: "It's up to you."

Seaver, to Fisk: "What do you think?"

Fisk: "You've got good stuff. You can get him."

Seaver: "Let's go."

Seaver, later in the interview room: "If you can't get up for the
one out that's going to get you 300, then you ain't never gonna get
up."

He brought the right arm—baseball treasure for all times now—
forward with the "top to bottom" motion that has been his glorious
trademark. One last time, he tried "to keep the ball active in the hitting zone." He did. Baylor lofted the ball high to left.

Halfway between the mound and the first-base line, Seaver
watched, hands on knees. Reid Nichols caught the ball. Shortstop
Ozzie Guillen did a Mary Lou Retton vault in short center. It was
over. No. 300. The ceremony of the 300th became a New York block
party. And Fisk was grabbing Tom Seaver and lifting him into the air,
to collide with the cheers. To find the marvelous sounds of an old romance.

Then Seaver was kissing his wife, Nancy, and daughters, all of
them crying their way into a rugby scrum. He embraced his 74-year-
old father Charles (Seaver: "I couldn't have him flying all over the
country at his age, waiting for me to get 300").

Fisk came over and got in on it, and Guillen. Then Seaver was
taking his cap off and smiling his kid's smile and showing the same
old mop of hair and the scoreboard said something about 300 and the
cheers and the noise, pushed by memory, just kept washing over him.

"A day I'll remember the rest of my life," Tom Seaver would say
later.

New York will remember, because New York has never forgotten
him, or the genius, or the magic. The 300th had to be in New York.

Had to be. The circle had to be completed here, the one that began on April 20, 1967.

Sport does not often get homecomings such as this. But then, sport is allotted just so many Seavers. He gave us one more afternoon of grace.

• *1985*

At 35, Gullett is too young to be old

T
•

he number was the same in all the wire service stories about the heart attack victim. "Don Gullett, 35" the stories read.

This was not about Gullett's uniform number. That was 35, too. But Don Gullett hadn't worn a baseball uniform in a long time. It was five years ago that the Yankees finally had to give him his unconditional release because his left shoulder was never going to get better. It was 10 years since Sparky Anderson said, "Don Gullett is going to the Hall of Fame" during the 1975 World Series. And it was 15 years since Gullett was a phenom with the Cincinnati Reds, a lefthanded Kentucky farm boy who could throw fastballs past the world.

Don Gullett, 35.

Ron Guidry has the highest lifetime winning percentage for a pitcher with more than 100 decisions, .694. Guidry's record is 154-68. Don Gullett's record was 109-50, a percentage of .686. Guidry is getting ready for another Yankee season. Don Gullett got off a tractor at his Lynn, Ky., farm Friday morning and had what the doctors across the Mississippi in Portsmouth, Ohio, called a myocardio-infarction, which means coronary occlusion. Heart attack.

Guidry was 22-6 last season. Gullett went on the disabled list in July of 1978 and never came back. Guidry and Gullett are the same age, 35.

But Gullett's luck went bad one day in 1978, after

years of shoulder troubles. The doctors found a double tear of the rotator cuff. His luck never got better. By 1980, the Yankees had to finally give up on him. Gullett went back to the farm in Kentucky. Friday Gullett's luck got worse. Thirty-five years old would make him a veteran pitcher, if the shoulder had not gone wrong for Don Gullett, but thirty-five is supposed to be a young man. Too young for a heart attack. Maybe once the fates start beating up on you they just can't stop.

He came up to the Reds as a 19-year-old, and struck out six straight Mets in a game. In 1971, at the age of 20, Don Gullett was 16-6. In 1973, at the age of 22, he was 18-8. He won his first World Series game for the Reds in 1975 at the age of 24. His record in the big leagues by then was 80-41. At the age of 24.

Ron Darling is a 24-year-old pitcher with the Mets. His future is bright, the way Gullett's was once. He read the heart attack stories about Don Gullett, 35.

"I didn't want that to be the right age," Darling was saying yesterday at lunch. "In this strange way, I wanted it to be a misprint, for him to be 45 or something instead of 35. I didn't want for us to have forgotten about someone that age, this quickly."

He came to the Yankees in November of 1976, after he had won one of the World Series games in the Reds sweep of the Yankees a month before. In the Imperial Ballroom of the Americana Hotel, it was announced that Don Gullett has signed a six-year contract worth $2 million. Gullett was one of the first of the big free agents. In '76, $2 million was perceived as riches beyond avarice. Gullett was supposed to be worth it. He was 25 years old. Now the lifetime record was 91-44, 2-0 in the Series.

On Nov. 18, 1976, in the Imperial Ballroom of the Americana Hotel, Gabe Paul called Don Gullett "a modern-day Whitey Ford."

But Don Gullett's shoulder was breaking down, had been breaking down for a long time. He had been an extraordinary high school athlete in Kentucky. But things happened once he got to the big leagues. A broken thumb here. A case of hepatitis there. Back spasms. By the middle of the 70s, the left shoulder hurt all the time. He looked big and strong as ever, but he began to play out a career between trips to the disabled list. He won 14 games for the Yankees in 1977, but spent a month on the disabled list. He was 4-2 in 1978. He pitched in Texas before the 1978 All-Star game, and never pitched another major league baseball game.

Gullett, kayoed at 27. Hard to believe.

"Every pitcher knows what happened to Donny Gullett can happen to them," Catfish Hunter said from North Carolina yesterday. "You can break something one day and never get it fixed. But pitchers can't let them think about the Gulletts, because if they do, they go crazy."

"The amazing thing about the kid was, he never complained, no matter how bad things got," said Yankees clubhouse man Nick Priore yesterday. "If he had a fault, it was that he smoked too many damn cigarettes."

After the mess with the rotator cuff and surgery by Dr. Frank Jobe (who put Tommy John's elbow back together), Gullett, the former phenom, became a series of headlines about false comebacks. "Gullett's coming back"—May 13, 1979. "Gullett takes the road back step-by-step"—Jan. 14, 1980. "Gullett strong in first trial at comeback"—Feb. 28, 1980. And on and on. But the shoulder never got better. Then, finally, this headline, on Oct. 25, 1980—"Yankees give up on Gullett's ailing arm."

Don Gullett was a former pitcher, a fulltime farmer.

At 11 a.m. Friday morning, working the fields with a friend named Milford Hunt, Gullett complained of chest pains and clutched his chest. "He wouldn't go to the doctor at first," Hunt was quoted as saying. After about half-an-hour, he agreed. "By the time we got to the doctor, Don was laying out across the front seat of the car." It was a heart attack. He was placed in the Intensive Care Unit of Scioto Memorial Hospital, and his condition labeled "serious." Yesterday that was changed to "stable" and they got ready to move Gullett out of ICU. He could be discharged within the week.

"He doesn't talk much about baseball since he retired," wife Cathy Gullett was saying yesterday from Scioto Memorial Hospital. "Every once in a while he'll be watching a game and say how much he misses the game, and pitching. But not very often. Don always has kept things bottled up. In fact, I think that's the problem here."

"I'm puzzled by what happened to Don, other than the fact that he's a smoker," said Gullett's physician, Dr. Grant Stevenson. "He looks the same as he always did, same as when he was pitching."

That is the problem. He is the same Gullett, for whom things always were going wrong, whose luck went bad and never did straighten out.

Don Gullett, 35.

• *1986*

Weaver salutes O's fans with 'battle cry' for 1980

BALTIMORE

I

t was all over now, and 108 wins, loud wins, had turned out to be one short. A light rain was falling on Memorial Stadium. There had been no miracle on 33d Street in Baltimore. In the Orioles' clubhouse, Wild Bill Hagy was trying some half-hearted cheers that no one was really listening to. But on the field, the season went on. There were some last, loud roars, the last vestiges of summer.

There were a lot of people out there, maybe a thousand, maybe more. They were standing in back of the Orioles dugout, and they were standing on the field. They were making a lot of noise. They did not want to leave. If they left, then the season was really over. These people wanted to hold onto the season for just a little while longer, here in the early morning. No one seemed to notice the rain.

Oriole players had been coming out in threes and fours to wave and clap and shake some hands, and each time they did, another roar would stretch out the season in Baltimore, carry on a wonderful little romance between a city and a team. The fans wanted to thank the players, every one of them, while they waited for the little man. No one was going anywhere until Earl Weaver came out and took a bow.

So finally a police lieutenant came into Weaver's office. He told Weaver about the people. "You gotta come, Earl," the man said. And here was Weaver, his cap back on his head, jogging through the runway, on his way to say goodbye to a season that fell apart in three games. He never did get the 109th win.

"Losin' one more than you win," Weaver had said a little earlier, "never did mean a ---- in this game."

"Have any of the players been out here?" Weaver said in the runway.

He was told that most of them had.

"Well, okay, then," he said, and charged up the dugout steps. Then the noise hit him. Weaver stopped, and turned toward the stands, and smiled. He took off his cap, and waved it. The cops tried to hold the people back, and couldn't. An hour after the season, chants of "Weaver! Weaver!" lit up Memorial Stadium. The little man stood there and drank it all in.

"1980!" he screamed at the people.

He turned to a small crowd of writers standing with him, and grinned. "I still get a contract for that year, I hope," he said. He waved his cap again, slammed it back on his head, and looked up into the stands.

"1980!" Weaver yelled.

A television reporter grabbed him, and a mini-cam moved into place. Weaver talked a little bit more about how it had all gone wrong, how his team had stopped hitting and the Pirates had started, how a 3-1 Series lead had been squandered for only the fourth time in all the history of baseball.

When the television reporter finished with him, Weaver stood in front of the dugout where he had worked his magic all season long, until his team stopped hitting, and choked away a World Series. For the moment, Weaver wasn't going anywhere. He did not want to let go of this season either. He put his hands on his hips in a familiar pose. He looked like he wanted one more shot, just one more, at the Pittsburgh Pirates.

"You know what the great thing about this game is?" he asked to no one in particular. "You know what it is? You get another shot next year."

He looked up into the crowd, blinking slightly in the rain.

"1980!" Weaver yelled. "We just got 102 wins to go!"

He seemed almost relieved to be back on the ballfield. He did not want it to end in an interview room, or in his office, or talking with Jimmy Carter, or handing the governor of Maryland an honorary Orioles cap. He stood there, tough and funny to the end, 10 feet in front of his dugout.

"Remember what I said after the fourth game?" Weaver had said in his office, having finished with presidents and governors. "I told all you guys that they wouldn't let us call ourselves world champions until we won that fourth game." He paused, and poured a little salt into his beer. "Why couldn't they make this damn thing three out of five, anyway?"

Earl thought he owned this World Series, on Saturday, in Pittsburgh. He needed one more win, and either Mike Flanagan or Jim Palmer or Scott McGregor was going to win it for him. But then the patchwork team which he had woven so brilliantly for all the 108 wins just fell apart on him, began to unravel; then the Pirates, led by a remarkable old man named Wilver Dornell Stargell just tore that patchwork team to pieces.

Stargell hit another home run last night. And in the eighth, a ballplayer named Eddie Murray, who was stripped naked in this World Series, flied out with the bases loaded. They weren't going to let Earl Weaver call his team the champs.

"You know," Weaver said in the office, "If Stargell don't hit that home run, and Murray's ball is down the line, you guys would be askin' me a million different questions, most of 'em about how smart I was."

Now he was on the field, and people were chanting his name, and Weaver wasn't noticing the rain, either. He waved his cap one last time, prompting one more thunderous cheer. He said, "I better be going now."

He walked down the dugout steps, turned and looked at the field one last time, headed down the runway. A friend came up and grabbed his hand. Weaver reached for his cigarettes.

"These bleepin' people are great," he said quietly. "In 1969, after the Mets cleaned our bleepin' clocks, they were all waitin' at the airport for us. Just great."

He was standing at the door of the clubhouse. "It's a great place to manage," he said, with a grin. "Even when you lose." He walked into the clubhouse, and a guard closed the door on a baseball season in Baltimore.

• *1979*

Baseball loses its headwaiter

I n the end, Bowie Kuhn walked into a room in Boston and brought more dignity to the job of baseball commissioner than the job deserves.

It won't change his record. It won't make him a great commissioner, because he never was that. Maybe his resignation yesterday was a bit of a grandstand play, since his head was about to be lopped off anyway. But he did leave with some style. You have to give the man that.

The only mystery he takes with him is why he wanted another term. Maybe he was worried about getting back into the law after being a glorified headwaiter for 14 years.

It has become a demeaning job, being commissioner of baseball, and Bowie Kuhn should have known better than anyone; if he did know, he never let on that he cared. You really do become a headwaiter to the owners, a well-paid greeter, a handshaker with portfolio. The owners give you enough power to dole out the odd suspension here and there, and they let you sit in while the networks tell how much they're going to pay to televise major league baseball. But what you really end up with are good seats at World Series and All-Star Games, and a chance to make a speech at Cooperstown every year. Bowie thought this was good work if you could find it.

He worked for the owners, not all of baseball, and they never let him forget it, and it only took five of them to do him in. Great job. Seventy percent of the bosses can be for you, and your head still goes rolling across the room. People like John Mc-Mullen and Nelson Doubleday, neither of whom knows a slider from an exploding scoreboard, went after Kuhn and got him.

It is because of Kuhn's opponents, people like McMullen and Doubleday and Ted Turner, that Kuhn became a hero as he tried to keep his job. Go up against people like that, and you walk away looking like the Pope. Kuhn was always a politician first and foremost—he came to the job in the first place on Walter O'Malley's coattails—but toward the end he damn near turned gallant in the public eye, mostly because he found himself in the ring with clowns and empty suits.

Kuhn is a good man; I am told that by friends, and people whose opinions I trust. They say he is decent and honorable, and I take them at their word. But not enough of that came across in his job. He was inconsistent, he was wrong a lot, he backed down and shut his mouth at the oddest times. Even considering the terrible strictures of his job, even though the owners want little more than a presentable bootlicker, it says here he could have done better.

It was a stupid, empty gesture to kick Mickey Mantle and Willie Mays out of baseball. He wouldn't let Edward DeBartolo buy the White Sox, because DeBartolo owned a racetrack and would have been an absentee owner. John Galbreath of the Pirates owned a racetrack. George Steinbrenner owned Tampa Bay Downs and was an absentee owner. But DeBartolo couldn't buy in. In its way, it was a classic Kuhn decision.

He let Steinbrenner come back early from the suspension following his felony conviction. He stopped Charles O. Finley from selling contracts that rightfully and legally belonged to him. It was always done "in the best interests of the game," or so he said. He tells us now about the growth of the game during his reign, but all during the reign he kept shouting about the dire economic future waiting for us down the free agent road. He wanted it both ways.

Maybe he couldn't have done anything during the strike in 1981. Still he disappeared without even trying to help. Then he supported that idiotic split season plan, which further cheapened an already shaky product. The end result was that the Cincinnati Reds had the best record in baseball and didn't make the playoffs, and the commish should have seen it coming.

He gets a lot of credit now for negotiating that new $1.2 billion television contract. Won't wash. You don't win that sort of money. It wins you. All the commissioner had to do when NBC and ABC started throwing money at him was this: Not drop it.

Maybe history will treat Kuhn more kindly than I have. Maybe he will look like a Greek god when a new headwaiter comes along. Again, he left in style yesterday.

But the bottom line today is the same as it was when he really lost his job a year ago: Since Kenesaw Mountain Landis there have been four baseball commissioners, and Bowie Kuhn was one of them.

• *1983*

Winter-time of dreams to future boy of summer

T he new bats were stacked neatly in the equipment room, down the aisle from the boxes and boxes of Bazooka bubble gum. There was an old list of "soups du jour" next to the bubble gum, but equipment manager Charlie Samuels said: "Forget the list, homemade soup every day this year." One brand new Mets cap sat on a box of brand new baseballs, as if standing guard. In the Mets clubhouse at the Joan Payson Baseball and Recreation Complex, it seemed like the baseball clock should read 20 minutes till pitchers and catchers.

The pitchers and catchers don't officially report until tomorrow. They don't officially take the field until Thursday. But it all seemed so close now in the Payson clubhouse. Mail neatly stacked in front of lockers (Gooden and Hernandez have the most; two for John Gibbons). Full lockers for the ones who are already here.

Giant apples don't fall here, the way they do on New Year's Eve in Times Square. Sirens don't sound, alarm bells don't ring. There will just be this big clatter of spikes tomorrow morning and you will be able to hear it everywhere.

In the equipment room, Charlie Samuels busied himself doing equipment room things. And in the middle of the clubhouse Sunday morning, down past where Hernandez will dress for 1986 and Gooden will dress and Darling and Carter and even Bobby Ojeda (No. 43, it's not too early to know), down where the orange stickers with blue lettering told of "Magadan, 65" and "Bautista, 67," there sat a baseball player. The bag said "Randall K. Myers."

He is a 23-year-old with a big left arm coming off a 5-9 minor league season, but the Mets like the arm. Maybe not for this season, but the Mets like the arm. The empty clubhouse at Payson was a fine, quiet place for Myers to ponder his own fine spring dreams.

The truck with all the Mets equipment had been unloaded Saturday. It was as if it had unloaded Myers—lefty trying to figure out when the future starts—too.

"I think everybody starts to get the itch after the bowl games on January 1st." Myers said. "I hit January and the world changes."

In the last week, Myers had been working out on his own at Payson with Roger McDowell, Doug Sisk, Bruce Berenyi, Mookie Wilson, Jesse Orosco, Randy Niemann, Ron Gardenhire. A lot of them had shown up earlier, before the gates opened, and probably would be back later. But Randy Myers, out of Clark Jr. College and Vancouver, Wash., with a fastball in the 90s sometimes, wanted to get some throwing in.

"You have to feel this way," he said. "You have to feel that if you explode, you can make the big club. If that happened, I don't know what I'd be doing—long relief, short relief—but I have to believe I'd be doing something."

Like everyone else, Myers knows the Mets could be obese with pitchers if Sisk and Berenyi are healthy. You have Gooden, Darling, Fernandez, Aguilera, Ojeda, Berenyi as starting names. Orosco, McDowell, Lynch, Sisk, Gorman, Leach, Niemann are bullpen names. Randy Myers, if you want to throw him in—on the chance that he will explode, you know—makes 14 names in all.

"Someone is going to get traded," Myers said. "You look at the numbers and you have to expect that to happen. But who would want to get traded away from this particular team at this point in time?"

The spring is full of possibilities; it is what the Lord himself, or Abner Doubleday, or somebody intended. Myers will be a Met or Triple-A player or traded. He did not really take pitching seriously until after his first year at Clark Jr. College. His career plans were to be a machinist or an auto mechanic. Then the summer he was 18 he had a big American Legion tournament and now he is "Myers, 48" across from "Sisk, 39" and about a hundred baseball miles down from "Gooden, 16." But Myers is dreaming his dreams.

"The brass here, they know pitching," he said. "If you do the job, even if you're coming off 5-9, you can get yourself promoted."

He wore gray sweatpants and high-topped white leather basketball shoes and when he opened his bag there was a lefthander's glove and a catcher's mitt; before it is official about pitchers and catchers, the pitchers carry catcher's mitts, just in case they run into somebody willing to have a throw. In this case, Myers' battery mate was Bob Costas of NBC Sports, who was in the area and came by to dip a toe into the baseball season.

In a little while, Wally Backman showed up on the field. Someone mentioned to the second baseman that he was a couple of weeks early.

"If you'd been shoveling the snow I've been shoveling in Forest Grove, Oregon," he said, "you wouldn't think I'm here early at all. I think last year I was here on the first of February."

When, Backman was asked, did he first get the itch over the winter?

"It wasn't the winter," Backman said. "It was the fall. I was ready to play again the month after the season ended. You think you need a rest, you think you need to get away, then you're sitting in front of the television set thinking, 'Damn, let's go!' "

Backman went and got into some sweats, got his glove, ran out onto the field at the Payson complex and began playing catch with Randy Myers in the perfect Florida midday sun. Backman got loose slowly and Myers' ball began to make bigger and bigger popping noises. In a while, Myers would throw Backman grounders. Met and aspiring Met alone on a ballfield. The baseball wheel began to groan and turn, ever so slightly.

Pitchers and catchers tomorrow. Officially.

Yeah.

• 1986

Gabe's golden anniversary

H• is first spring training was in Monroe, Louisiana, in 1928, with the Rochester Red Wings, who played in a ballpark whose name Gabe Paul no longer remembers. Paul was 18 years old that spring, and was sent with the Red Wings by the sports editor of the Rochester Democrat-Chronicle, who needed someone to work cheap and send back stories as a stringer. Gabe Paul liked the job, apparently. In Monroe, Louisiana, he began a life of baseball.

"I was ambitious," Gabe Paul was saying now. "Once I got there, I started sending back stories to all three papers in Rochester. Not too bad for a kid. When spring training was over, Warren Giles offered me a job fulltime with the Red Wings, and that was that."

In the warm, clear Arizona afternoon, all sun and green grass, Paul adjusted his big straw hat and chuckled softly.

"When I told my father I was getting paid for watching baseball games, he asked me when I was going to get a job and go to work," Paul said. "And if he could see me now, after all these years, he'd probably ask me the same thing."

He was sitting in back of home plate at Hi Corbett Field, wearing the big sun hat and a pink Lacoste shirt and blue cotton slacks the color of the sky, and he was watching the touring Japanese team, the Taiyo Whales,

76

playing the Indians. At the age of 70, Gabe Paul's life in baseball continues, with both charm and vigor. The Indians are his team. And this is his 50th spring training.

Since 1928, he has missed just two baseball springs—those he lost to World War II. Other than that, there have been 50 years of afternoons like this one, in Monroe and Orlando and Tampa and Fort Lauderdale and Tucson: 70 degree afternoons, with a soft wind blowing across the outfield, from left to right, and Paul watching a baseball team take shape before the April trip north.

"This is it, my golden anniversary year," he said. In the shade the hat provided, there was just a trace of a smile. "It's still not such a bad job, is it?"

On the field, Indians righthander Steve Narleski had gotten a fastball up to Skip James, one of two American players on the Japanese team (the other is old friend Felix Millan, who did not make the trip to the States). James hit a hanging liner toward the gap in leftcenter. Sadly, the ball and Indians leftfielder Mike Hargrove missed connections, and the ball rolled to the wall. Paul interrupted his conversation only briefly, leaning across a visitor and poking his general manager, Phil Seghi, with a finger.

"He was playing too shallow," said Paul quietly. "Then he takes a step in when the ball's hit."

In his 50th spring, Paul was asked what appeals to him most about this baseball cerem. "Oh, I guess it's still watching the young fellows come along and develop," he said. "You see this kid come along who's green as grass, and all of a sudden you have a polished gentleman and a proven performer."

He stayed with the Red Wings from 1928 to 1936, scrambling for Giles, learning all parts of the operation, doing every office job you can do: Traveling secretary, scouting sometimes, running the concessions. In October of 1936, he went to the Reds as a p.r. man. He stayed for 24 years, finally becoming general manager in 1951. He became general manager of the Indians in 1961, president in 1963.

He was Baseball Executive of the Year in 1956. He was accorded that same honor in 1974, after he had come to the Yankees and started them in the business of becoming champions again. When George Steinbrenner came to New York—you can find out about this in the Book of Genesis—he had one powerful natural resource with him: Mr. Gabe Paul. Do not ever forget that.

And now Paul is back with the Indians, his real love. He returned as president and chief executive officer in 1978. The reasoning, Paul explained, was quite simple.

"This is," he said, "my final challenge in baseball. That's it, exactly."

It is a healthy challenge. The Indians play in the American League East, which has other tenants known as the Orioles, Yankees, Red Sox, Brewers and Tigers, all of whom must be considered good bets, in the spring anyway, to finish ahead of the Cleveland Indians. And the Indians had a 81-80 record last season, closing 38-28 after Dave Garcia replaced Jeff Torborg as manager. The AL East is going to be Afghanistan.

"I think we'll be better," is all Paul will say. "I think we have this thing moving in the right direction. Other than that, who knows? If there's one thing you can't do, it's worry about the other guys. It will drive you crazy."

So Paul, without the Yankee money now, keeps tinkering with his team. Bobby Bonds goes to St. Louis, and John Denny and Jerry Mumphrey come to the Indians. Then Mumphrey goes to San Diego for Bob Owchinko, a 25-year old lefty whom Paul thinks is going to win a lot of games in the American League. More tinkering: Paul signs Jorge Orta, a free agent who can hit. He'll play rightfield for the Indians, after playing second base for eight years in Chicago.

The outfield will be Orta in right, Rick Manning, coming off a poor year (.259-51 RBI-67 runs year), in center and Hargrove (.325 for the Indians in 100 games) in left. The rest of the lineup is pretty well set: Gary Alexander and Ron Pruitt catching, Andre (26 homers, 93 RBI) Thornton at first, Duane Kuiper at second and Toby Harrah at third. There is a very big fight going on at shortstop between a lot of consonants. Rookie Jerry Dybzinksi is pushing incumbent Tom Veryzer.

"Dybzinksi's a local kid, out of Cleveland State," said Paul. "And he's got a real good chance. Veryzer has played good ball for us here, but it's gonna be a helluva battle."

Pitching? Gabe Paul needs pitching. He has probably been talking about pitching across all 50 years. Rick Waits, who won 16, is his best. Denny and Owchinko will probably be in the rotation. The remaining spots will be fought for by 6-4 Len Barker (down to 220 from 240), Mike Paxton, Wayne Garland, Dan Spillner and Rogelio

Moret. Sid Monge, one of the best relief pitchers in baseball, is still the gem of the bullpen.

"Garcia's run a very good camp," said Paul. "We're going to be better."

In front of him, spring moved along, unhurried. Opening Day, in Anaheim, was still weeks away. The team was taking shape. The green kids were trying to become gentlemen. In Gabe Paul's 50th spring.

It was now 3:25 in the afternoon at Hi Corbett Field. The Taiyo Whales led 6-4. Only Gabe Paul noticed it was time for the seventh inning stretch.

"C'mon," he said. "Everybody up."

• *1980*

We hope you've enjoyed your stay at Cross Keys Inn

ST. LOUIS

When we last left Billy Martin as manager of the New York Yankees, the little disciplinarian was in a hallway at the Cross Keys Inn, Baltimore. Martin was in his boxer shorts.

According to an eyewitness from the *New York Daily News*, Martin was also drunk. His broken arm was at his side, but he was still screaming for pitcher Ed Whitson to come out of his room and fight some more.

"I know what room you're in!" the manager of the 1985 Yankees yelled in the hallway of the Cross Keys Inn. "I'll fight you right here!"

Martin had already tried to fight Whitson in the bar of the Cross Keys, then the parking lot, but, what the heck, the night was still young.

It was Martin's idea of the way you do it in a pennant race.

"There's a way Yankees are supposed to act," Billy always says.

Well, there you go.

Billy Martin is clearly the man to lead the Yankees back to baseball's promised land, now that he is back as Yankee manager for the fifth time.

Steinbrenner has hired Martin. Now there is an idea that has always worked real well in the past. It is like Gary Hart trying to patch things up with Donna Rice. It is like Jim Bakker going back to the motel with Jes-

80

sica, booking the same room, it holds so many wonderful memories.

Steinbrenner and Martin? It has turned the New York Yankees into the Benny Hill skit of baseball.

Billy Martin, the broadcaster, was considered such a positive force around the Yankees the last couple of years that he was kept quarantined from the ballplayers on the road.

Maybe Steinbrenner should consider trying it now that Billy is manager again, so he doesn't end up in the hall in his boxers this time around.

It would have been a nice picture to put out there with his plaque at Yankee Stadium, you bet.

Martin was quoted as saying how excited he was to have the chance to bring exciting and winning baseball back to Yankee Stadium. If the Yankees are as exciting on the field as Billy is at the hotel, they are going to be more fun than the Metrodome.

Steinbrenner's Yankees. They win 90 games a year, and they still have become a baseball joke. A Benny Hill skit. You think the Homer Hankies are dumb? Really? Did you watch Steinbrenner on "60 Minutes"? America thinks New York's baseball season, in the form of the Yankee principal owner, is dumber.

Think about it. You get done with the Homer Hankies, you can throw them away. Yankee fans are stuck with George Steinbrenner.

He is never out of season.

He gets on "60 Minutes," he tries to tell everybody that his butting out of the Yankee season is what knocked the Yankees out of first place. You remember how it really happened, the hysterical statement he issued in Detroit, you laugh.

You can't call the man a liar, because he believes this material. You wonder why the man doesn't look to be in better shape, the way he tries to throw around material like this.

He likes to parade all the people who come back to the Yankees. Tommy John and Rick Cerone. Gene Michael as a scout. Bucky Dent as a minor league manager. Steinbrenner gets them back because no one else wants them, he overpays them, then kids himself into believing that they are loyal to him.

And there isn't a ballplayer in the room who would step forward for Steinbrenner. They just take his money.

He talks about building character in ballplayers, making them strong, like he's the No. 1 Boy Scout of the world.

Steinbrenner talks about the fact that the Yankees have won

more games than any team in baseball the last 10 years, but he gets rid of managers because they don't win the World Series. There is a different bottom line for them, a different bottom line for him.

He makes up the rules as he goes along. He wins. The Yankees lose.

The Yankees have won more games than any team in baseball the last 60 years, too. What's the man's point?

Steinbrenner paints himself as a baseball Patton, but doesn't have the heart to break ranks with the other owners and sign Jack Morris or Tim Raines, or Andre Dawson, any one of whom might have gotten the Yankees through the hard times and won them the American League East.

He doesn't have the heart of the ballplayers he criticizes.

He doesn't have the heart to face the press when he brings Martin back to manage.

Now the Yankees are the other team in New York. The Mets drew 3 million fans, probably will do it again next year. The Mets got all the important headlines. Now Steinbrenner props up Billy Martin, plays Gary-and-Donna. Jim-and-Jessica.

In the midst of the World Series, he brings Billy in from the Cross Keys hallway and puts him back in the manager's office. Piniella goes upstairs; Woody Woodward, a decent man, goes out the door.

So it is a big day for George Steinbrenner. He's got a shipbuilding company whose stock was dropping long before yesterday and a fourth-place baseball team, but look at the headlines he gets one more time with Billy Martin.

Look at the time he got on "60 Minutes." Where does he go from here? Landmark status?

• *1987*

Shooting from the Lip I

The Sunday column is a lot of fun...and more work. It gives me a chance to touch on about thirty different things, instead of one. There are column ideas that turned out to be worth just a couple of lines, jokes, lines I hear from athletes or friends, impressions of things happening in books and movies and all parts of the newspaper. Some people love the non-sports references, some hate them. Interestingly enough, a lot of the mail I get on "Shooting from the Lip" is from women, whatever that says.

Anyway, I've decided to include some of my favorites in this collection. The joy of the one-liners is their immediacy; they're not supposed to have a terrific shelf life. But since they are a big part of what I do in the *Daily News*, I thought some of them might as well be preserved.

*****

Afternoon baseball in the middle of the week is like summer camp for grownups.

Larry Holmes looks like he's been locked inside the Haagen Dazs factory since he lost the title to Michael Spinks.

New Orleans is the Times Square of cities.

To book an act older than the Niekro brothers, you'd have to reunite Kukla, Fran and Ollie.

What if Columbia University is allowed to recruit dumber players and still loses?

From what I saw of the chests of Tim Witherspoon and Tony Tubbs, Dolly Parton should have done the blow-by-blow.

Pinklon Thomas and Trevor Berbick were fighting underwater, right?

Looking back, it probably would have been to much to expect Navy to beat Libya and Duke the same week.

Did the Indians win 10 straight or did the American League lose 10 straight, that's what I'd like to know?

You hear a lot of people in saloons talking about the Goodwill Games?

Sometimes I think I'd like Mike Tyson's next fight to be against Ronald Reagan, Jr.

Irving Fryar and the missus, I'm thinking, aren't exactly Lucy and Ricky for the '80s.

When Jesse Orosco announced he wanted to be traded, it wasn't like they had to get Frank Cashen's head out of the oven.

I guess you ought to hear this from me: Oil Can Boyd's mother is named Sweetie.

How come when a sports figure is arrested for drunk driving there isn't the same thunderclap of noise on the sports pages as there is for dope?

At least professional boxing keeps Roberto Duran off the streets, right?

If the golfers at the U.S. Open thought the Shinnecock Hills crowds were tough, I'd like to see them play 18 holes at Madison Square Garden in front of New York Rangers fans.

A tennis player's idea of heartbreak is when the courtesy car is late.

When St. Louis Cardinals owner Bill Bidwill finally leaves Busch Stadium, they'll have to spray his office.

Teaming up Vin Scully with Tim McCarver would have been like putting Bob Hope with Letterman.

Let me get this straight: The Rangers traded for a goon and his name is Petit?

AUSSIES, GRASS COURTS, STREETFIGHTERS, CLASSY LADIES...

I sometimes joke that I have done a lot of hard time covering tennis, that a lot of those Chris Evert matches didn't exactly induce labor. But I love the one-on-one of tennis, the closeness of the two players, the grand, theatrical setting a place like Wimbledon provides. The tennis columns I like best are the ones from Wimbledon. The Aussies have always seemed to cover the sport with a flinty class, from Hoad to Laver to Cash. Jimmy Connors is simply one of the great subjects a columnist could ever have; Connors and I are the same age, and I have seen his whole show. The classy lady is Miss Evert.

•

Part 4

Fate kept Hoad from being one of greatest

e sat quietly at the end of a bench in a special section for members of the All-England Club, watching Martina Navratilova play Dianne Fromholtz on court No. 1, below him. He wore a navy blazer and gray slacks, and his tie was undone around a thick neck as big as the rest of him. The hair is still as blond as it was when he was the golden boy of tennis, and Wimbledon, but Lew Hoad is 43 years old now.

So only the old members sitting on the bench with him, and a few young ones, knew who sat with them, that this was the great Lew Hoad who once, when he was young and the back had not yet betrayed him, could beat anyone.

The old player Gardner Mulloy spotted him as he was leaving the match, which Navratilova now had well in hand in the third set. Mulloy smiled at the sight of him. This was Hoadie, the man who could hit tennis balls like no other man, and one who would have a beer with you. Lew Hoad, you see, also knew how to live a life.

"How's the back, all right now, Mate?" Gardner Mulloy asked. Last September, after more than 20 years of pain, Lew Hoad finally had a back operation. It was too late to save what would have probably been the greatest career ever in tennis, but enough to enable him to get out of bed in the morning without a knife in that back.

"It's fine, now," Lew Hoad said.

"Ready to play?" Gardner Mulloy asked.

"I doubt that," Lew Hoad said with a smile.

In a day at Wimbledon which centered around a young star named Tracy Austin and a champion named Billie Jean King, it seemed right that Lew Hoad should be on the grounds of the All-England Club, watching tennis. He once owned the All-England Club, and Wimbledon. Lew Hoad was the Mickey Mantle of tennis, a big, strong, good-looking blond-haired monster who could simply do everything there was to do in tennis, do it with silly ease. That was before the back and injury took it away from him, all of it, too soon.

Hoad was asked yesterday if it still hurts him that he was able to play only five Wimbledons.

"I don't think about those things," said Lew Hoad quietly. "I just remember that I had a pretty good run."

He had a pretty good run. He and his buddy Ken Rosewall came out of Australia to play Wimbledon in 1953, when they were both 18, and they won the doubles here. Later that year, he and Rosewall would team up to beat the United States in the Davis Cup, and the world began to hear about these kids Hoad and Rosewall. Mostly they heard about this golden boy named Lew Hoad. They heard how he made tennis into child's play.

At 21 he won his first Wimbledon, beating Rosewall in the final. That was 1956. He almost won the Grand Slam (Australia, French, Wimbledon, U.S. Open) that year, but Rosewall beat him in the final at Forest Hills. In 1957, he won Wimbledon again, beating Ashley Cooper, ruining him, 6-2, 6-1, 6-2 in the final.

Wimbledon had never quite seen anyone quite like this Lew Hoad, who could run and hit all the shots, hit them with power and precision.

And then, afterward, he would go out with you and drink as many beers as you wanted to drink, and maybe sing some songs.

Hoadie.

"He was the most virtuoso tennis player I have ever seen, for sure," says Lance Tingay, the distinguished tennis correspondent for London's Daily Telegraph. Lance Tingay has not missed a day of Wimbledon tennis since 1932. He knows what he is talking about.

"He was a brute with an iron wrist," Tingay continued. "That one year, 1957, no one could have beaten him. If he played that way this year, no one would beat him still. Lew Hoad could do everything."

At the Wimbledon Ball that year, Hoad raised a drink at the end of the evening, and yelled that he'd be toasting them all again next year. He would never play Wimbledon again until the late 60s, in a last hurrah.

He turned pro the next year, for a lot of money, and played a couple of years on that night-to-night, city-to-city circuit that Jack Kramer put together. Pancho Gonzales was with him, and Pancho Segura, and Frank Sedgeman and Rosewall and Ashley Cooper. Hoad played in 1958 and 1959 and into 1960, winning some, losing some, the back getting worse and worse on the hard indoor courts, turning each serve into a tiny piece of hell.

He'd first hurt it at Wimbledon in 1956, but played on, saying nothing, winning the tournament. "That's the way we did it in those days," he said. He would eventually see doctors all over the world. No one helped him, not really. He tried traction, he tried acupuncture. He tried everything. The back kept getting worse.

"They just didn't know about backs in those days," he said quietly yesterday.

In 1960, Lew Hoad retired from fulltime tennis. He would play a little here, a little there, filling in. In the late 60's he even came back to play Wimbledon and the Open. But Lew Hoad was done in 1960. He was 26 at the time.

He says now he doesn't know how long he would have played tennis, even if he'd been healthy. "I'm not built that way," he said. "I wanted to live." But 26 was too soon.

Last fall, he finally had two discs removed from his back in a four-hour operation at the New York Hospital for Special Surgery. When the surgery was over, Dr. Richard Frazier said this to Gene Barakat, Hoad's lifelong friend: "How did the man walk around this long?" The discs were a mess.

Hoad was asked at court No. 1 yesterday afternoon if, when he was young and healthy, anyone could beat him. Hoad thought for a moment.

"Not really," he said finally, then got up to tour the grounds of the All-England Club, which he owned once.

• *1978*

A time for hello, goodbye

S. uddenly it was match point at the grandstand court of Louis Armstrong Stadium, and Lori McNeil was getting ready to say hello to this U.S. Open as Chris Evert said goodbye. Lori McNeil, a 23-year-old black woman, came to the moment all the way from public courts at MacGregor Park in Houston. Evert came to the moment from one of the grandest histories the Open, the sport, has known.

It was the third set of the quarter-finals of the Open. McNeil had five games, Evert had four. Evert had 15-40 on her serve, McNeil had two match points. McNeil was young, Evert was not. Evert had made it to the semifinals of the Open 16 straight times. But she had not been able to hold her serve against Lori McNeil for what seemed like an hour, or a year.

In the quarterfinals of the Open, on the grandstand court, Chris Evert was the past trying to hold off the present. The ball went into play. Now here came the ball shoulder high for Lori McNeil, backhand side. Like a hanging curve. She did not so much hit a winner as dismiss the ball the way she had dismissed the great Evert over the last two sets.

At an Open where there has been so much talk and theory about why there are no American kids doing anything in tennis, and no black Americans doing anything at all, Lori McNeil made the semifinals by beating Chris Evert, 3-6, 6-2, 6-4.

The two women shook hands at the net when it was over, and the applause at the grandstand court was for both of them, winner and loser, upstart and champion, MacGregor Park and tennis legend. Hello and goodbye. Lori McNeil stopped to do a television interview after the rackets had been packed. Chris walked into the shadows between the grandstand court and the stadium court. She handed a red Wilson racket bag to a man named Don, who wore a white shirt and red Wilson suspenders. "I'll go straight to the interview," she said, and handed him her wristbands.

Lori McNeil was on the court, in white shirt and black skirt, white towel around her neck, soaking wet, drinking in the day. She finished the television interview, went over and hugged John Wilkerson, her coach. John Wilkerson runs the tennis program at MacGregor Park, has for a long time. He saw something once in two black children, one named Zina Garrison, the other Lori McNeil.

First Garrison came to MacGregor Park, then her friend. Wilkerson first saw Lori McNeil hit a ball when she was 10. The other day, McNeil had to beat Zina Garrison to make the quarterfinals. It was a splendid match, relegated to court No. 3. Perhaps it was too colorful for the stadium or grandstand.

Even yesterday, it was still the grandstand for Lori McNeil. Tomorrow, she will finally get to play the big room at the U.S. Open, against Steffi Graf. As Arthur Ashe said yesterday, "They can't keep her out of the stadium now." Then Ashe said Lori McNeil's win over Chris Evert was the biggest thing for black tennis players in this country since he, Ashe, beat Roy Emerson in Forest Hills in 1965.

In the interview later, someone asked Lori McNeil if she had "arrived." The 11th seed smiled and said, "All I've done is arrive in the semifinals." All she wanted to talk about was tomorrow. John Wilkerson said, "All I'm thinking about is tomorrow."

While Lori McNeil went to get a shower, Chris Evert went to the interview room. It was no easier in there than it had been against McNeil. She would not have the chance to win a Grand Slam tournament for the 14th consecutive year. She would not make the semis of the Open for the 17th straight time. For only the second time in her life, she had been beaten before the semifinals of a major. People wanted to talk about all that.

She was the legend who could not hold her serve, and lost. Lori McNeil came in on first serves, second serves, anything. She pounded forehand approaches, she found this angle and that angle for volleys, she put it all in reverse and got underneath famous Evert lobs and knocked them away. Evert was not an immortal yesterday, just a 32-year-old woman fighting to stay near the top of her sport.

Chris Evert made wonderful gets in the last few games. She picked up short balls and knifed a couple of old-time backhands cross-court. But she could not hold her serve. McNeil was over her, every point, like a full-court press. Then at 15-30 in the last game, Chris had a short forehand, easy forehand, the kind that used to make her seem like a terminator.

This time, she just looked 32, going on 33. She golfed it long. Old golfers miss short putts. Old tennis players hit sitters long. It was match point. Then came the backhand volley from McNeil, and goodbye.

In the interview room, someone said that Evert didn't seem as disappointed as she had a year ago, when she was beaten by Helena Sukova in the semis.

Chris Evert said, "What do you expect me to do, start crying in front of all these people?" No one expected that, not from her. Someone also talked about streaks ending, chances for more history lost, questions that were really about her being so close to the end.

"I'm sure all those things will hit me later on," she said. At the side of the room, Colette Evert stood on tiptoes, heard her daughter say, "As hard as I tried, I couldn't get my body to do the things I wanted it to do." It is what happens with aging athletes, every single one.

When Lori McNeil got to the interview room, someone wanted to know about her being broken when she served for the match at 5-3. McNeil said, "I'd been breaking her serve all along. I figured if I kept coming in, I could do it again."

Then Lori McNeil said, "There is so much history behind it." She meant beating Chris Evert at the Open.

When Evert left the interview room yesterday, she did one more television interview between the grandstand and the stadium. The man with the red suspenders still had her racket case. There was Colette Evert, and Chris' boyfriend, Andy Mill. A few other friends. There were a couple of photographers. They all walked underneath the stadium, and the people lined up above began to applaud Chris Evert, thank her for a lot of yesterdays at the U.S. Open.

Just then in the stadium, out in the sunlight, Steffi Graf was being interviewed on television. Graf had just beaten Pam Shriver. Like Lori McNeil, young Graf talked about tomorrow.

- *1987*

Connors slams death's door shut

T•here were three match points now for Jimmy Connors at Centre Court, at the finish of this match that was like his career. He had been as good as he could be against Mikael Pernfors, despite losing the first two sets, 6-1, 6-1. He had given as much as he could give. Someday, Bjorn Borg will wonder if he could have done more with his skill. John McEnroe wonders already. Connors will never wonder.

Jimmy Connors has gone the distance. Connors has squeezed this one extraordinary tennis game bone-dry. One more time yesterday, in one more big match, he forgot what year it was.

Billie Jean King said later, "Jimmy will never wake up in the middle of the night when he's 45 years old and ask, 'What if?' "

But there was still the last point to be won at Centre Court, at the end of an afternoon Centre Court will not forget. Connors is that big line from "The Untouchables": Never stop fighting until the fight is done. Connors knows. His right thigh was cramping. He is 34 years old, too old in a young man's game. He is an American man when they don't win anything in tennis. He took a last deep breath at Centre Court and served at Mikael Pernfors, and grunted as he came over the ball, and got ready to make sure the fight was done.

In the interview room, Connors was asked if the

right thigh, which began to cramp in the fifth game of the fifth set, ever made him think he would not be able to finish. Connors threw a look at the questioner that was like a punch.

"I was always gonna finish," Jimmy Connors said. "Even if I had to crawl."

The serve went over the net and it came back and then here was Jimmy Connors leaning into one last backhand crosscourt, one of those backhands that magically got longer and meaner when it was 6-1, 6-1, 4-1 for Mikael Pernfors. Pernfors could have chased the backhand out of Centre Court and out to Church Road and never caught it.

It was over, after three hours and 39 minutes, at 7:56 on a London evening, as the last of the sun disappeared behind the Old Vic of a tennis theater. In one of the greatest comebacks in Wimbledon history, in tennis history, Connors had won, 1-6, 1-6, 7-5, 6-4, 6-2. Against all odds, against a player good enough to make the final of the French Open last year, Connors won his 91st singles match at Wimbledon and played himself into the quarterfinals.

"He is such a great hustler," Pernfors said. "If he gets the opportunity to come back, he's gonna take it."

"It has to be," said past champion Lew Hoad, "as good an effort as anybody has ever given here."

Connors is a champion. He is not a nice champion. But there is no rule to say you have to be. Connors has defaulted matches in his career. He has quit because of injuries. He has been vulgar, every bit the guttersnipe McEnroe has been at his worst. He has been a graceless loser and a snappish winner. There is a lot of Billy Martin in Jimmy Connors.

But across a career that really began in 1972, there has been so little quit in Connors. Borg was more talented. Borg had more serve, more speed, more topspin. McEnroe had all the shots the Lord can give; McEnroe was the whole orchestra. Connors was a groundstroker with heart, the way Chris Evert has been a groundstroker with heart. McEnroe beat up Borg; Borg didn't want to play any more. McEnroe became unstable, took a sabbatical, has a career in eclipse at the age of 28.

And Jimmy Connors keeps going. He is a tennis player. He keeps playing. Borg came along, then McEnroe. Connors was dismissed. Connors came back and won Wimbledon and the Open in 1982, eight years after he'd won his first Wimbledon, his first Open. Now he is 34, close to 35. He was the last American in the draw at the French Open. He is the last American in the draw at Wimbledon. He plays Slobodan Zivojinovic in the quarterfinals today.

"I can still play," Jimmy Connors said in the interview room.

He did not sit in a chair in the interview room. He did not want the leg to begin cramping again. He leaned forward into the microphone.

"What I did today is all fine and good," he said. "But all it means is now I'm in the hunt."

He was asked another question about the comeback and said, "The best thing I did today was grind and fight."

We had heard it all before, in press rooms all over the world. It is easy to joke about Connors talking about grinding and fighting, spilling blood, all that. It is a routine. There is phony in Connors. It is too easy to remember him grabbing his crotch, swearing at umpires, walking off the court against Ivan Lendl in the Lipton tournament last year. It is easy to remember him skipping a ceremony for past champions at the centenary Wimbledon in 1977.

He could have done it better off the court. There could have been more grace, less mean spirits. But maybe those mean spirits helped make him great, a champion, an American tennis immortal. The wonder boys go away. Connors keeps carrying the flag. Others would have curled up into a little ball at Centre Court yesterday. Connors' tennis obituary was being written in the press box: "Jimmy Connors, age 34, perhaps made his last appearance at Centre Court yesterday..."

And Connors began to squeeze another day out of his tennis game, another day out of this Wimbledon. He gave himself at least a chance to win one more Wimbledon at a time when he has been counted out again.

At Wimbledon, they will always talk about Jimmy Connors and Pernfors and Connors making his stand after Pernfors had won 16 of the first 19 games. The first set took 29 minutes. The second set took 29 minutes. It didn't take Pernfors long to get to 4-1 in the third. Then Connors made his stand. Go figure the man's heart.

"I didn't have enough time to get embarrassed the first two sets," Connors said. "I was getting my butt beat."

But he came back and won yesterday. Once more, he filled Centre Court with his moxie, his grunting, his mouth, his groundstroking game, his heart most of all. The other guy had the lead. The other guy was 23. Didn't matter.

When it was 6-1, 6-1, a British reporter turned to me and said, "At least you're here for Connors' sunset." Ten minutes after the match, the sun set behind Centre Court. It went down. Not Connors. The twilight of his career is just like his career. Billie Jean is right. When it is over for Connors, there will be no questions, no might-have-beens.

• *1987*

Ashe recovering like champ

"Your first reaction is, Wait a minute, I can't be having a heart attack. I'm young. I'm skinny. I eat right. Heart attack? Me? I went to the gym yesterday."

—Arthur Ashe

aniel Castro, the attendant, pushed the bed carrying Arthur Ashe through some double doors and out of the Paul Felix Warburg Cardiac Care Unit, on the fourth floor of New York Hospital. It is one of the intensive care units of the hospital, specializing in heart ailments, and heart attacks. Arthur Ashe, a 35-year-old tennis player, had spent the last four nights in Room 421 of the Warburg Unit because last Tuesday Ashe suffered a myo-cardiac infarction of the back wall of his heart. He had suffered a heart attack. A real heart attack. Him.

Now, on Saturday afternoon, Ashe was being moved out of intensive care, out of Room 421, to another room, on the 15th floor. "The place for normal people," Ashe said in the morning when nurse Mary McConnell told him he was moving. Ashe grinned. McConnell took the IV needle out of Ashe's left arm.

Then he said to Nurse McConnell, "Can you believe that I had a heart attack?"

Castro pushed the bed into a long freight elevator. Another attendant followed, pushing a cart loaded with flowers, and cards, and Ashe's huge cassette player. Ashe wore blue pajamas. Resting on his stomach was his reading material for the past few days: a folder filled with literature about myo-cardiac infarctions.

"This is about right," Ashe said. "The patient is supposed to show improvement within two to five days, as the blood system carries the damaged tissue away."

No one in the elevator said anything.

"How'd the Yankees do last night?" Ashe said.

He was told they'd lost, 1-0.

"I figured there was no way they could play baseball last night," Ashe said quietly. "Such a tragedy. Such a waste."

A friend in the elevator asked Ashe how his father, Arthur Sr., was. Ashe put his arms behind his head, and closed his eyes. When he spoke, it was in a quiet, tired voice.

"My dad gets out of the hospital Tuesday," he said. "After his *second* heart attack." The elevator doors opened at the 15th floor, and Daniel Castro pushed Ashe toward the room at New York Hospital where he will spend at least another week while his doctor, Steven Sheidt, closely watches the great heart of Arthur Ashe.

Ashe has always been a great tennis player. This year, he made a marvelous comeback from heel surgery and eye trouble. But Ashe has always been more important as a man.

He first felt pain in his chest Monday night. It was severe; he thought he was just sick to his stomach, having gas pains. Heart attack? Don't be silly. On Tuesday, perhaps the most murderously hot and humid day of this murderous week, he did two tennis clinics. The first was for Vitas Gerulaitis' Youth Foundation, in the Bronx. People there thought he did not look well.

"I think something might be wrong with Arthur," Vitas said to his mother. "Look at him sweat. The guy never sweats like that."

But Ashe was scheduled for another clinic, at the East River Tennis Club. He was going. Ashe fulfills commitments, always has. He is the greatest tennis ambassador there has ever been, one who has understood best that you must give something back to the game.

"All he does is give," his friend Mike O'Shea said at New York Hospital yesterday. "I've never seen anyone like him."

At East River, the pain in his chest became worse, much worse than Monday night: "It was constant pressure, terrible pressure, like someone had stuck a fist down there and closed it around everything." There happened to be a doctor at the club. He examined Ashe. Then Ashe described the pain he had felt Monday night, the pain he was feeling at that moment. The doctor sorted everything out for him.

"You're going to the hospital," he said.

"Let me tell everyone I'm leaving," Ashe said.

"You're going to the hospital, now," the doctor said. The doctor drove him to the emergency room at New York Hospital. Ashe walked in. He was admitted. Within minutes, he was in the Warburg Cardiac Care Unit.

"I am a lucky man," Ashe said. "Usually, when someone suffers this kind of heart attack...if they're not in the shape I'm in...well, they don't walk into the hospital. They're *brought* in."

He was lying on a bed in the large private room on the 15th floor. The window to his right offered a view of the East River. There was a television in the room; he could watch television again. Daniel Castro placed the flowers on a table in the corner of the room. Ashe asked the nurse to shut off the air conditioner. The nurse did that for him, and left.

"Well, here I am," he said casually. "Just your basic myo-cardiac infarction of the old back wall of the heart."

The doctors did not confirm it was actually a heart attack until Friday afternoon, after three days of tests. On Thursday, he was injected with a special radioactive material that showed there was indeed damage done to his heart. The next afternoon, Dr. Sheidt came in and told Ashe he indeed had suffered a heart attack. It wasn't the end of the world, Dr. Sheidt said. He was a young man, Dr. Sheidt said. He shouldn't worry. He would get well. But it was a heart attack. The words came into the room like a bomb.

"You are stunned," Ashe said. "That's all. Stunned. It can't be happening to you. Not at 35."

It is felt now that the problem may be a congenital one. There are the two heart attacks his father has suffered. Ashe said yesterday he has asked to see the records concerning his mother's death, in 1950. His brother, a Marine, will undergo extensive examination.

At the hospital yesterday, Ashe was asked if he will play tennis again.

"I think I'll be able to play...next year," he said carefully. "I've pretty much written off this year."

He paused. The nurse had come back, bringing with her a pitcher of ice water. Ashe sipped ice water. He stared out at the East River for a moment.

"This is kind of hard to accept," he said. "Tennis was such fun again. I'd come back from 257th in the world, all the way back to eight. But I can do it again. Dr. Marshall (John Marshall, a friend) says that I've just got to rest it, really rest it, but then I can start conditioning it just like I would any other muscle. He told me about Dave

Stallworth (ex-Knick, also a heart attack victim), and the way he came back."

If a special, gifted man named Arthur Ashe is getting better, then maybe everyone is lucky. There has been too much death lately. We keep losing people, young people. Troy Archer is killed in an automobile accident. A 28-year-old football player named J.V. Cain drops dead at the St. Louis Cardinals training camp. And on Thursday, a 32-year-old baseball player, Thurman Munson, is killed in an airplane accident, a death that still has the city of New York in mourning.

On Tuesday, Arthur Ashe, in so many different ways the most significant tennis player of his generation, suffered a heart attack. It was a terrible thing to happen, something only understood fully by the man with the fist in his chest, the man who cannot believe it is happening to him. But Ashe survived it. He is going to be all right. He says he will play tennis again. In a week colored by death, Ashe won one. We all did.

Give an ovation for that.

• *1979*

The greatest

T he night before he had made a personal appearance in Milford, Conn., autographing racket covers and tennis balls and old copies of his book, "The Education of a Tennis Player," promoting his clothing line. It was raining in Milford and the night was cold, but the people had come out to see him. A lot of people. They came to see Rod Laver.

Tennis is the sport with the weakest links to the past and the worst memory, but they remembered Laver. Even though his glory was right before the big money and the big time, they knew that he is probably the greatest there has ever been.

"I guess the name still means something," Laver was saying the other afternoon. "I mean, it was just a store appearance, you know, nothin' special, but there must have been 1,000 people there. I was very complimented that that many people would come out on a Monday night, and a wet one at that."

He will be 40 this year, Rod Laver will. He won his first Grand Slam (Australian, French, Wimbledon and U.S. championships) the year Tracy Austin was born, 1962. He won his second Grand Slam in 1969, the year after open tennis brought the sport into the 20th century. In all, he won three Australian Opens, two French, three Wimbledons and three U.S. Opens, though barred from all of them in his prime because he was a pro. Laver won everything.

Laver has graced tennis with his flair and talent in three decades. He is still a treasure. The hair is still carrot-red, and the lefthanded strokes pretty pictures. In 1978, those with memories that go somewhat past the first million-dollar challenge match can still watch Laver play and appreciate what they are seeing.

"You can thank team tennis for that," said Laver, player-coach for WTT's San Diego Friars. "It's the perfect outlet for my competitiveness. Oh, every once in awhile I'll come off the court after catching it pretty cleanly, having gotten that extra thrill out of playing and I'll think, 'Well, maybe I should play a few more tournaments and show these kids I can still play.' But then I realize that's silly that I'm interested in prolonging a career now, and WTT is perfect for that."

Laver was sitting in Felt Forum in the afternoon, watching his team practice for the evening's match against the Apples. Behind him, a workman painted the scoreboard. At the end of the court, some security cops waited for Laver to warm up. But he was reminiscing about the barnstorming days of pro tennis, the '60s, when the one-night stands were not as glamorous as in World Team Tennis, and the money was practically invisible.

"We'd come in in the afternoon and lay the court ourselves," said Laver, speaking warmly of the days. "Me and Hoadie (Lew Hoad) and Pancho Gonzales and (Ken) Rosewall. In the old Garden, when we used to come in there, we'd get 60-40 split on the gate. At the end of the night we'd end up with maybe $1,000. We'd cut it up four ways."

Laver is no pauper. He became tennis' first millionaire in 1971. But he must know that if he were in his prime now, when millionaires are made weekly and Bjorn Borg can skip a shot at $100,000 because of a blister, he could be making enough money to remain constantly dizzy.

"Nah, I'm happy I came along when I did," said Laver. "I don't begrudge the world today anything. I feel privileged in some ways. I was able to play my game my way. There was no pressure on me moneywise. I was allowed to keep my flair, hit the ball with a lot of spin, play the game the way I did best. And eventually that gave me an advantage. In today's world, everybody seems to play the same. Everybody's (Harold) Solomon and (Eddie) Dibbs. Stay back and don't make mistakes. I always thought you should be an individual out there."

He was always that, with his topspin and his song of a backhand, and the serve that surely couldn't be coming from the little body. The other night against the Apples' Vitas Gerulaitis, the new WCT champion, Laver showed that the talent is still there. He beat Gerulaitis 7-5, offering a little bit of everything, from the bow-legged walk to the big shots to the old anticipation.

In the middle of the set, Gerulaitis hit a perfect lob to Laver's backhand corner. Even as Gerulaitis was hitting it, Laver was moving, and when he got to the ball, his back to the net, he sent a backhand from about 1962 screaming down the line for a winner, just to give the fans at Felt Forum a taste, just to remind them just who it was they were watching. Rod Laver.

• *1978*

McEnroe turns boos into cheers

H
•
e had finally pulled his head out of the green towel, got out of his chair, and now John McEnroe was standing next to Peter Harvey, the umpire, while Bjorn Borg shook hands with the Duke of Kent on Centre Court, then shook hands with the Duchess of Kent, then put both his hands on the huge gold cup that means you have won Wimbledon.

All afternoon, the stage had belonged to Borg and McEnroe, McEnroe and Borg, as they played a Wimbledon final the likes of which Wimbledon had never seen. Now the stage belonged to Borg alone. Borg had won 28 games, McEnroe had won 27. Borg was holding the cup over his head, kissing it. McEnroe leaned against the umpire's chair, and looked down.

Peter Harvey said something to him. McEnroe did not look up. Peter Harvey tapped him lightly on the shoulders. Borg was moving in a small circle now, showing the trophy to the different sections of Centre Court, being greeted by a new wave of cheers, each of which seemed to roll across the five years during which that trophy has belonged to him.

"John, could you sign my book please?" asked Peter Harvey. He was talking about the official scorebook in which he had charted the points of the match. McEnroe looked up, then took a pen from Peter Harvey, and signed his name.

"Thank you," said Peter Harvey.

"Don't mention it," said John McEnroe.

McEnroe walked out to receive his small runner-up medal from the Duke of Kent. And as he did, a tremendous cheer rose up out of Centre Court. The cheer was for John McEnroe, a man they had booed when his name was introduced at the beginning of the match, the first time anyone could remember a man being booed before a Wimbledon final. They had never much liked McEnroe at Wimbledon: scorned his temper: jeered at his histrionics on the court. They had mistaken his fighting character for childishness, or boorishness. Now, they cheered him as loudly as they had the victor, Borg.

John P. McEnroe Jr., of Douglaston, Queens, had changed a lot of things over his four hours on Centre Court with Bjorn Borg, he had not won. Borg had beaten him 1-6, 7-5, 6-3, 6-7, 8-6. But when McEnroe comes back to Wimbledon next year, and the year after that, and the year after that, he will come back a hero, because the people here remember players who come back to the All-England Club and combine talent with heart, even when they lose.

When McEnroe heard that big roar, he looked up, startled, then smiled. He had given the people a message with his tennis. They were giving him a message back.

"I don't think they should have booed me at the start," he said. "But it was nice to hear that cheer."

He was sitting in the interview room when he said that, answering the questions in a quiet, painful voice, fidgeting with his hair, patting it, smoothing it, looking down at the table as he answered the questions. He was not "superbrat." There was no bravado. He was a 21-year-old tennis player who had lost the Wimbledon final by the barest of margins. He wore a purple T-shirt, and dungarees, and yellow sneakers, and he tried to answer the questions as best he could, find the right words to disguise the hurt as well as he could.

"I tried as hard as I could, that's for sure," he said.

Someone asked him another question, about the fourth-set tie-breaker, which lasted 22 minutes, which McEnroe somehow won, fighting off five match points in the process.

"I tried as hard as I could," John McEnroe said again.

"I gave it my best. I can't complain."

He leaned back in his chair, squinted into the television lights, played with his hair a little more, shuffled his feet. This was going to be his day. He had played his finest tennis under the most excruciating circumstances of pressure against the best player in the world, the greatest Wimbledon champion of them all. He was going to stop Borg's streak. At 21, he was going to win Wimbledon, add that title to his WCT Championship and his U.S. Open and his Davis Cup. He was going to force Borg to make room for him at the top. And it had gone wrong at the end. He had to talk about it.

He was asked about the way Borg had lifted his game after watching McEnroe fight off two match points before the tiebreaker, then five after that.

"It would have gotten me a little down," he said, and grinned weakly. "It didn't seem to get him down."

How to describe that tiebreaker? How to describe the way McEnroe kept coming off the ropes with the big punch, again and again. He would not crack, not when Borg led 6-5: not when Borg led 7-6: not when Borg led 10-9 or 11-10 or 12-11, he hit backhand winners and forehand volleys and big first serves. There had never been a tiebreaker like it in a final, never been a comeback quite like McEnroe's. You do not fight off match points against Borg like that, not at Wimbledon, not in a final. It is just not done. McEnroe had done it.

He was asked a lengthy question about the match. It would be called the most exciting in the history of Wimbledon, the most dramatic, the best ever. Was there ever a sense for him that he was involved in such a match?

"Sure, you can maybe sense that it's a helluva match," he said. "But mostly what you're trying to do is win."

John McEnroe tried to win Wimbledon yesterday. In a way that will not soon be forgotten. After he beat the seven match points in the fourth set, he would beat seven break points in the fifth set. He growled and dove around and kept hitting winners. He would not crack until the 55th game of the match, and even then, he did nothing about which he should be ashamed. He was beaten by marvelous shots from Borg. No one had ever hit shots like them.

Someone asked him if Borg was the greatest player of all time, and McEnroe said "He's won this thing five times, that should be a hint." Then he got up from his chair, and moved over to a BBC television show. There would be more questions about an unforgettable final, a day which had gone wrong at the very end for John McEnroe, who at least heard the cheers he deserved.

• *1980*

A touch of Sherry
flavors the U.S. Open

I
•

t all ends very quickly, and then you're just the 29th victim in a row for Chris Evert Lloyd at the United States
Open. All the anticipation is gone, and so is the high-
pitched ring of nervousness that never quite went away.
The fleeting thrill of taking a set off Evert Lloyd is history.

The crowd stands and applauds, briefly and politely,
and the crowd files out of the stadium. You sit down to
the left of the umpire's chair, and adjust the thin, brightly
colored headband. You put the Wilson racket back in the
cover, and you wait for Evert Lloyd to have her picture
taken, and then the two of you walk out of Louis Armstrong Stadium.

That's it. Your name is Sherry Acker. You've had your
biggest day at your first Open, you've taken that shining
set, and now you join a list in a record book. You are the
45th victim for Chris Evert Lloyd in her Open career.
You're the 29th victim in a row. In the end, it all goes
very quickly.

"It's on your mind, constantly, that it's her over
there," Acker would say later, in the players' lounge. "And
it's on your mind that you're in that stadium. I never
wanted to look up at that humongous stadium. I just
wanted to pretend that it was a practice court, out back
somewhere."

Acker's hair was still wet from a shower. She was

meeting someone for lunch, and was late. She carried a small leather handbag. She was wearing navy warmup slacks, and a "Colgate Series" T-shirt. And she was talking softly, in a little girl's voice, about her afternoon in the big stadium with Chris Evert Lloyd. The day before, in the same lounge, she had been asked what you do on the day before you play Evert Lloyd at the Open.

"You go to St. Patrick's Cathedral," Acker said, and laughed.

Sherry Acker is 20 years old and lives in Kalamazoo, Mich. Her heroines are Jane Fonda and Gilda Radner, and she does not think Burt Reynolds is so bad, either. She has already seen Radner's Broadway show once while she has been in New York, and says she will go again if she gets the chance. She has been a pro since January.

She won one tournament on the Avon futures circuit, in Atlanta, and made the finals of another, in Boise. For a few weeks, she played on the Avon championship circuit. The night she won her first match on the big circuit, in Seattle, she took a couple of beers to the top of the auditorium there and sat for a while, watching other people play. It was official that night. She was really a pro.

These are some things to know about Acker, who lost yesterday, but who did well on her big day at the Open, and who was a little bit more than just another victim—number 29—for Evert Lloyd.

"It's funny," she said afterward. "You're not sure how to react. Like, I don't want people to think I'm real happy just because I won the first set (6-4, and Evert won the next two, 6-0, 6-2). I wanted to keep doing well. And I don't think I fell apart or anything over the next two sets. Chris just picked her game up. Boy, did Chris pick her game up."

Chris has done that a lot at the U.S. Open, ever since she came to Forest Hills that first time, in her 16th summer. For her, yesterday was just another afternoon at the Open, with Evonne Goolagong and Billie Jean King, then either Tracy Austin or Martina Navratilova still ahead if she wants to win her fifth straight title. It was not just another afternoon for Sherry Acker of Kalamazoo, who did just fine.

"You try to turn the nervousness into something positive," she said 30 minutes before the match, waiting for Roscoe Tanner to finish playing Tim Gullikson in the Stadium. "But you still know it's Chris out there waiting, and you know she's beaten so many people one-sidedly..." She went back into the locker room to wait.

Evert Lloyd would eventually beat her one-sidedly over those last two sets. This is the new, streamlined Chris, looking leaner and hungrier than she has in a long time. She is running down the tough ball, coming to the net more; she just seems more active on the court, more colorful, as she goes about the business of not missing any balls. Over the last two sets, she gave us the entire show—from the baseline, with the angles and lobs, with the consistency.

But for the first set, Acker made her work, work hard. "I couldn't find a weakness in her game the first set," Chris would say after the match. Acker, a big girl with real quickness, was all over the net. She got up a break, then another, then held on at the end. The electronic scoreboard at the top of the stadium suddenly had a "6" next to her name, and a "4" next to Chris'.

Before this Open, Acker had not made it past the third round in nine consecutive tournaments. Last week, at a tournament in Mahwah, N.J., she did not get out of the qualifying. But she won three matches in this first Open in which she played singles, and for a few minutes yesterday afternoon,was a set up on the Open champion, the first set Evert Lloyd had lost since the '75 final. Acker will take some memories from the afternoon, even with the beating she took over the last two sets.

At the press conference, Acker sat there smiling while Chris did most of the talking. At one point, Chris wondered out loud if they had ever played before. "Doubles," Acker said quietly, "not singles." A friend standing near the table at which Evert Lloyd and Acker sat asked Sherry if she wanted a beer. She smiled and held up two fingers.

She took her time walking to the clubhouse, signed a few autographs. Now it was time to hold on to the last parts of the afternoon. A female reporter interviewed her when she got back to the locker room. Sherry Acker showered, and came out into the lounge, and more reporters waited. She talked to every one of them. A great afternoon at the U.S. Open stretched out a little more for Chris Evert Lloyd's 29th consecutive victim. Lunch could wait.

• *1980*

Aussies help Chris drink in defeat

LONDON

T. hey sat at the long table with a kind of quiet, painful class, using small talk to mask hurt. Yes, they would have to discuss hotel accommodations in New York for the U.S. Open.

No, there would be no set dinner plans for the evening. Colette Evert asked Chris Evert when the car should come to take them back to the Inn on the Park, their hotel. Chris Evert said to her mother that maybe the car should come in an hour.

"What's that drink called with beer and lemonade?" Chris Evert suddenly asked her companions in the Players' Tea Room, an elegant saloon at the All-England Club.

"A shandy," Lew Hoad said happily. "Somebody get Chrissie a bloody shandy."

An hour after Martina Navratilova beat her at Wimbledon yesterday, Evert sat at this long table with the only sensible crowd of people with whom to share a terrible defeat: a crowd of Australians drinking beer. The Aussies know how to deal with such things as Evert's 2-6, 6-4, 7-5 loss in the finals of Wimbledon.

"Yes" said Fred Stolle. "Get Chrissie a beer."

Hoad sat at the head of the table, his great stomach not hidden by a baggy white tennis shirt and falling over his belt. Tony Roche was on his right, and on his left were Stolle, three times a loser in the Wimbledon finals, and

Ray Ruffels. All had huge pint glasses of beer in front of them. Tea would not do for an occasion like this, nor would coffee. Colette and Chris Evert had iced coffees and croissants on their trays.

But then the Everts are not used to dealing with defeat, at Wimbledon or anywhere else. That is why the Aussies were so perfect for her in the Tea Room yesterday afternoon. They, better than anyone else in their sport, have always understood about mortality.

"I hate beer," said Chris Evert.

"The lemonade kills the taste," said Stolle, "and the beer just gets the job done." Stolle went to get Evert a shandy. He stopped halfway to the bar, and said, "You know what they say about a day like this in Russia?"

"I don't care what they say in Russia," Evert said with a smile.

Stolle uttered an expletive loudly, in a Russian accent. Only when Evert laughed did her table of Aussies explode into laughter. There are certain rules for these wakes.

When the laughter stopped and the noise was gone for the moment, the hurt came back to Evert's face. It was in the eyes. But she handled it with class. All during Wimbledon she had said she did not know if she was tournament tough, and in the final which began a few hours before, she had found out she was not. "Right now, Martina is tougher," said Evert. "At this point, this week she's tougher than I am." It was not an easy admission to make.

It is toughness that has always set her apart. She has lost some of it, maybe in the four-month vacation she took at the start of this year. At her press conference yesterday, which she handled beautifully and with such style, she was asked if she can get the toughness back.

"If I want to be No. 1, I'll have to want it more," she said slowly, wanting to make every word right. "The desire to win Wimbledon was there this year, but it was never there like it was in the past. The intensity was not there. I'm going to have to look inside of myself, and figure out how to get it back if I'm going to be No. 1 again."

She left the press conference, then went to BBC television, and was terrific there, then went to BBC radio and gave the same thoughtful answers. Defeat was new to her. She articulated it calmly.

"Calm, control, that's what I wanted," she said in the Tea Room, "I wasn't going to break down. Last year after I lost to Virginia Wade, (in the semifinals), I just wanted to cry."

She did not cry after the Wade match. She did not break down yesterday. Chris Evert dealt with defeat. Dianne Fromholtz came by and said something quietly to her. Evert signed a couple of auto-graphs. John Lloyd, the English player, hunched down next to her and talked for a few minutes, and JoAnne Russell came by and tried to make her laugh, and Brigitte Cuypers, another player, told her, "I lost 10 pounds on you."

"I'm sorry," Evert said. She was serious. Stolle came and set the glass of shandy down in front of her. "One sip," she grinned. "I'm not trying to get away from anything." She meant that, too. Along the ta-ble, all the Aussies, Hoad and Roche and Stolle and Ruffels, raised their glasses.

"Cheers, Chrissie," said Lew Hoad.

"Cheers," said Chris Evert, picking up her glass.

• *1978*

GYMS

I am a frustrated basketball player, I think from the time Bishop Guertin High School went 3-17 my senior season and the only thing I had to show for all that were 14 broken pairs of glasses and a seven-stitch cut in my forehead. But I have never gotten the gym out of the system. The Final Four of college basketball is my favorite sports event, year in and year out. Ernie DiGregorio is my favorite player of all time, next to Cousy. And, as you will see, I have always thought coaches made pretty good columns. After two games on the Knick beat in 1975, at the age of 23, I second-guessed a move Knick coach Red Holzman made. After the third game, someone in his office asked a question. Red looked up at me and said, "Why don't you handle that one, Mike, you've been around this game a long time."

Red and I got along famously after that.

•

Part 5

Dropping his shield, Knight regales and disarms the press

NEW ORLEANS

The press conference in this big ballroom at the Hyatt Regency had gone past 90 minutes now. Bob Knight was still yacking. If there is a Good Bob and a Bad Bobby, this was the good guy all the way. It looked like somebody from Hyatt security would eventually have to fight him for the microphone.

Knight had talked about Syracuse, Syracuse coach Jim Boeheim, the Big East, Ted Williams, Vince Lombardi, John Bench, John Havlicek, the 3-point basket, Red Auerbach, Col. Red Blaik, Pete Dawkins, Pete Newell and Henry Iba and Clair Bee, national championships, winning and losing in general, the movie "Hoosiers." He had talked about basketball and the state of Indiana, about a state of hoops attached to one small town after another.

Knight had been funny, needling. He had gotten laughs and casually iced two mentions of "Season on the Brink," the bestseller that has been written about him. Knight told the sportswriters in the room that he had already finished writing his syndicated column for today's newspapers. He joked with Steve Alford and Rick Calloway and Dean Garrett while they were on the podium with him. It was no act. Knight is many things, but dishonest is not one of them. He approves of artifice the way he approves of zone defenses.

Now he was asked a question that went like this:

"Doesn't it bother you that there are a lot of people out there who think of you as a bigger, older McEnroe?"

Bob Knight said, "I'm comfortable with who I am."

This was not Knight's type of setting. He is no talk show host. Knight is most comfortable with five or six friends at some Bloomington pizza parlor at one o'clock in the morning after Indiana has just beaten somebody, discussing a game he coaches like an immortal. But still Knight was compelling yesterday, and fun. For 90 minutes on the day before he would try to win his third national championship, Knight opened the door and let everybody visit for a while.

On the Sunday afternoon before the finals of college basketball— third time Knight's team has played in the last game—Knight closed up a little of the distance between private reality and public image.

Johnny Bench, a Knight friend, spoke to the Indiana players Friday night. Knight introduced Bench by telling his players "rarely do you get to meet somebody who's the best at what he does." The people in the big ballroom were listening to someone yesterday, Knight of Indiana, who is the best at what he does.

Knight talked about Williams being his "all-time sports idol." He said that when Williams walked down the street, people could say "there goes the greatest hitter who ever lived." Someone asked Knight if he wanted people to talk about him that way as a basketball coach.

"No," he said. "Because I know there are people who were better than I was. But I would like them to say, 'There goes a guy who got the most out of what he had.' " Later on he said, "Victory, winning, has never been a particularly satisfying thing to me. It's always been how we played."

Knight has a temper. He has always abused players verbally. There was something in the papers Sunday about Bob Hope having five p.r. men. If *Bob Hope* has five, how many does Bob Knight need? Knight will always have that incident with the Puerto Rican cop, there will always be telephones to bash and officials to berate. "Season on the Brink" is apparently not flattering and will be read by millions. He is a volatile man in a public job.

"My mistakes," he said yesterday, "are always in front of at least 18,000 people. That doesn't justify anything, or say I'm right or wrong, but when I get mad, it's news."

With all that, he is also funny, intelligent, a student of history, an intensely loyal friend, and he is a genius at what he does, elevating the job of coaching to an art. His players go to class; Knight's academic standards are stricter than the NCAA's. It doesn't mean you have to like him or approve of him, but if you could have gone the 90 minutes yesterday at the Hyatt Regency, you would think about giving him a shot anyway.

I asked him to name his heroes in coaching and managing. He said he would give three or four people, no particular order. He ended up giving seven.

Knight said Lombardi "gave a meaning to playing as well as you can." He said Paul Brown brought "qualities of organization to leadership and coaching." Red Auerbach? "He was a psychologist," Knight said, "with an approach that was like inner arrogance." Then there was Red Blaik, and the three basketball coaches about whom he always talks with reverence: Clair Bee, Peter Newell, Henry Iba.

"I got to know them all well," he said, "except Lombardi." He said he went to visit Bee near the end of Bee's life up at Bee's farm north of Roscoe, New York, in the Catskills. Bee, who in addition to coaching wrote the marvelous Chip Hilton books for boys, was 85 years old and blind at the time of his visit. Knight said Bee wrote out a note for him anyway.

It read: "Clair Bee and Bob Knight do not think repetition is gospel." So Knight has taken from the philosophies of men he considers matters, refined, kept his players passing the ball and giving him ball-you-man defense, and here he is tonight at the Superdome against Syracuse.

Knight was happiest yesterday talking about losing Steve Alford. Not because he doesn't love Alford as a kid and as a shooting assassin, but because next year he will have to move Keith Smart into Alford's No. 2 guard spot, and that will present new coaching challenges.

"I'm really looking forward to using Smart as a shooter," Knight said. "I'm just like a guy who likes putting pieces of a puzzle together."

He has done it again at Indiana with Alford, two junior-college transfers (Garrett, Smart), a rather soft forward named Daryl Thomas, and Rick Calloway, who is an All-American next year if his knee holds up. Now he is tonight's game away from the national championship hat trick. Everything would be perfect about that chance, he says, except the line that says you get three points if you can make a shot from 19 feet, nine inches away.

"I enjoy the machinations of the game too much," Knight said. "There's not too much involved with it (the new rule) that's traditional to basketball."

The press conference finally ended. Rick Brewer, the North Carolina publicity man who had moderated it, told the writers to stay off the Superdome court after the championship game was over.

"That doesn't include coach Knight, of course," Brewer said.

It was time for Bob Knight to go coach an Indiana practice. It was time to start getting ready for Syracuse. But already he was thinking about moving Smart into Alford's spot. Smart isn't as good a shooter as Alford, but he can drive better, post up more.

It will be a very good puzzle.

• *1987*

Ernie D. a great act, but nobody's buying

PROVIDENCE

H.

e wore a torn yellow sweatshirt that said Fleet Feet on the front, and old green gym shorts, and dirty Adidas sneakers. And everyone stopped playing to watch him, as though E.F. Hutton down there dribbling the ball. It was as if the stands were not empty, as if this were not just another pick-up afternoon in his exile from his game. He was back at Providence College, it was 1973 again, he was his season's Larry Bird, and he was showing a doubting basketball world that he really was a genius, one of a kind.

Ernie D.

As soon as they walked into Alumni Gym, to play three-on-three games or wait to play or watch, someone would poke them, then point wordlessly. Ernie D. was in the gym; Ernie D. was back home; he was down there making all those passes; he was the littlest kid out there, the one with the ball. The others couldn't take their eyes off him.

Ernie DiGregorio.

He still made the silly, perfect playground passes from behind the back, hitting teammates in the back of the head. He still came off the dribble, in traffic, with that soft little push shot. Of course, he still saw openings only he could see and sent breathtaking passes through them, special delivery. And every once in awhile the other afternoon, in this noisy, busy old gym, players in other games would stop and applaud something magical DiGregorio had just done. For the briefest moment, he would smile. Then his three-on-three game would continue.

"See," Ernie D. would say later, leaning against empty bleachers between the grueling 50-basket games. "I can still play, and enjoy myself. Lemme tell you: I have a lot more fun playing here than sitting on the bench in Chicago or Philadelphia."

DiGregorio grinned, a smug, kid's grin. At 28, currently retired from pro basketball, he is still the game's perpetual boy.

"You know," he said, "I still kinda have the knack of doing something out there other people can't do."

Most afternoons, he still does these things. He does them at Alumni Gym on the Providence campus, or at the Boys Club down the street, on Branch Ave., or outdoors, on the Smith Street playground, the place where he spent all the hours as a kid, making himself into something special. That is it. Ernie D. has no team. There is no place for him in the NBA.

At a time when the NBA drowns in mediocrity and inspires total boredom, no one wants to give Ernie D. the ball. At a time when Bird is treated like a visitor from another planet because he can pass wonderfully and is unselfish and sees the court whole, all the time, everyone seems to have forgotten that Ernie D. is the same player, in miniature.

But there is no place for him, except maybe on the end of a bench somewhere. For Ernie D., that is unacceptable. If you have ever once played the game the way Ernie D. has, you cannot tolerate being a bum in a bum of a league. The Lakers put him on the bench last season and then the Celtics did, and Ernie D. finally went home to Providence.

"I can do what I can do better than anybody else," DiGregorio said matter-of-factly. "But if I'm not gonna be allowed to play the way I can, why should I bang my head against the wall? Why should I buck the system."

He paused.

"I won't sit on the bench," he said. "To do that would be against all the principles I've stood for my whole life. I've worked too hard to get what I've gotten to be able to play the way I can. I'm tired of showing up people who don't believe in me."

All his life, he has heard that he was too small at 5-11 to be a great player. And every time a team has given him the ball, he has played himself big, set himself apart, showed himself to be one of the most distinctive players ever. In 1973, after a great college career at Providence, people still had to be shown. As a senior that year, in the NCAA playoffs, he showed them again.

He and Marvin Barnes and Kevin Stacom took Providence to the Final Four. If Marvin had not hurt his knee against Memphis State in the semifinals, Providence would have surely gone against Bill Walton and UCLA in the finals. But up until then, the tournament was Ernie's show. He threw behind-the-back passes from halfcourt to the cutting Barnes. He threw passes between his legs. He dribbled out the clock when it was necessary. He was Cousy. He was his year's Larry Bird.

By summer, Ernie D. was a millionaire. The Braves made him the third pick in the NBA draft, and paid him $2.5 million over five years.

"College," he said the other day, "was the best it ever was for me. I'll never forget any of it."

He was Rookie-of-the-Year for the Braves in 1974, then hurt his knee in 1975. In 1976, still at Buffalo, he found himself on the bench for the Braves, but came back to have a brilliant playoff series against the Celtics, just as he had done in 1974. But by 1978, he had moved to Los Angeles, where Jerry West had no use for him. Toward the end of the season, he was waived to Boston. When the Celtics would not offer him a no-cut contract before this season, Ernie D. retired. He plays pick-up games now.

The other afternoon, he sat in Alumni Gym and talked about the past, and the future.

"If I don't play again, I won't look back with any regrets," he said. "Hey, that's the way it goes in the big world. You gotta have fun. The last couple years, I didn't have fun.

"So now, I wonder. I wonder what the future holds. The future's funny."

Then Ernie D. went out to play again. Three-on-three, on a Tuesday afternoon. First team to 50-baskets wins. And after about three baskets, Ernie DiGregorio was cutting right to left at the top of the key, and a guy on his team broke open underneath, and Ernie flicked a pass to him without looking, a bullet, and the guy got a lay-up. Ernie grinned, and signalled for the ball. It was winners out.

• *1979*

Marvin jailed; Lula, Debbie weep

T he 10 little girls from the Wheelock Elementary school sat in the last two rows of Courtroom No. 8, with notebooks opened, eyes fixed on the judge sitting high above them. They were watching him almost as closely as three people sitting in the front row of the courtroom: Mrs. Lula Barnes, her daughter Alfreda, and a tiny young woman named Debbie Santos, who bore Lula's son Marvin a child. This was no school assignment for them. This was about Lula's son Marvin going to a jail.

It had now come down to this for Marvin Barnes, the wealthy young basketball player who was once found guilty of assault, and who violated his three-year probation for that by carrying a gun through an airport some months ago. He had surrendered to the Supreme and Superior Court of Rhode Island. Now he was sitting at a table 20 feet away from Judge Anthony Giannini, and he was waiting in the terrible quiet of a courtroom to find out if he had to start serving a year's sentence in jail.

Giannini flipped through papers in front of him. His voice was even. You could not tell good news from bad in the sounds he made. He talked about the request of a continuance made by Barnes' lawyer, James Feinberg of Detroit, whom Barnes had retained only Sunday night, hoping that late move would get the continuance. Anthony Giannini was having none of that.

"Let the record show that the motion for continuance has been denied," Giannini said, still in the even voice. Marvin Barnes put his head down and adjusted the silk square in the pocket of his sports jacket. Even he, who has never dealt so well with reality, knew what was coming next.

"Any further motions like that," said Giannini, "can be filed while the prisoner is incarcerated." There it was. Incarcerated. The word came into the room like a bomb falling. "The guards can take Mr. Barnes now," said Giannini.

Deputy Marshall Joe Spiver came over to Marvin Barnes and led him out of the courtroom. In an anteroom, Spiver put handcuffs on Barnes. Then he took him down some back stairs to a cellblock on the second floor while Lula Barnes and Debbie Santos sat in the front row and began to cry.

In the cellblock, Marvin emptied the pockets of his expensive tan outfit, then walked through a metal detector. He had not spoken since he left the courtroom. His possessions were placed in a large manila envelope. Then Barnes, the Providence All-American, the $300,000-per-year player for the Pistons, was put in a small cell, to wait there until there was another marshall, Lt. Peter DiBiase, available to drive him—still handcuffed—to the Adult Correctional Institute in Cranston where he would begin serving the year's sentence. He will be eligible for parole in four months.

For a while yesterday, there was none of the grimness of jail and prison sentences on the sunwashed street in front of the old courthouse where a large crowd had gathered to wait for Barnes. It was as if this was one more crazy game for Barnes, one more careless lark. He was supposed to appear before Giannini at 10 a.m. He did not. The principal deputy clerk, Thomas Luongo, then announced that Marvin had called and would be late.

This was perfect. Marvin Barnes, who in his short career had been late for games and practices and airplanes, was now going to be late for jail.

"I think he's coming from Boston," said Luongo, "so if he comes by car, expect him in 45 minutes. By bus, maybe longer." Actually, Barnes had been calling from the Providence Airport, where he had flown from Detroit.

"I hope he shows," smiled Alton Wiley, a black Providence lawyer who would find out when Barnes arrived with Feinberg that he was not representing Marvin anymore.

Finally, at 1:30, Barnes and Feinberg came walking down South

Main St. toward the courthouse. Marvin was more subdued than he has ever been. "No comment," he said before anyone asked a question. A woman trailed by a television camera pushed in front of him and said, "Marvin, did you ever think this day would come?" Marvin gave a little smile and said "No comment" again.

Forty-five minutes later it was over. Feinberg went into chambers with Giannini and asked for the continuance because he had come into the case so late. It was denied. Then Giannini, who'd said earlier, "You'll get my decision in open court," went into open court and gave it.

Now it was back to the street, to wait for the drama to be played out. Lula Barnes stood by the van that would take her son the seven miles to jail. "This is like a funeral," she said, " 'cept Marvin ain't dead."

At 3:30 Marvin came out in handcuffs, led by three marshalls. "Let me kiss my mama," he said, and did. He was put into the blue van, and the door was slammed shut and locked. He turned once to wave to Lula Barnes, then the blue van headed down South Main St. and was gone.

• *1977*

Red's lit up our lives

T
•
here was no other way for it to end. It had to be the Boston Celtics and the Los Angeles Lakers, and it had to be Game 7 of the NBA finals. It had to be Boston Garden, the ratty shrine on Causeway Street. One last time, it had to be Arnold (Red) Auerbach, the greatest basketball Buddha of them all, sitting underneath the championship banners, hard by the parquet floor, one last cigar in the pocket, waiting for a championship and a light.

Ultimately last night, the seventh game of this Celtic-Laker series which has done so much to bring magic and luster back to pro basketball would belong to the players. But in many ways it has been for Red Auerbach too, because he is stepping down finally as general manager of the Celtics, after all the years and all the championships, all the days and nights when he has brought honor and genius to the NBA. This column is for Red Auerbach too.

"It would have to be the Lakers, wouldn't it?" he was saying yesterday afternoon. "Yeah, and it would have to be here."

He was in the famous office on Causeway Street, surrounded by the clutter of mementos and souvenirs of his extraordinary Celtic lifetime, killing time, answering the phone, waiting to go to lunch, waiting for Game Seven against the Lakers. As Celtic coach, there were two games just like it; Auerbach's teams won them both.

127

There was another after he became general manager; the Celtics won that too. In all during Auerbach's grand tenure on Causeway Street, as coach or GM, the Celtics have played eight finals against the Lakers. They had won all seven before last night. Auerbach waited yesterday to see if the Celtics could win their eighth against the Lakers, their 15th world championship since he showed up with the cigars.

"I might as well be hanging around here," Auerbach said. "What the hell am I going to do? Go home? What the hell am I going to do at home? Be nervous there? I'm happy enough right here."

Whatever happened last night, he was proud of this Celtic team. Whatever happened, this latest Celtic army, led by Larry Bird, had played Celtic basketball. Just that. Celtic basketball.

Tradition is a word too overworked in sports. Here, at the end of Auerbach's active career, these new Celtics had embraced all the traditions of the old Celtics. They had played with heart. They had not died. They had come back. They had given him one last seventh game.

"They sure have showed some character," Auerbach said. "You've got to give them that."

He gave them that. Across 30 years, he has become a unique and dominant personality in his sport, has made the Celtics into the New York Yankees of the NBA. He has made mistakes, he has cursed and been stubborn, he has seen owners come and go; he saw the Celtics fall completely apart, and into disgrace, under the ownership of John Y. Brown, and then he got Bird, and he built them again. But he has always been Red Auerbach, plotting and growling, intimidating and coddling, keeping the only real family he has ever known together. He has always been a couple of steps ahead of everyone else. There will never—never—be anyone remotely like him.

He says he will still be active as team president, that at 65 it is finally time for him to turn the day-to-day operation of the team over to younger men. If that is true, the game will be poorer, because from bench or front office, he has been the NBA's enduring giant. But you must wonder. You must wonder if there will be a game next season, or the one after that, a game at Boston Garden, when Auerbach thinks his team is getting a bad deal. You must wonder if we won't see the balding, round little man walking out of the stands, spewing venom, going after a ref or a coach or even a Moses Malone. You must wonder if retirement will change Arnold Auerbach at all.

They will always be his Celtics, you see. They always have been. Against the Lakers. Against the world.

• *1984*

Pearl casts his magic
spell one more time

utside, the high school game on the Garden court was
over. You could hear the pounding of the disco music
over the public address system. Almost time now. Earl
Monroe adjusted the elastic brace on his right knee. He
opened a green-and-red box that said "Seamless Ankle
Supports," and carefully pulled heel-to-ankle rubber supports over his white socks, right foot then left. Mike
Saunders, the Knicks trainer, came walking over to Monroe's locker. Twenty-five minutes until gametime now.
Saunders wanted to make sure everything was just right
with Earl Monroe.

"Mike, do you suppose you could get me another pair
of white shorts?" Earl Monroe asked. "These are a little
tight."

"How can they be tight?" Saunders asked. "They're
the same size you always wore."

"This body is old," said Monroe, smiling brilliantly.
"Very old."

"But how's the mind?" said Butch Beard, the Knicks
assistant, from across the locker room.

"My mind," said Monroe, "is not what fits into these
shorts."

So Saunders got him some new white shorts, and 35-
year-old Earl Monroe put them on, then carefully took
some white sneakers out of a box, and put the sneakers
on. He noticed the shorts were wrinkled. He smoothed

130

them out. Most of the young Knicks were in the locker room now, waiting to take the court for warmups. Monroe, the old magician, stood up, and stepped to the middle of the room. He seemed to be wearing a tuxedo.

"How do I look?" Earl Monroe asked.

One more season, his last probably, was a few minutes away; one more New York basketball evening would be graced with his style. Once more, on a Garden court, one of the city's fine love affairs would continue: The one between the city and Earl Monroe. There is no old hero quite like him left in New York sports, no natural resource that we have tapped for such a long time. Once more he would walk into the Garden, shoulders and elbows back, hands dangling loosely at his sides, and hear the cheers.

The chemistry would be the same as always. The crowd would add its cheers to his talent, and charm. The combination, of course, would be magic. He was out of shape, and there would be no oldtime Magic Show on this night back. On this night, the people did not care. The Pearl was joining another season.

In New York, there is no active player revered as Monroe is. Not Guidry. Not Espo. Not Chinaglia. They hear cheers. Monroe hears something louder.

"Long ago, these people here seemed to realize the types of things I was going through," he said. "My knees. Bad feet. Maybe they knew I was holding myself back a little. And I guess they saw that I was able to maintain some degree of excellence while doing so. They *appreciated* me. And over the years, I think it's gone from appreciation to respect to making me one of their own."

He was asked if he remembered his first game as a Knick.

"I think it was Nov. 11, 1971," he said. It was. "I think we were playing one of the western teams (they were: Golden State). We lost that night. I threw a couple of nice passes. I musta played about 20 minutes, and scored eight or nine points (right again; twenty minutes, nine points). But what I really remember about the night was that the crowd was with me on everything I did. Every move I made."

It has been that way ever since, through a championship, through some very thin years when the only reason to come to Madison Square Garden was to witness the elegance of Earl Monroe. Those nights when he alone lit up the Garden are his personal legacy for the 70s. Now, as the 70s were ending, as his last New York season was beginning, people in the Garden were waiting for him to dust off his top hat, flick some lint off the shoulder of his tuxedo, and give them as much of the old show as he could.

The Knicks filed out of the locker room, into the hall, and began moving toward the disco music inside the Garden. In the hall, Monroe smiled.

Magic time, right?" he said.

The place exploded when he took his first practice layup. John Condon introduced the entire Knick squad, and saved Monroe for last. The people were on their feet before Condon ever spoke his name. The organist played "Old Times." The young Knicks surrounded Monroe. When he finally took off his warmup jacket with 8:43 left in the second period, the people rose again. This time they chanted "Earl...Earl...Earl." For one of their own.

He was rusty on this first night. There were no tricks. Even with the people trying to will every shot into the basket, he shot only one-for-eight. But that will change. The old magician will make some shots, and stabilize the young Knicks, especially down the stretch, and help them. Even on a one-for-eight night (six rimmed out), he shuffled around like an old sand dancer and got his shots.

"We were happy when he missed the first couple," said Phoenix assistant coach Al Bianchi. "We didn't want him to make those people crazy."

After the game was over, and the young Knicks had won by four, Monroe said he was relieved to have the first game under his belt. He said he felt much better the second time he was on the court. He smiled and said he thought the shooting percentage would get a little better. He said he would have to get into game shape in a hurry, now that his left leg was healthy. He talked about this season being another challenge for him, perhaps his last.

"But you know," he said finally, "if I had to do it over again, maybe I'd be a tennis player. I probably would have been the same in tennis. Not a hot dog. Just a lot of style."

The last reporters left. He stuffed the last of his uniform, his tuxedo, into an equipment bag. A bus was waiting. There would be a trip to the airport. A flight to Baltimore. Frankie Blauschild, the Knicks' road manager, handed Monroe an itinerary for the short trip. Monroe, the old magician, smiled as he read it. A season was beginning.

• *1979*

Red's showing the kids how to fill Garden

H•e has been getting up in the morning and going to gyms for a living since 1945, when the Rochester mornings were cold, and the practices were held at the Edgerton Sports Arena, and Red Holzman played guard for the Royals. There were years when he scouted, and a couple of years when the Knicks had nothing for him to do. No mornings then, no gyms. But the best part of Red Holzman's long life in pro basketball has started early in the day. He has written most of his great story at the Lost Battalion gym in Queens, or at Alumni Hall at St. John's, or at Fordham, or at Pace University, anyplace where there was court time and two baskets, and a team to teach, all-black, all-white, or brushed denim.

"You teach in the morning," he said.

It was 10:30 of another morning, in the downstairs gym of LaGuardia Community College in Queens. Holzman was sitting in a pulled-out row of bleachers, waiting for the Knicks to assemble for an 11 o'clock practice. At the other end of the court, Bill Cartwright, his gifted rookie center, was practicing hook shots. A workman swept the court. Mike Saunders, the Knicks trainer, rolled out a cart filled with basketballs. LaGuardia students watched Cartwright through windows on the gym door. Red Holzman smoked a cigar through an orange holder, squinting through gray smoke as he read some notes on a piece of yellow legal paper.

"Every day is a different day," he said. "Every day, there are differ-ent things to go over."

The little man is still around. He no longer wears gray suits to practice; the outfit yesterday included a leather jacket and a turtle-neck, and some beige jeans. It also included a small black leather handbag. Holzman was a little embarrassed about the bag. "Oh, well," he said, lifting it. "I gotta relate, right?"

The Cleveland Cavaliers cut Walt Frazier the other day, and when they did, Red Holzman was the only one left from the 1970 championship team. The players are all gone. Only Phil Jackson is still active in pro basketball, as an assistant coach with the Nets, but Jackson was hurt in 1970. Frazier and Reed and DeBusschere and Bradley, the heroes, the big men, are gone. The little man outlasted them all. He still has the gyms. In 1979, Holzman gets up in the morning and drives from Cedarhurst to Queens and goes to practice.

"I'm the only one left?" Holzman asked. He took the cigar out of his mouth and laughed, the sound loud in the near-empty gym. "Back in '70, we probably thought it was gonna be the other way around. Everybody thought that, me included."

In what might be his last year of coaching, he has an ideal team for him to coach, a team of hungry, talented kids who are willing to listen, and learn ("They seem to buy the act," Holzman said with a grin). Holzman does not know how good this team can be; he doesn't know how long he will be with them. But he is enjoying himself with these Knicks, enjoying the challenge of starting over, 12 years after starting with another group of young Knicks and carefully molding them into champions.

"When I took over in '67, those guys, they were hungry to win," he said. "They hadn't won anything yet, and they were real hungry. They liked it. The kids here now, they seem to like it. These young fellas, they're anxious to make their mark and show they're gonna be here for a while. That's always a good thing. Can't hurt."

More players began to filter into the gym. Sly Williams. Larry De-mic. Toby Knight. Holzman took off his leather jacket and folded it neatly, placing it on the bench beside him. He re-lit the cigar.

"You know, they're gonna have to earn those seats at the Gar-den," he said. "They're gonna have to fill 'em up by what they do on the court. That's what we're tryin' to do here. Lemme tell you: you never own any fans. New York's got the best basketball fans in the world. If you give 'em something, they'll come out."

Holzman says they are "good kids," high praise for him. He likes Cartwright, thinks he is going to be "one helluva player." He is delighted with the improvement of Michael Ray Richardson. He is happy with the size of his team: "We got some beef. Beef helps you run." He is highly amused about this week's big New York discovery, that his team has 11 black players (one august journal printed pictures of all 11 players the other day, just to prove this vital fact). Mention this fact to Red Holzman and he says, "So?" For him, that about takes care of the issue.

"I'm fired up about this team," he said. "But you're always fired up. You always try to do the best you can with what you've got. I'd like to get this team to the point where they're gonna have some respect around the league, and respect themselves. How far they go, what they accomplish, that's up to them."

Even with the empty seats right now, there is real hope for the Knicks for the first time in years. Sonny Werblin takes a lot of cheap shots in New York, but his unloading of the immortal Robert McAdoo was a dramatic move that had to be made. The Knicks got draft choices for the immortal McAdoo. One of those draft choices was Bill Cartwright; he is the immediate dividend. How the other kids turn out remains to be seen.

"But even if it's only Cartwright," Holzman said, "that's a helluva start."

For now, the kids belong to Holzman, and that is a lucky thing. Al McGuire might have put people in the stands, but Holzman can teach. He can teach better than anyone.

The gym at LaGuardia Community College was filled with his players. It was 11 o'clock. Holzman butted out the last of his cigar. He took one last look at the piece of yellow legal paper, and stood up. He walked to the middle of the court in his shuffling gait. Another morning of basketball was beginning.

"Could we have some layups to start off?" Red Holzman asked.

• *1980*

The name's Jimmy V., as in victory

ALBUQUERQUE, N.M.

immy Valvano followed the NCAA man out the door and up the ramp and into the mean cold of the Albuquerque night. The press building is next door to the arena called The Pit at the University of New Mexico, and that was where Jimmy V. was heading, and for the first time all night, he was away from the heat of the building where his remarkable team had shoved Houston out of the way and climbed to the top of the college basketball mountain. His tie was undone, his sweaty hair was matted to his scalp, his eyes were State colors, red and white. The eyes were shaded more by tears than the flu he had been fighting all weekend, the way he had been fighting the odds for a magical month that will be remembered as long as college basketball is played.

His voice was a rasp hurrying toward a whisper. When the wind hit him, he coughed and hunched his shoulders, and took a sip from the soft drink in his right hand. Then he grinned his flinty, gym rat's grin.

"I had always hoped to catch double pneumonia on the night I won the national championship," Jimmy Valvano said, and tried a laugh before it died in his sore throat.

He got to the top of the ramp, and broke into a trot toward the press building.

"Phi Slama Jama!" he yelled into the night and over the sound of the wind. "Phi Slama Jama. Tell me about that jive now."

An old friend from New York came up the ramp from behind him, touched him on the shoulder, and said, "Congratulations, V." Valvano, known as V. to friends, stopped and grabbed the man in something that was part handshake and part embrace.

"You know what the amazing thing is?" Valvano said. "It shoulda been easier. It shoulda been bleepin' easier." Then he ran into the open door of the press building and went to the podium, where he would talk with triumph and humor and emotion about the greatest night a gym rat can know. He will coach a long time and he will laugh a lot and win a lot more, and he is going to give Dean Smith one hell of a run in the state of North Carolina from now on. But nothing is ever going to touch this Monday night in Albuquerque, when North Carolina State pulled off the biggest upset the NCAA final has ever seen, thanks to the damndest finish of them all.

Maybe it shoulda been bleepin' easier than having Lorenzo Charles pull a prayer out of the air just one tick away from the buzzer, then jam it through the basket to give State its improbable 54-52 victory over Houston and its impossible national championship. But Valvano will take it. Yeah, he'll take it. He has been in the business of coaching for 16 years, and he knows about the ups and downs, and he knows about all the famous men who have worked sidelines with skill and heart, but who have never won the title and never will. He got his chance. He saw the brass ring there in The Pit, and he grabbed for it like he was in Corona and it was a subway strap on the Flushing Line.

The gym rat got it all Monday night. By now, the details of the miracle are well-known. The Phi Slama Jama people from Houston got one dunk all night. The way Guy Lewis of Houston coached, his team would have had a better chance to win if he had stayed home. With 10 minutes left and Houston up seven and about to blow State all the way back to Raleigh, Lewis had his team go into a semi-stall and blew the game. As one coach would say afterward, "Lewis spends $90,000 to recruit this amazing team, then has them play like Princeton." So Valvano had help from Houston.

And he had help from his own gritty champions from N.C. State. The Wolfpack were a hungry bunch of street fighters. Down the stretch, Sidney Lowe and Dereck Whittenburg and Terry Gannon made this incredible series of bombs—from no closer than 20 feet—to bring State back to a tie with a minute left. Then Valvano came running down the sideline and screamed at Whittenburg, "Foul the freshman." He meant Alvin Franklin. Whittenburg followed orders.

Franklin missed a one-and-one. State ball. State held. Whittenburg threw up a 30-footer with four seconds left. Everyone stood and watched, except Charles. He jumped. He had never had a chance to catch a national championship before.

When someone asked Whittenburg about his missed shot, Valvano whispered to him before he answered. Valvano does the jokes for everyone. Whittenburg said, "I assume you are referring to my pass."

All along their extraordinary journey, Jimmy V. told his team to have fun; he didn't want them to stop now. He had always had fun, all along the way, from Corona to Seaford, Long Island, to Rutgers and Johns Hopkins, to UConn and Bucknell, to Iona and finally State. Gym rat with the jokes. He became a better coach year by year. The funny lines became a little funnier. He kept dreaming about the day he would have it all.

They said he could never take North Carolina away from Dean Smith. He did that this year, beating Carolina twice, then winning the ACC tournament. They said a team with 10 losses had no shot at winning the national championship. Valvano said, "Why not?" Finally, when everyone except the Valvano family said he could not beat all the amazing skill of Phi Slama Jama. But Valvano could see the brass ring too closely now. It was his. The gym rat had it all.

So here he was late Monday night, on the podium, talking and talking and talking as only Jimmy V. can. And in the back of the room the old coach, Rocco Valvano, father of the national champion and a longtime coach in New York high schools, said softly, "Next to the day I was married and the days when my children were born, this is the happiest day of my life."

• *1983*

And Larry Brown stands by Kansas

Y
•

ou know the reputation. He is supposed to have gotten into more getaway cars than Bonnie and Clyde. He is Larry Brown. See the name and you are conditioned to think of a cloud of dust. Larry Brown? You hear him saying goodbye as soon as he says hello. He grabs his coat, gets his hat, leaves his worries on someone's doorstep.

Other coaches have moved more. Gene Bartow, who left Memphis State for UCLA and left UCLA for Alabama-Birmingham and is currently dickering with USC, comes to mind. He jumps in like Michael Jordan. Stan Albeck is a walking boarding pass. But Larry Brown —four head coaching jobs in 14 years—has become the Hester Prynne of coaching basketball. Scarlet letter deal. "L" for leaving.

"I can deal with people always referring to me leaving," Brown said yesterday morning from Lawrence, Kan. "I have moved. I don't hide from that responsibility. When I'm big news, they talk about the jobs I've left. I think it's old stuff."

Larry Brown is news again. For the second time he is taking a team to the Final Four. Once it was UCLA. This time it is the Kansas Jayhawks. You want to make Larry Brown Public Enemy No. 1 because he only stayed two years at that great UCLA job (five coaches in the 11 years since John Wooden packed it in) and only stayed two years in that great New Jersey Nets job (five coaches, 10

139

NBA seasons). Do it. Have a ball. But don't forget that there are very few people alive who can coach a basketball team better than he can.

Larry Brown leave? Yeah. The opportunities are always going to be there for him because what he mostly does is win. This he has done with a 35-3 Kansas team that is No. 2 in the country. For those of you keeping score at home, Brown is in the third year of a four-year contract. The fourth year will find him at Kansas. He will be coaching the Jayhawks next season, not the Knicks.

"I will definitely be here," he says.

Good news for Jayhawk fans. Very bad news for Knick fans, who thus finish a distant second in Browns.

See, there are more important numbers with Larry Brown than four jobs, 14 seasons. His lifetime record, ABA and NBA and college, is 571-303, a winning percentage of .650. His record in five college seasons stands at 125-38 (.767 winning percentage). Now he is one of seven men in history to coach in the Final Four with two different schools. He is a great coach.

Brown resigned at Denver after coaching the same team for seven years, whipped emotionally, at odds with team president Carl Scheer. He was working on one-year contracts when he left UCLA, just as Gary Cunningham, Bartow and Larry Farmer left UCLA. The contract he walked was in New Jersey. Brown could have done better there, much better (even if he never forgot that Joe Taub was ready to fire him after a 3-12 start in Brown's first season at the Meadowlands). He took the Kansas job with the Nets on the verge of the playoffs, Taub told him to beat it rather than finish the season; the young Nets, feeling betrayed, died.

He acted badly in Jersey and knows it. It doesn't change the part about him being a great coach.

"I'm very proud of what we've accomplished here with these kids," said Larry Brown. In three seasons under Brown, Kansas has won 81 games and lost 21. In Lawrence, they care more about what they see from Larry Brown than what they've heard. Last night they saw Brown and his team getting on a plane for Dallas.

In 1980, Brown took Kiki Vandeweghe and Mike Sanders and a bunch of freshmen to the championship game in Indianapolis before losing to Louisville. Saturday, a Larry Brown team will be back in the big show.

"The first time (in '80), I didn't realize how difficult it was to get there," Brown said. "We just kept winning, and all of a sudden we were right there. This time, I realize how lucky you have to be. Hey, little did we know back when we played the pre-season (Big Apple) NIT that three of us (Kansas, Louisville and Duke) would be reconvening in Dallas."

It almost didn't work out that way for Brown. In the semis of the Midwest Regional Friday night, Kansas was down two points to Michigan State with two minutes left. Ron Kellogg of Kansas received his fifth foul; it was generally acknowledged to be a phantom call. L. Brown got testy. He got too close to a ref named Bobby Dibler. He was so close his rolled-up program had a collision with Dibler's whistle. Scott Skiles would shoot a one-and-one, plus two free throws for the T. Fortunately for L. Brown, Skiles missed the first shot of the one-and-one. Kansas didn't go down six at that point. Kansas survived and won in overtime.

"You know how people say you can see your whole life passing in front of you when you're drowning?" laughed Brown. "It was like that on the T. One freeze frame after another. I saw the program hit the whistle. I saw the whistle begin to spin. I knew it was gonna hit him in the nose. I knew I had the T. But even then, I didn't think we'd lose, even if Skiles made all the free throws. I've had a feeling about these kids since October."

In Dallas, because of the way the draw worked out, No. 2 Kansas plays No. 1 Duke Saturday afternoon. Duke won by six in the Big Apple NIT. That was in November. Not much has separated the teams since. Duke is 36-2, Kansas 35-3. Duke is 16-2 against teams that were in the NCAA tournament, Kansas 15-3. Kansas has Danny Manning, Duke has Johnny Dawkins. Brown says the game will be very, very close.

"We can't give them second shots the way Navy did," said Brown. "We can't turn the ball over, because Dawkins hurts you a lot more in the transition game than he does shooting jump shots. We've got to be seven points better than we were in November in the NIT, because the season has come full circle."

The career of Larry Brown will only come full circle if he coaches someday at alma mater North Carolina, or with the Knicks, since he grew up in New York. But for now he is at Kansas. He will be at Kansas next year, winning. He is one of the very best. Yeah, Larry Brown left Lawrence yesterday. For another Final Four, which figures.

• *1986*

Road can take a strange turn

T here are no real road maps for these things, despite all the business about the road to the Final Four. You just kind of end up there.

Rony Seikaly was born in Lebanon. His family moved to Athens when he was 10. He had this aunt in Syracuse. He visited his aunt one summer, he went to coach Jim Boeheim's basketball camp. Then one day Seikaly walked into Boeheim's office and said, "I want to play." Boeheim, whose eye for detail is a bit keener than his sense of humor, noticed right off that Seikaly was 6-11. Boeheim said: OK, Zorba.

And four years later, in the last two games of the East Regional, Seikaly plays maybe the best two games of his life, scores 33 against Florida and 26 against North Carolina. Syracuse finally beats Carolina, 79-75. Syracuse is going to the Final Four for the first time under Boeheim. The big Zorba carries Boeheim the last few yards, and is named MVP of the East Regional.

Syracuse hadn't been to the Final Four since 1975. They weren't supposed to go this year, despite the No. 2 seeding in the East. Seikaly changed all that. He goes to New Orleans by way of Lebanon and Athens and Boeheim's camp and Boeheim's office and East Rutherford, N.J.

Kenny Smith, of course, doesn't go at all. And when

he left Lefrak City for North Carolina, Smith must have thought he would go all the time.

"Surprised?" he would say softly outside the Carolina locker room when it was over. "Yes, that's a good word. I am disappointed and surprised."

Smith, from Archbishop Molloy, was the best of some great city guards who came out of high school in 1983. There were Mark Jackson and Pearl Washington and Kenny Hutchinson, who ended up at Arkansas. Smith, it seemed, made the smart play. North Carolina had won the national championship two years before. Smith, another New York guard headed down to Dean Smith, would be handed the ball at the most consistently excellent program in the country.

He had the ball for four years. And after the loss to Syracuse yesterday, Smith had never played on a North Carolina team that won the ACC tournament. And Kenny Smith never made it to the Final Four. A lot of guards went from New York to Chapel Hill to a Final Four somewhere. Kenny Smith was good as any of them. He never made it. Again, there are no road maps. Kenny Smith is an All-America, he was named Player-of-the-Year by "Basketball Times," he is talked about as a Lottery pick in the NBA.

It's just that March never gave him anything.

Dean Smith said, "This has been a great North Carolina basketball team, one of the best we've ever had." But Syracuse went 8-0 at the start, Carolina never did get the lead, and Seikaly (11 rebounds) and Derrick Coleman (14 rebounds) just kept beating Smith's team up inside. Smith tried to change it all. He got his team back into the game with a three-pointer that started Carolina out of a 53-38 hole. He would score 20 in the second half.

But the three-pointer that could have tied it at 76 with a minute left bounced off the back of the rim, and when the ball landed in Howard Triche's hands, so did Kenny Smith's last chance.

In the interview room, Smith said that losing the big game in March "is not characteristic of your growth as a player or person. . . . A certain game doesn't indicate how a player has grown."

One year it was Indiana in the Round of 16 and another year it was Villanova in the Round of Eight and last year it was Louisville in the 16s. Now Syracuse. This one was hardest. Smith is a senior, the game was in Jersey, a group of 50 supporters—friends and family—was at Meadowlands Arena.

"I had a little following," Smith said.

Outside the locker room, William Smith, the father, hugged him, and Ann Smith, the mother, kissed him. Kenny Smith said, "Got to shower, I'll be quick." His mother smiled and said, "He's kidding about quick."

Smith sat in a corner of the locker room. He talked about the second half, when he almost brought the Tar Heels back by himself. The first half was bad, just five points. But after the Tar Heels got behind by that 53-38, it was Smith for three, Smith on a drive, Smith to Dave Popson, Smith scoring when Coleman goaltended. Now it was 55-51, and the game was on.

Finally, the three from the corner bounced away, and the game was over. Smith said he would watch the Final Four on television. He said Billy Donovan, against whom he played in high school when Molloy got after St. Agnes (Rockville Centre), is a friend.

At 7 o'clock, Boeheim and Seikaly were still in the interview area. Kenny Smith and Dean Smith walked out onto the empty court. Kenny Smith found his parents. Some of the 50 who had come from Queens to watch were still in the stands. When they saw Kenny Smith, they began to applaud. The road had ended close to home, anyway.

• 1987

THIS JUST ISN'T CRICKET

Like I said at the start. I get 200 or so columns a year. They aren't always going to be about the Olympics, or big games, or sad songs. Sometimes I just sit down and decide to have some fun. And I write about baseball games that take 604 hours, or cricket, or Cyndy Garvey.

By the way: I went back to Wimbledon in 1986. I still don't understand cricket.

•

Part 6

604 hours later, it's finally over

In a game that took 604 hours and 15 minutes, the Kansas City Royals finally defeated the New York Yankees 5-4 yesterday, before an announced crowd of 1,245 at Yankee Stadium.

In the first game of the doubleheader, played in courthouses in both the Bronx and Manhattan, Judge Joseph Sullivan of the Appellate Division of the Supreme Court of the State of New York bested Judge Orest Maresca of the State Supreme Court 1-0 in a tight, exciting pitchers' duel. Judge Maresca was relieved by lawyer Roy Cohn, the feisty little former relief hurler for Sen. Joseph McCarthy, in the ninth inning. The judges wore black, by the way. Roy Cohn wore lavender.

After the doubleheader, it was announced that George Steinbrenner, the principal owner of the Yankees, had optioned Judge Maresca to Columbus of the International League, but both Steinbrenner and the judge were unavailable for comment.

Or something like that.

Anyway, it is mercifully over now, after the 604 hours of a game that began around two o'clock on July 24 and ended about 6:20 on August 18; after a George Brett home run that was, then wasn't, then was; after a bat that had a lot of pine tar on it went from Yankee Stadium to the American League office to Detroit by Emory Air Freight and then into history; after one class action suit

147

and one individual suit and an injunction for one judge and another judge going into legal history by actually yelling "Play Ball"; after 10 pitches from Royals' reliever Dan Quisenberry ended this Marx Brother fiasco once and for all. A home run is still a home run. Lee MacPhail, the AL president, is still the most decent man in baseball. Royals 5, Yankees 4. Finis.

All we know for sure now about the national pastime is this: The opera ain't over 'till the judge at the Appellate Division of the State Supreme Court of New York sings.

The end of the Tar Wars Saga was supposed to be a happening, an event, a piece of baseball history. There were supposed to be so many thousands and thousands of people pouring through the turnstiles at Yankee Stadium that the U.S. Marines wouldn't be able to handle crowd control. I read somewhere that because of reduced security at the Stadium, we might have "another Diana Ross concert on our hands." Well, the whole scene at the Stadium was about as dangerous as a Diana Ross rehearsal. And if there were 1200 people there, well, my name is Judge Orest Maresca. Try about 500. The thing began silly and ended silly, and in the end they gave a Pine Tar game and no-body came.

Still, the last chapter almost wasn't played out. This Judge Maresca of the Bronx, who obviously left judge's school after he got to the part about Joe DiMaggio's 56-game hitting streak, tried to en-join the AL from playing the game yesterday morning. Judge Maresca, a shining light in his profession clearly, did this because of law suits brought against the Yankees by ticket holders aged six and seven and 14. The six-year-old and his seven-year-old brother handled the first suit. It was class action. The 14-year-old handled the second. It was individual.

I would have sentenced these little brats to a lifetime of watching indoor soccer, but not Judge Maresca, who was obviously auditioning for a spot on "The People's Court."

"Yankee pinstripes are the end-all and be-all of young and some-times old Yankee fans," the judge wrote in his breathtaking decision. My decision is that he and the brats should be sent to their rooms un-til Thanksgiving.

After that, the American League appealed, and down everybody went to the Appellate Division on Madison Avenue, where we found the true star of the day, Judge Joseph Sullivan, who is forever more my hero. He watched while the lawyers representing the AL, Robert

Kheel and Lou Hoynes, kicked Roy Cohn (representing the Yankees) and his daring lavender outfit around for awhile. Cohn and his guys, who kept trying to act like victims, tried to worry the world about security at the Stadium, but Judge Sullivan, my hero, was having none of it. He really did say "Play Ball" at the end.

It was on to the Stadium. The Royals had flown into Newark Airport, sat around for a while, then came to the Stadium not knowing whether they would play. They got the word from Judge Sullivan: Play ball. They did. Billy Martin, the FLG (fiery little genius) tried to protest about Brett not touching all the bases 600 hours before. Ump Dave Phillips pulled out a notarized statement from the original umpiring crew that basically said: "He touched all the bases, fiery little genius." Hal McRae went out for the Royals. Don Mattingly, Roy Smalley and Oscar Gamble went out for the Yankees. It was over, 604 hours and 15 minutes after it began.

Gee, isn't it amazing how time flies when you're having fun?

• *1985*

How Lupica 'did in' Giants

Here are some things I thought contributed to the Giants failure to defend their Super Bowl title this season:

The players strike. George Young's refusal to seek out quality scabs. The strike. Karl Nelson getting cancer, Chris Godfrey getting hurt, Brad Benson not blocking anybody. Joe Morris getting off to a very bad start. Raul Allegre missing a field goal in Giants-Cowboys I and Phil Simms not missing Too Tall Jones with a couple of passes in Giants-Cowboys II.

Now I find out there were more sinister forces at work with the defending Super Bowl champions.

Tape recorders.

I find that the fact that Bill Parcells and lots of Giants players and even strength coach Johnny Parker doing books started the Big Blue on the road to ruin.

So I'm here to take my share of the responsibility for the 1-6 record the Giants took into last night's game with the New England Patriots. I wrote Parcells' autobiography for him.

The tape recorder I used was a Sony Cassette Corder TCM-858.

Call it Exhibit A.

Forget about Raul Allegre missing the kind of field goal he made in the Giants' big run last season. Forget cancer. Forget the rotten pass Simms threw right at Ed (Too Tall) Jones (I was surprised Jones didn't catch it in his teeth).

Forget all that.

My tape recorder did it to the Giants. And tape recorders belonging to Dave Klein, who wrote Leonard Marshall's book, and Hank Gola, who teamed up with Jim Burt, and Dick Schaap, who hooked up with both Simms and McConkey; and David Falkner, who got together with Lawrence Taylor for that how-to book about hitting 5-irons and conquering addiction to drugs and alcohol.

Here is how we did things to the Giants that no one in the National Football League did last season: We got Parcells and Taylor and Simms and McConkey into rooms and turned on the tape recorders and made them talk about themselves.

You can imagine what an ordeal that must have been for people associated with professional sports, and the celebrity that comes with winning a Super Bowl.

Sometimes I made Parcells talk about himself for a full two hours at a stretch in March before his coaches would show up and he would go to work.

It was probably in these early sessions, when Parcells was talking about his first coaching job in Hastings, Nebraska, that Parcells' team began to unravel.

Somewhere in Jersey, Dave Klein of the Star-Ledger was doing the same thing with Marshall. Schaap, he was probably in Manhattan, ruining Simms and McConkey the way he once did the Green Bay Packers, after he wrote that first book with Jerry Kramer.

"The other teams in the NFL asked me to write a book with Simms and McConkey, Dick Schaap said yesterday. "I guess they thought it was the book I did with Namath that ruined his knees."

As it turns out, we were doing more damage to the Giants than the most inept group of scabs in the history of strike-breaking.

Later on, the players appeared on talk shows and talked more about themselves. Parcells didn't do any talk shows, or any appearances of any kind; it is why "Parcells II: The Year We Nearly Finished Behind Dartmouth in the Ivy League" is somewhat unlikely from Bonus Books of Chicago, Illinois; Bonus Books didn't think Parcells was such a good sport.

One day at training camp, Parcells stood behind a podium, answered some questions, posed for a couple of pictures, went back to coach his team. Is he a salesman or what? Stop it, Parcells, you're killing us.

But it was the tape recorders, and the talking, and then having to take the time to read the manuscripts in galleys that were listed Sunday as the first Daily News reason—chronologically—that the Giants were in the fix they were in last night as they got ready to play the Patriots.

Distracting, the books were.

This is pretty funny, even for New York.

I would suggest cancer is more distracting than a Sony Cassette Corder TCM-858; but then, I'm a suspect here.

I say that all defending champions in sports, whether the team has a lot of authors or not, come back flat, and then don't repeat. That is without cancer, holdouts (Gary Reasons), a strike, missed field goals, a fourth quarter collapse in Dallas, things like that.

The Giants started poststrike season 0-5, and were lucky enough to get the St. Louis Bidwills first. The Giants, who had struggled before the strike, came back not having solved their problems, just postponed them, and it is a fact they played like chokers last Monday night.

The Giants were thin in the secondary before they told Elvis Patterson to have real good luck with the rest of his life.

"You were a great team last season," I kept saying to Parcells in his office.

Parcells kept saying: "We *finished* great. I think we were a very good team and everything broke right for us when we were getting that winning streak started." He kept talking about how different things would have been if the Giants had lost those close games to the Vikings or Broncos or 49ers.

Now things have gone all wrong. That is Parcells' problem, not mine, he's a big boy. The real Giants were 1-3 before last night, the scabs were 0-3. The Mets had hernias and rehab. The Giants have had Karl Nelson and a strike. The Mets had 162 games to try to get over hernias, rehab, all the sore arms.

The Giants came back from the strike with 10 games, needing to win nine.

Talk to me about the unfairness of that, if you think it's unfair. Talk to me about the choke against Dallas. Talk about Morris and Benson and Allegre's miss and Simms' lousy pass.

Don't talk to me about a Sony.

I mean, you think somebody should warn the Twins?

• *1987*

England's 'Boys of Summer' do it up dull

LONDON

S
•

omewhere, across the ocean where the sun shines and there is such a thing as summer, there is a baseball season. There are stories about Reggie Jackson hitting home runs, and Pat Zachry shutting out the Pirates; the Yankees padding their lead and the Mets scratching towards .500. Phil Rizzuto, God bless him, is saying "Holy Cow!" Joe Garagiola and Tony Kubek are describing games on Saturday afternoons. Tommy John is throwing ground balls. Mike Schmidt is taking someone deep. And I miss it all.

And I sit in front of a television set while it rains on a city constantly being punished, one called London, and I watch a silly game known as cricket. I specifically watch something called the Corn Hill Test, between an English all-star team and one from the West Indies, in a stadium named Old Trafford. Then the next morning, I pick up the newspapers and I do not get game stories by my man Bill Madden or Jack Lang or Phil Pepe. This is what I get instead, from a man named John Woodcock, who writes for *The Times* of London:

"Thirteen wickets fell for 188 runs when the third Cornhill Test match started at Old Trafford yesterday. Having been put in, England was bowled out for a miserable 24 runs. When England fielded the initiative remained with the bowlers, West

153

Indies being 38 for three when, to England's frustration, bad light removed 90 of the day's last 100 minutes."

Catch your breath for a second. It gets better. Woodcock continues:

"The only batsmen on the two sides to make more than 11 were Rose, Gatting and Richards. The reason for the low scoring was not, I think, any inadequacy in the pitch, new though it is, as much as the relentless pressure applied by the fast bowlers and the heavy cover of the cloud which allowed ample movement off the seam."

That must give you a pretty clear idea of how the Cornhill Test match went on Thursday. But just in case you have any questions, Woodcock sums things up late in his story:

"In Marshall's next over Rose was bowled off his pads and Willey behind his legs. In his last nine test innings, Willey had made 82 runs. Knott, called for a single to backward square leg by Botham, the non-striker, hesitated in the call and was stranded far from home. This was a wanton waste."

West Indies ended the day 112 runs behind England. I am not sure, but I think Knott's single to the backward square leg and Willey going behind his legs had a lot to do with this.

Before I tell you a little more about this thrilling match, let me take you around the league. Bad news for Middlesex fans. Middlesex, with six first inning wickets in hand, is 128 runs behind Hampshire. In *The Times*, this was Alan Gibson's opening paragraph about that slugfest:

"Since, during the previous three days of cricket I had attended, there had been a total of less than an hour and a half's play, I was glad to see some yesterday—not that either the cricket or the weather were exhilarating. After lugging my overcoat around on a succession of damp, close days, I had left it in Summerset on a grey and cold one."

Well, there you go. Middlesex is in all kinds of trouble against Hampshire, and poor Alan Gibson left his overcoat in Somerset.

I have been watching cricket for seven summers now. I have even gone to cricket matches, and had some poor, crazed English devil who actually likes this sport try to explain it to me. I watch it because there is a man who throws a ball and a man who tries to hit it, and people in pants who try to catch it. It is played on green grass, occasionally in sunshine. And I have not a clue about what is going on.

All I know is that a match begins around tea time on Tuesday, and by the end of the day, someone is leading by, say, 542 to 3. But the match doesn't end on Tuesday, or Wednesday, or Thursday. By tea time on Thursday, the team that was losing 542 to 3 catches up. Then it rains for a couple of days, and by the following Tuesday I am told that someone has won by two measly wickets. I consider all of this especially wonderful.

You can imagine how excited I am about this Cornhill Test. I sit and wave my souvenir Union Jack for Graham Gooch and Ian Botham and all my other favorite players on the English side. This is a big grudge match for us, because the hated West Indians beat us by two wickets last winter in our test match in Melbourne, Australia. I said "Wait till next year" when I heard about that one. I just know we're going to fix them at Old Trafford.

We've just got to take the initiative with our fast bowlers, and keep those wickets from tumbling. If we can keep it close—within 200 runs or so—I think Graham Gooch can take one of the West Indians deep.

Here are some other observations I have made about cricket after studying the sport intently over 7,897 consecutive rainy afternoons in London:

1.) The pitchers (known as bowlers) are ahead of the hitters. This is mostly because they can take a running start from what would be the second base area in baseball. Then they're allowed to bounce the ball right before it reaches the batter. The batters then hit a lot of ground ball outs, or so it seems to me. But then the BBC cameras cut to the crowd, and everybody is waving Union Jacks, and suddenly the score is 33-0.

So I wave my Union Jack.

2.) It must be hard to cheat in cricket. This I have figured out because when something isn't nice in England, someone says, "That isn't cricket."

3.) Cricket is a great sport for England, a country in which people just go from one queue to another, waiting for something to happen. Despite all those fabulous run scoring innings in cricket, there is a whole lot of standing around by guys in white pants.

4.) Foul balls must be brilliant. Every time the guy with the bat hits a ball behind him and I think the count should be 0 and 1 the camera cuts to the crowd again, and everybody is waving Union Jacks. If the ball hits the batter in his shin pad, and he misses it completely, they practically stop the match and have a ticker tape parade. Churchill comes out of the sky and announces the war in Europe is over.

Incidentally, it does not look good for our side against the hated West Indians. We looked to be in the driver's seat after Thursday's play, when we were ahead by 112 runs. Then this old guy named Clive had a big day at the dish for West Indies, and by the time it got dark on Friday, we were behind by 69 runs. But let my man Woodcock of *The Times* tell it:

"A belt of rain reduced play in the third Cornhill Test match in Old Trafford yesterday to three hours and ten minutes—80 minutes in the morning and another 110 minutes after tea. In that time, West Indies in their first three innings, advanced from 38 for three to 219 for seven.

"This marks a decline in England's fortunes after they had taken the fifth West Indian wicket, the vital one of Richards, when the score was only 100. They had the advantage of bowling with the wet ball for awhile and of finding Clive Lloyd in fine form. Willis has also bowled with a drastic lack of success: In fourteen overs he has been hit for no fewer than 21 fours."

Somewhere, in a baseball season, in a wonderful place called New York City, Lee Mazzilli has begun to tattoo the old horsehide. Ron Guidry won his 10th, in Texas. I am told that Craig Swan went up against Bert Blyleven at Shea Friday night.

But right now I've got to get back to the Cornhill Test match. I think England gets to bat around tea time today. I don't know what happened to Alan Gibson's overcoat. I hate cricket.

• 1980

Shooting from the Lip II

I say the Spinks brothers just go ahead and open a darn driving school.

Mary Beth Whitehead is a fertile little scamp, isn't she?

Susan Butcher won the Iditarod Sled Dog Race for the second year in a row, so who the heck says you can't repeat in sports anymore?

If the NFL tested for steroids, the Super Bowl would have to be 5-on-5.

Dick Enberg can stay on NBC's No. 1 announcing team when it comes to pro football, but it's time for Father Murphy to go back to the prairie.

I give you this news item straight: "A new Polish translation of A.A. Milne's classic children's book 'Winnie the Pooh' switches the sex of the lovable bear from male to female." Whoo. Look out Heidi, is all I can say.

I saw the closing numbers of CBS's New Year's Eve show with Gladys Knight, the Pips, and Brent Musburger, and I tell you this as honestly as I can: I do not think Brent Musburger makes a very good Pip.

Lawrence Taylor really isn't a Larry, is he?

The new layout for *Sports Illustrated* makes it look like a bound version of *USA Today*.

I feel it is going to be very difficult for Bess Myerson to get her consumer column back in the *Daily News*.

I like Kevin Loughery, but there's something you need to know about him: The Bullets need to go on an 152-game winning streak for him to get to .500 as an NBA coach.

I think I understand the judicial system of San Diego, California, now: Every month or so it tries to give Gene Klein another $5 million of Al Davis' money.

The Denver Nuggets uniforms look like they were designed by Cyndi Lauper.

Favorite USA *Today* headline, Feb. 6, 1987: "Volleyball coaches refute Wimp's digs at their sport." This one could get ugly before it's through.

Any Mets get arrested since you started this?

If that basketball player Lloyd Daniels has to go to jail, it might give him time to work on that elusive high school diploma.

Professional boxing, interest-wise, is professional bowling, just with more creeps.

Sugar Ray Leonard versus Marvelous Marvin Hagler was that last *Road* movie Hope and Crosby never got to make.

The rivalry between Martina and Chris, at the end, is like *The Honeymooners*. Same 39 original episodes, over and over and over again.

By the way, if you've been reading the gossip columns, it's hard to tell whether Chris is setting her sights on the Grand Slam, or a seat next to Chuck Woolery on *Love Connection*.

Steve Carlton talks more than Kris Kristofferson did in *Amerika*.

When I open up the Baseball Encyclopedia, it gives off a beam of light.

I was reading about Gerry Cooney in the Miami *Herald* the other day and he said he was in great shape, and my question is: Relative to what?

FIGHTERS

I don't get to the racetrack as often as I should. And the *Daily News* has a gifted boxing writer named Michael Katz, so I don't see as many big fights as I used to. But I have never gone to the track and come away without the makings of a column. Same with fighters and fights. The chapter is headlined "Fighters"? You bet. Read about Ron Turcotte and tell me the little guys aren't as tough as the guys named Vito.

Part 7

Spinks put Gerry away
for all time

Michael Spinks had Gerry Cooney in the middle of the ring now, hitting him with everything and beginning a public service. There was no place for Cooney to hide anymore, not behind a phantom rotator cuff or his addict brother or free enterprise or love of country or Dennis Rappaport or all the ones who have always made him something he is not, which is a boxer. Or a champion.

The time for hiding was over. Michael Spinks just kept hitting Cooney. It was easy. These were not combinations. This was just a session on the heaviest bag in boxing.

In the second row of the VIP section at Convention Hall, Sugar Ray Leonard got up on his chair and began to dance. As he danced, he threw punches, straight lefts and overhand rights and then uppercuts, along with Michael Spinks. Spinks was getting ready to knock some slugs named Cooney and Rappaport out of the sport, and Sugar Ray Leonard kept dancing and smiling and shouting, "Yeah!"

"See," he said to Mike Tyson, who was next to him. "I told you."

Sugar Ray Leonard yelled, "Get him, Michael." He meant Spinks, but up in the ring Michael Spinks needed no further encouragement. The getting was easy.

Before the fight, Donald Trump—the organizer of Spinks-Cooney in Convention Hall—asked Leonard who would win. Leonard, who fought with Spinks on the 1976 Olympic boxing team and who knows champions when he sees them, said to Trump, "Michael. Don't worry about Michael. Michael is a pro."

Now it was over. Cooney sat down. He dragged himself up. The ref stepped in and looked at him, but the ref couldn't help Gerry Cooney, not unless he was suddenly going to give Cooney a boxing lesson. Tyson, who did not stand up on his chair, did not get a very good look at the last few seconds of Cooney's sorry career. It did not matter much to Tyson. He would have made a lot of money if Cooney had won. Now he will make more vs. Spinks, which will be the most interesting heavyweight matchup since Frazier-Ali I.

In the third row of the VIP section, Tyson's co-manager, Jimmy Jacobs, just shook his head and pointed to Cooney, in his neutral corner and doing what he has done for most of this decade: Sitting.

"It is one thing to fight straight ahead," Jimmy Jacobs said. "It is another thing to keep walking in there without any plan whatsoever."

I said to Jacobs, "Spinks knocks that guy out of the sport, right?"

Jacobs said, "I would think so." Jacobs went and collected Mike Tyson. Tyson is one who fought, who earned the title, who has ducked no one. Tyson is for real. Jacobs told Tyson they would meet in the lobby at 9 in the morning and he would take Tyson to the airport and Tyson would fly to New York. In New York yesterday, Jacobs probably made the first phone calls about a Tyson-Spinks fight that probably will not happen until next year.

Jacobs just smiled last night when Atlantic City was hailed as "the boxing capital of the world."

"Small world," he said.

And when Spinks was introduced as "heavyweight champion of the world," Tyson, one row up and a few seats to the right of Jimmy Jacobs, laughed and started clapping.

"What's so funny?" Sugar Ray Leonard asked Tyson. The two of them were dressed in white. Ray looked pretty good. Tyson looked like the Good Humor man with an attitude.

"I don't know, it's funny," Tyson said.

Spinks will not be as funny for Tyson down the road. Even with the consideration that Cooney is the heaviest possible bag, Spinks still hit him with more than Larry Holmes did. Spinks looked like a heavyweight in Atlantic City, hit like a heavyweight, took a couple of hooks from Cooney and survived a cut. Maybe it is time to wonder what exactly you have to do to beat Michael Spinks in a boxing ring.

Somebody asked Jimmy Jacobs before the fight who he thought would win.

"I wouldn't bet the fight," said Jacobs, who is a smart, pleasant man. "But if you put a hundred dollars on the table and told me I could have it if I correctly picked the fight, I would reluctantly take Cooney."

He was a little bit wrong. The way the betting line—7-5 for Cooney? *Gerry Cooney?*—was wrong, and the way all the boxing writers who've sold Cooney for years have been wrong.

Sugar Ray Leonard knew the line was wrong, because Leonard knows champions. The rest of us will probably keep underestimating Michael Spinks as he continues to win big fights into 1990.

We keep him now. We get Spinks-Tyson. I don't care so much about boxing, and was in Atlantic City for other business, but I would very much like to see Spinks-Tyson—in Convention Hall, as a matter of fact.

As for Cooney, the sensitive and misunderstood fellow I've been reading about for so long—well, he goes away now. He goes away for good. He takes his sweaty manager Rappaport with him. Give Rappaport credit. He made a lot of money out of very little boxer, if you discount Cooney's size. He sold whiteness, he appealed to the worst in everybody, and showed again you can make millions doing that. Rappaport made big money and was small-time all the way. Spinks knocked Cooney out and he knocked this Rappaport out, and I think you give Spinks back his IBF title for that.

Mike Tyson also got up on his chair one time Monday night. It was when Cooney climbed into the ring. Others clapped or booed. Tyson just stared. It was as close as he will ever get to Gerry Cooney in a boxing ring.

"Where you going?" Sugar Ray asked.

"I want to see Cooney," Mike Tyson said.

At least he got to see him. Most heavyweights never did.

• *1987*

Vito: The champ of Mulberry Street

T he old men yelled at each other in Italian on sun-washed Mulberry Street, and tiny old women carrying cloth purses hurried past them into Most Precious Blood Church. Mulberry was beginning to smile and sing again after the storms. Across the street from the church, most of the regulars were back at Le Bella Ferrara: Pepino and Madaldo Ciarcia and Dominic DeLucia, who will be 100 soon and honored by a block party. Mary, who works the pastry shop side of La Bella Ferrara, was there, and Vic, who works the cappuccino side, and the owners, the Angelieri brothers. Cha-Cha was there, as always. Only Vito Antuofermo, the boxer, was not there.

"When Vito's fightin', " said Nicky Angelieri, "he don' wanna know nuthin' from nobody."

On this morning they were all talking about Vito, the middleweight who has become the king of Mulberry, the first fighting hero they have had in many years since Nino Bevenuti retired. Here at this pastry shop across from the famous church which is the first landmark of Little Italy, they ate the cannolis and the tortonis and the rum cake, sipped cappuccino at the little marble tables while the songs of the great Mina filled the room, and talked about Antuofermo, whom they have adopted.

"Vito fights right here in the street some o' the time," said Cha-Cha Ciarcia, who is the son of Mafaldo and thinks of himself as the mayor of Mulberry. "The last

Monday in June it was, Italian Unity Day. John Condon brought the boxing ring down from the Garden and the San Gennaro Band played, and Vito fought a coupla rounds right here for his people.

"If he wasn't trainin', Vito, he'd be here right now," said Cha-Cha, wiping cream from a cannoli off his mustache. "He'd be havin' some coffee and maybe some sflogliatelle, his favorite pastry, and before you know it 30 people be right here. And you wouldn't see Vito bein' able to pick up no checks."

"He always try," said a man named Ronnie from another table.

"Yeah," said Pepino, "that Vito don' wanna be takin' no handouts from nobody."

Autuofermo is 25 and has a left hook. He was born in Bari, Italy, and now lives in Brooklyn. But because he is a boxer who was born in Italy, he really is of Mulberry Street and Little Italy. The reason he was not at La Bella Ferrara on this morning was because he wants to take a middleweight fight from a Philadelphia fighter named Briscoe next Friday at the Garden. If he wins the fight, he will probably get a shot at the world middleweight championship held by Rodrigo Valdes. In La Bella Ferrara, they are planning a big party for after the Briscoe fight. If it was the spring, it would be in the street.

"He goes through Briscoe like he don' see him," said Cha-Cha. "He puts him away in five, maybe six if he don't get cut. And then, after what I seen of the Briscoe-Valdes fights, Vito gonna bring some left hooks and finish Valdes' career for him."

There used to be a lot of stories about fighters like Vito Antuofermo, in other days of boxing. Came to America when he was 16. Grew up on Flatbush Ave. in Brooklyn. Ran with gangs. Caught by the police in a gang fight when he was 16. Cop takes him to a gym instead of the precinct house at Flatbush and Snyder Ave. A trainer named Joey LaGardia takes him over. Wins the Golden Gloves two years running. Turns pro. Marries neighborhood girl. Fights himself into shot for a championship while working as a mechanic.

"The cop asked me if I was a fighter," Antuofermo was saying the other day after a workout at Gleasons' Gym. "I said, 'Yeah.' I just wanted to stay out of trouble."

He has fought 44 times as a pro and has lost three times, twice because of cuts. The fights are in his face, especially above the eyes. But if he can stay away from cuts over two more fights, it is thought the left hook might make him champion of the world. He already rules Mulberry Sreet.

"Those people," said Antuofermo quietly, "have become such a big part of what I do. It's the glory they give me. If you don't have the glory, you can get so tired."

"We gon' have us a world champ-een," yelled Pepino at La Bella Ferrara yesterday morning. The old men cheered. Cha-Cha waved for more cannolis as a Sinatra song eased into the room.

• *1978*

Holmes must kayo
shadow of Ali

LAS VEGAS

 e is the heavyweight champion of the world and has never lost and has knocked out all the miserable pugs sent his way. And yet there is still so much of him that is sparring partner, making $500 a week plus room and board from Muhammad Ali, waiting for a chance to show his stuff.

Larry Holmes will tell you how much he loves the woods of Easton, Pa., and the quiet and being left alone. Then he will turn around, like a man playing a theater-in-the-round, and tell you how much he loves Vegas, loves the action, loves the tables, even loves Ali for agreeing to fight this fight with him.

"Don't you see?" Larry Holmes, the heavyweight champ-een of the world will say. "Ali is making you KNOW me." He will tell you how strong he is and full of energy, how he is going to knock Ali out in an early round, then suddenly he will look around his hotel suite and ask, "How many people in here really think I'm gonna win this fight?"

Holmes tries to call Ali a chump, tries to do lines about how old Ali is, and says all the right things about Ali being washed up, but somehow the words do not sound right. And, in the next mouthful, he is telling you that Ali has been a great fighter and a great athlete and a great human being and that, by God, nothing is going to change his mind about all that. Then he tells you that a legend is only something men write.

Larry Holmes never had any say in the scheduling of the acts, you see. He never asked to come out after Ali. Holmes is the singer of ballads who had to come out after the naked dancers were lowered from the ceiling. And it has confused him. And he does not feel like a champion. And he has sensed that nothing he does in a boxing ring will ever be enough. On Wednesday afternoon, as Holmes graciously entertained a platoon of media people in his suite at Caesars Palace, someone asked him why he finally gave up the $500-a-week job as Ali's sparring partner, back in 1975.

"I couldn't follow him around and be a sparring partner all my life," Holmes said.

But he is still that sparring partner, because he perceives himself to be that. Only on Thursday night can he end that particular career. It does not matter that his hands are as fast as Ali's ever were. It does not matter that he can throw combinations that are like hot jazz riffs. It does not matter how many men he has knocked out in succession. Larry Holmes, a good man, has to beat Muhammad Ali so he can get on with the business of being heavyweight champion of the world. A long time ago, Joe Frazier had to do the same thing. Larry Holmes wants to own the title, not the lease.

"I want to get this monkey out of there as quick as I can," he was saying Wednesday. "One round won't be too soon. I know the bottles will fly and the beer cans will fly, and I don't care. I'm young, I'm strong, I'm full of endurance, and he knows it. He's old, he's washed up, he's had it. When I whup Ali, they're all gonna say I whupped an old man, and they gonna be right."

Holmes had been down in the big room at Caesars shooting craps. Don King had been with him, and Angelo Dundee had been at the other end of the table, and all of them had put on a show for the crowd that gathered around the table. Dundee made pass after pass and kept shouting at Holmes. Then Holmes did the same thing, to cheers. A heckler shouted that Holmes should save his money, that Ali was going to retire after Thursday night. Holmes grinned and said, "Go ahead, bet on that old fool."

After a while, Holmes turned to the writers pressing around him and said, "Y'all ever seen a press conference at a dice table before?" King announced that the party was moving to Holmes' suite. Now

Holmes was sitting on a purple couch in the suite's main room, hold-ing his six-month-old daughter Candy in his arms, talking about a fight with Muhammad Ali.

"I never thought I'd get the chance to fight Ali," he said. "He avoided me for a couple of years. Why is he fightin' me now? 'Cause there's no other one for him to fight. The only way he can get the proper money is through me and Don King."

Across the room from Holmes was a lifesize poster of Ali, one on which a lot of artwork had been done. The poster looked a lot like the side of a New York subway train, and above Ali's face was written "Dark Gable." On another wall, off to Holmes' right, was a drawing of the mansion he plans to build in Easton. Next to the drawing was this list, handwritten:

"First: My Wife.

My Children.

My family.

My house.

P.S. My pool."

Someone asked him about the stability of his life, as opposed to the chaos of Muhammad Ali's.

"Don't mistake my kindness for my weakness," Larry Holmes said firmly. "I change when I get into the ring. I'm like the weather. I'm good one minute, bad the next."

Then he talked a lot about Ali. Holmes said that the night Ali won the title from Sonny Liston, he was probably at St. Anthony's Youth Center "rasslin'. " That he first met Ali in 1971 when Dundee took him up to Deer Lake for a training session. That he always knew he could beat Ali, even when he was a sparring partner. That he would not be fighting when he was 38 years old. That he would not even be fighting when he is 32. Holmes will be 31 next month.

Should Ali be fighting at 38, someone asked.

"I always say, a man's gonna do what he wants to do," Holmes said. "When I'm 38, I won't be a fighter."

He was asked this: What if he lost on Thursday night?

"We not gonna if, if, if in here," Holmes said quickly, nearly cut-ting the questioner off. "If the world comes to an end, we all gonna be in trouble."

Someone mentioned Ali's various careers, his interest in other fields besides boxing.

"I don't know about history or geology," Holmes said. "I just know about knocking suckers out."

If he can knock out a sucker named Muhammad Ali tomorrow night, then Larry Holmes, the heavyweight champion of the world, can win the heavyweight championship of the world.

• *1980*

Solar boxing club is facing the final count

E xcept for Jose Miro, the gym was empty in the middle of the afternoon, lit only by the sunlight that fought its way through dirty gray windows. Miro wore street clothes and a fur hat and heavy boots, which made rough noises as he circled the heavy bag, throwing awkward combinations and talking about Teo Stevenson's fight on television the day before.

Other than Miro, an old man who likes to come to the Solar Sporting Club in the afternoons, the place was empty. No gunfire from the fast bag. No bells. No slap of rope hitting the floor. There was none of the music of a boxing gym. The Solar S.C., the best gym in New York, is dying. And, in the afternoon, before the kids came from school, it looked dead already.

Jose Miro, lost in dreams of youth, stalked the heavy bag. He threw a long right, a left hook, another straight right hand. He shuffled around on his heavy work boots, exhaled sharply, threw another combination. The sound of a car horn blowing on W. 28th St. rushed in through the Solar's one open window.

"How's that for a skinny guy?" asked Jose Miro, loudly. "You see those punches? You see 'em? I shoulda started boxing when I was a kid, I always knew it."

Jose Miro went off to work on the fast bag, which in the Solar hangs in front of a yellow poster for the second fight between Muhammad Ali and Joe Frazier, the one in

1974. Frazier trained in the Solar for that one. The spectators lined the walls in the afternoon, and the kids from Golden Gloves sat and stared while Frazier sparred in the corner ring. The Solar was bright and loud and alive, and the kids must have thought that the big shots would come around always and the gym would live forever.

And now the Solar is dying. The gym is on the fifth floor of a building at 146 W. 28th Street. The building has just been sold. The new owners want to turn it into an apartment house. Jaran Manzanet, the owner of the Solar since 1973, has been told to be out by the end of the month. Manzanet has been looking for an alternative site in the neighborhood and so far has been unable to find one. On Feb. 28, another part of New York's rich boxing history will be ripped away. And 175 boxers, most of them kids, will be looking for a gym.

"The minute I tell a landlord I want to open a gym, they say, 'No,'" Jaran Manzanet said. "I try to tell them about the kids, and they say, 'No way' again. I try to go to everybody for help. I try to go to the mayor, to the governor. I try to tell people about all these kids I got comin' from the Bronx and Brooklyn and New Jersey, more kids than all the other gyms combined. But nobody wants to help me."

Manzanet was asked how much money he will lose if he is forced to close his gym for good. Manzanet laughed.

"Who makes the money running a gym?" he asked.

"He's just a guy scuffling to keep boxing alive for kids," said John Condon, boxing vice president at the Garden. "The other place (Gleason's) has the reputation. This guy Manzanet, he's got boxers."

On a wall at the Solar the color of dust there hangs a bulletin board. On the bulletin board are two long sheets of yellow legal paper. At the top of one is written, "Solar S.C., Home of Champions." Listed one by one are all the famous fighters who have trained there: Ali and Frazier, Foreman and Duran, Emile Griffith and Larry Holmes and Jimmy Ellis, Ken Norton and Wilfred Benitez and Carlos Palomino. Sugar Ray Robinson and Jose Torres and Jake LaMotta have visited. Rocky Graziano filmed a commercial there; that's written on this piece of yellow legal paper.

But it is the second piece of paper, the one on the right, that is more important. Carmelo Negron's name is on that one; he trained for the Golden Gloves at the Solar. And Jimmie Cruz, he trained for the Junior Olympics. And one after another are all the other kids who trained for the Gloves and John Condon's Kid Gloves program and even the Olympics (Howard Davis). The names on the paper are

the reasons why the Solar is a treasure and must somehow be preserved.

"We got everything here," said Ray Rodriguez, who will be 15
years old a week before Manzanet is evicted. "We got showers and so
many bags. We got a mirror and a ring. Now they tell us that they
might close it down. We might find another place to go, but it won't
be the same, I don't think."

Rodriguez sat in a corner of the Solar's tiny dressing area, taping
his own hands. He is from the Smith Project on the lower East Side,
near Catherine Slip. He weighs 110 pounds and wants to fight in the
Kid Gloves. He speaks positively about the Golden Gloves, "someday." Every afternoon, he takes the subway to the Solar and goes to
work.

So does Cruz Bonilla, a 16-year-old from Bushwick High in
Brooklyn, who takes the "J" train to the Solar every day; and Joe San-
tiago, a former professional featherweight who works in a Wells Fargo
bank on Wall Street and dreams of a comeback; and Nelson Payana, a
22-year-old welterweight who talks about the Golden Gloves "next
year."

"I'm trying to find a place somewhere in the neighborhood," said
Manzanet. "Someplace between 23d and 31st that's easy for these
kids to get to. 'Cause if this gym dies, these kids are gonna be hurt."

So the gym should not die. So the 175 people who train there
should not be forced to find another gym. Always, gyms like the Solar
have been the foundation of boxing in New York City. We should not
lose another one. Mayor Koch does commercials and preaches that
businesses should stay in the city. Boxing has always been a fine business here. The mayor should do something to help Jaran Manzanet.

He can reach him at the Solar Sporting Club, W. 28th St. The
Mayor should try to reach him before the end of the month, when the
gym will die and a little more of boxing's music will die with it.

• *1980*

Wepner fought with a champion's heart

A s the evening wore on, the toughest fight crowd there is, the one at Madison Square Garden, began to fall in love with Chuck Wepner, who would not fall down. This is a March night in 1975. The live bouts were over. On the giant screen in the middle of the Garden smoke and noise, you could see that Chuck Wepner, from 54th St., and Kennedy Blvd. in Bayonne, planned on going 15 rounds with Muhammad Ali in Richfield, Ohio.

It was supposed to be an Ali crowd at the Garden, because it always was. He was the champ again, having beaten George Foreman in Zaire. But Chuck Wepner just did not have the good sense to fall down.

Round by round, he stood right in there with the champ, and he supported this dream he'd worked out over 20 years in bad arenas with the help of good cut men. In the Garden, where I watched, they began to cheer Chuck Wepner's heart. They cheered in Richfield, and in closed-circuit houses everywhere. Ali was listless, and Wepner, from Bufano's Gym in Bayonne, was making him work. And in the ninth round, Wepner hit Ali with a left jab, followed it quickly and smartly with an honest right to the heart, and the champ went down.

Ali would complain after the fight that Wepner stepped on his foot, tripping him. It was no trip. It was the right.

"I dropped him clean," Wepner says.

Wepner almost went the distance with Ali, who finally won on a technical knockout 14 seconds from the end of the 15th round. "He didn't knock me out," Wepner says. "I was just exhausted." He was 35 years old. He just missed carrying his heart the whole 15 rounds.

All along, in the weeks before the fight, Wepner had been telling friends, "I just want to look good. I don't want to look like a bum." On that March night against Ali, Wepner had been no bum. Chuck Wepner, from 54th and Kennedy, from Bufano's Gym, from the Western Electric Co., in Kearny, N.J., had fought well. The long road had been worth it.

"Every punch I ever took on the way up was worth it," he says now. "Every lousy arena and every lousy payday was worth that fight with Ali. To this day, I'm known nationally. People come up to me and say 'Great fight.' I grin and say, 'which one?' and they say 'Ali.' "

Wepner fought 145 times, amateur and pro. He doesn't remember his won-lost record as an amateur, but in the pros he was 39-14-2. There was nothing elegant about him; he was just a big man who could hit, and take a punch. He cut easily. He bled. They called him the "Bayonne Bleeder." When they finally got around to rebuilding his nose, the operation took a tidy seven hours. Wepner tells people now that with his new nose he looks like Debbie Reynolds. He looks like 145 fights. He looks like 20 years of shots to the face.

He fought four heavyweight champs, and eight men in all who'd been in title fights. In his one title fight, with Ali, he went 14 rounds, 166 seconds. And tonight, at the Felt Forum, the Garden is doing something fine. The Garden is going to honor Chuck Wepner.

Wepner is retired now. His last fight was over a year ago. He lost to Scott Frank, the current New Jersey heavyweight champ. At the age of 40, there are no more punches, no more cuts, no more stitches, no more hurting mornings. But the Garden is giving him one more fight night. They are calling it "Chuck Wepner's Farewell to Boxing." That may sound a bit overblown for a man whose record was 39-14-2. But we are talking here about a very good man.

Wepner will be presented with a silver plate bearing this message: "To Chuck Wepner, a champion to the millions of boxing fans he thrilled during an outstanding career."

"I wanted to get the word champion in there," says John Condon, a Garden boxing vice president, one with enough class to think of honoring Wepner, who inspired this little boxing movie called "Rocky."

Wepner has moved away from 54th and Kennedy. He still lives in Bayonne, but in a condominium. He works as a salesman for Majestic Wines & Spirits, and is active in various youth programs in Hudson County. And next year, when Jersey City Mayor Tom Smith runs for governor, Wepner will work with him. In New Jersey, Wepner's name cannot hurt you.

He remembers everything about the Ali fight, from the time a newspaperman called to tell him about it ("I didn't mind getting the news second hand"). He remembers training in a hotel in upstate New York, the first time he'd trained anywhere except at Dom Bufano's Gym. He remembers training for the first time in his life; up until then, he would run in the morning, go work as a security cop at Western Electric, box at Bufano's at night. He remembers how he began to feel strong. He kept telling people that he'd show them: he wasn't a bum.

So he fought Ali. When he knocked him down in the ninth, his first instinct was to laugh. "Me," he says. "From Bayonne. I hit Ali with a right and now he's lyin' there. I really did wanna laugh." Ali went to work on him after that, used Wepner's face as a fast bag. Wepner wouldn't go down. Between the 12th and 13th rounds, the referee came over to his corner and put two fingers in front of Wepner's bloody face.

"How many?" the ref asked.

"How many guesses do I get?" asked Wepner.

Tonight they honor Chuck Wepner at Felt Forum in the Garden. This is the way it ought to end for him. It's a good arena. They are going to cheer for him. No one can mess up his Debbie Reynolds nose. No one can foolishly try to knock him down.

• *1980*

Workaday wonder

He stood on a patch of grass between the paddock area and Aqueduct's outside track, his arms folded casually, waiting for an assistant trainer, Jose Valentine, to help him onto a horse named Happy Linda.

A whip dangled lightly from Steve Cauthen's right hand. He wore black-and-gold silks and a gold cap and a half-smile as old as horseracing as he surveyed the grandstand, where bettors hung over the railing, staring at the mystery of the paddock, 10 minutes before post time.

"They goin' to work, too," Jose Valentine said to Cauthen. "We're all workin.' "

In back of him, across the track, was the tote board saying Happy Linda would go off at 5-2, and beyond the board was a pond reflecting the day's sunlight. This was Cauthen's home. A track, any track. He looked so perfectly natural where he stood waiting for his horse, so relaxed and confident and young, that it seemed Aqueduct had been built around him.

Cauthen is coming off a year like no jockey ever had, a $6-million-dollar year. Yesterday he was four days past his first Kentucky Derby win, which came in his first Derby. He is teamed with a horse, Affirmed, that maybe can win the Triple Crown. All he cared about in the paddock at Aqueduct was Happy Linda. It was the only ride that interested him. The $6 million was a number, the Kentucky Derby pleasant history, the Preakness a rumor. Steve Cauthen, just 18, was going to work.

"Like I've always said," Cauthen was saying in the jockeys' room before the race, "it's nice to do something you enjoy. I think about that every time I walk out of the shadows in the tunnel and head out into the paddock area. Take a day like today. I'm going to ride for a lot of owners today. One of them, say, is gonna win $6,000. I'm gonna get as much pleasure out of winning that $6,000, maybe for somebody that really needs it, as I do winning anything else. I like to ride, and I like to win. It's a good game."

Cauthen likes to ride, and brings magic to the rides. But the magic makes the pressure on him keep building. Because of the dream year, because of 1977, he brought pressure enough into 1978. Now he has taken the first big step towards a Triple Crown.

He is besieged constantly for interviews, and early each morning must set up times for the media: 12:50, 1:10, etc. "He don't care if you're Jesus Christ," said one attendant in the jockeys' room. "If he didn't set up no time, forget about it."

But for an 18-year-old, he handles himself magnificently. He is a kid genius in a complex sport, one involving animals and filled with variables. It may be harder to be Steve Cauthen than any other athlete ever. But he goes easily from ride to ride, at Aqueduct and Churchill Downs and Santa Anita, eerily maintains the poise of a 50-year-old, and says he feels no pressure.

"Pressure," said Cauthen, mouthing the word as if it were an obscenity, "breeds mistakes. I can't even think about pressure. The way I look at it is that you just do your best, hope everybody can see you doing your best, and then let things take care of themselves."

Obviously, it is silly to call him a kid any longer. Cauthen was born grown-up, and with a gift for horses that the NYRA's Pat Lynch calls, "the touch of gold." Cauthen rides like an adult and acts like an adult. Only occasionally does he act his age. He did yesterday when asked if the Kentucky Derby was his biggest thrill yet, the best part of his short, glorious career.

"You know, it was," Cauthen said, brightening. "It really was. I didn't know until it happened, until I was in the winner's circle with the roses and my family. Then I knew. There was my mother and father, and they were getting a chance to share in the Derby, in the glory. That was something you can't buy. That was great."

By now it was time for Cauthen to go to work. He picked up his whip and walked out of the jockeys' room. Cauthen is slight and has delicate features, but has a smooth, regal walk. He moved briskly through the tunnel and into the paddock, looking neither left nor right. He then waited for Jose Valentine to hoist him onto Happy Linda.

Cauthen won with Happy Linda. When the race ended, Jose Valentine, standing at the first level of the clubhouse, took off his Yankee cap and waved it. "We lucky to have Steve," said Valentine. He meant Happy Linda's people, but he could have been talking about the whole sport.

• *1978*

Scent of roses brightens Belmont

T he morning had no glamor at Barn 54. The temperature was in the 30s and a mean wind blew rain across the walking track that led from Belmont's three training tracks, forcing the exercise riders to lean low and hard into their horses. Trainers walking alongside the horses in the mud jammed hands into jacket pockets, their breath coming in angry white bursts.

"Fifth of May," said trainer Doug Peterson, squinting into the wind and rain as he slid open the door to Barn 54. "Damn morning like this on the fifth of May."

This was the real business of horses, the morning business, light years away from the week's elegant celebration in Louisville. The only connection to the 104th Kentucky Derby was at the end of this barn, in Stall No. 2, where the horse named Seattle Slew cooled down from his workout.

A year ago the 103d Derby, these two words, "Seattle Slew," bright and lyrical, were on the lips of more horseplayers than "mint julep." Conversations about Slew were filled with curiosity and anticipation. The 3-year-old was unbeaten, the glamor horse of the Derby, and there was the feeling that he might be special. And of course the horse was special, one of sport's priceless treasures, a Triple Crown winner.

But a long year later, three lifetimes in horseracing, here was Slew standing in the hay of Stall No. 2, neighbor to a horse named My Bill, relaxing after galloping 7/8 of a mile on a sloppy track. He was far from Churchill Downs. It was a quiet corner for a hero one year removed.

"Good morning, Mr. Slew," said the 26-year-old Peterson, who replaced Billy Turner as Slew's trainer in December. Peterson opened the gate to the stall but kept three chains in front of Slew fastened. The playful horse leaned his head over Peterson's right shoulder. Even under the stall's dim yellow light, Seattle Slew looked terrific.

"Hello, big kid," Peterson said cheerfully, brushing the forelock away from his horse's eyes, trying to be helpful to a photographer. "Let's get you into the light, Mr. Slew."

The photographer got into position, his back against a window. Peterson stood by the door to the stall. He tugged on Slew's shank, turning the horse's head toward the camera. Then Peterson let go of the shank. The head did not move. Seattle Slew, so used to having his picture taken, looked right into the camera. The year had not dimmed his memory.

"You ham," said Slew's exercise rider, Mike Kennedy. "You big ham of a horse."

"He's been in a good mood, lately," said Peterson, a tall, sandy-haired Colorado native who learned his trade working horses at a track called La Mesa in New Mexico. Peterson patted Slew's head gently. "He can tell he's comin' around right and healthy. He can smell it. He knows what's goin' on."

"He's as good as ever," said Kennedy, who has been with Slew since the horse was a 2-year-old. "Maybe he's a little better than he was."

Life has not been so sweet for Slew since he won the Belmont last June to become racing's first undefeated Triple Crown winner. At Hollywood Park last July, Slew suffered his first loss, to J.O. Tobin in the Swaps Stakes. Slew has not raced since. In January at Hialeah, Slew was found to be suffering from a mysterious virus/blood ailment which threw his once-bright future into a quicksand of doubt.

But now Seattle Slew is fit. His speed work has been excellent lately. Last Sunday, on "Seattle Slew Day" at Aqueduct, he ran 5/8 of a mile in 57.2. He will be given a vigorous workout tomorrow morning, and then Peterson will know for sure when the horse can race again. Peterson is pointing toward the Metropolitan Handicap on May 29.

"Last year at this time he was getting ready to start something,"

Peterson said. "Now he's ready to start a new series. He's making it all look easy again, the stride, the changing speeds, the pull."

Outside, the morning still attacked the stable area. But it was time for Slew's valuable legs to be washed down. Peterson led the horse down the row of stalls toward the door to Barn 54. Even though the Derby week which belonged to Slew once now belonged to horses named Alydar and Affirmed, and the glamor was a long way away, this great animal looked fine and happy, and that lit up the barn and the morning.

"This work here, horse work, is seven days a week," said Peterson, walking ahead of Seattle Slew. "But to get full enjoyment out of it, you gotta be in action. Isn't that right, Mr. Slew?"

• 1979

Turcotte battles odds to get back to horses

H
•

e won two Kentucky Derbies, one on a horse named Secretariat. He won over 3,000 races and more than $28 million in purses. He says that he loved riding horses, just riding them, more than anything else. He did it professionally for 16 years. He sat in a wheelchair in his dream house in Oyster Bay Cove and discussed the nightmare moment when it ended. The wheelchair was in front of a huge brick hearth. The crackle of the fire richocheted around the kitchen and was louder than Ron Turcotte's voice.

"I came out of the gate on a horse named Flag of Leyte Gulf," he said. "I was in the three stall...and, uh ...in the two stall was a horse named Small Raja. Four hole had a horse named Water Malone...and, uh...it happened 20 yards out of the gate, maybe 30 yards. The three of us were running abreast, then, uh, Small Raja and Water Malone started to move out a little. I was in the middle...and, uh...Small Raja started to drift into me.

"Jeff Fell was on the horse. I started to holler. 'Jeff, Jeff, Jeff,' I yell. The horse kept coming anyway. Four, five times I holler...and, uh...he kept drifting and then he bumped my horse across Water Malone's heels."

Turcotte cleared his throat.

"My horse goes down headfirst," he said.

It was the feature race on July 13 at Belmont. Eighth

race. Five-thirty in the afternoon. Ron Turcotte flew over the head of Flag of Leyte Gulf. He landed on his back, somersaulted, and lay still on the track. He says he never lost consciousness. What he had lost was the use of his legs.

Gaetane Turcotte moved her husband's wheelchair closer to the fire. She handed him a coffee cup from the kitchen table and sat down next to him. She did not interrupt him.

"The wind was knocked out of me," Ron Turcotte said. There was no inflection in his voice. He could have been reciting a laundry list. "I reached for my belly and tried to get some wind...and, uh...it was like punching a water balloon. All the muscles had let go. They felt like they were just floating around. Then I reached for my leg. It was like touching someone else's leg.

"Bobby Barberra, the outrider, came riding over and dismounted. 'Is there anything you want me to do to help you?' he said. 'Don't do anything,' I said. 'I think my back is broken.' "

As he sat in the wheelchair, Turcotte looked immaculate. His wavy hair was neatly trimmed. There was not a wrinkle in the red silk shirt. His gray patent-leather boots, placed neatly on the footstand of the chair, matched almost exactly the color of his slacks. His expression was as neat as his outfit. He looked straight ahead.

"Do you want to see the videotape of the fall?" he asked. "I don't mind. I have it." No one in the room wanted to see it.

Turcotte was operated on eight hours after the accident at Long Island Jewish Hospital. Effectively, his back was broken. "One crushed vertebra, two broken right?" Turcotte asked his wife. She nodded. He had lost feeling below his abdomen. For three days, doctors held faint hope that the paralysis might be temporary. But the feeling did not come back. Before two weeks had gone by, he had survived a hematoma (blood burst through his stitches) an attack of meningitis, and more surgery to remove the rods inserted in the spine during the original operation. He lost 20 pounds, down to 90.

There were times when it was thought the 37-year-old Turcotte might not live.

"There was a couple of times when you coulda gone either way," said Gaetane Turcotte. She smiled at her husband.

Now doctors have told him there is little hope he will walk again. For 16 years, Turcotte was one of the great riders of his generation. Not a Shoemaker or an Arcaro, but a gifted pro who in addition to the Triple Crown on Secretariat won another Derby, another Preakness and a Belmont. Turcotte now braces himself for his hardest ride, in the wheelchair, one he hopes will eventually find him back on his feet. He is not listening to the doctors. Turcotte says he will walk.

"I hope," he says, the doctors say no, "but I hope."

From Long Island Jewish he was moved to New York University Hospital, then to Manhattan's Rusk Institute. He lives at Rusk during the week, and is allowed to go to his elegant home on weekends. The Racing Form is delivered to him each morning at Rusk. He has been to Aqueduct three times the last few weeks. He was asked if this a sign of great progress.

Turcotte smiled for the first time.

"I don't know," he said. "This is the first time around for me."

At first, he could only lie on his sides, so the back could heal from the inside. The next stage of progress was sitting up, first at 70 and 80 degrees, finally 90. Then came exercises, simple ones so as not to strain the back while bringing back muscle tone to arms that once looked like they belonged to a weightlifter. "His arms had become nothing," his wife noted.

At Rusk, he undergoes therapy from nine to four every day. Technically, the therapy is called "Activity of Daily Living." Turcotte has learned to transfer himself from wheelchair to bed; from one chair to another; and in and out of a bathtub. He has learned to move from his wheelchair into an automatic chair lift which takes him upstairs in the home in Oyster Bay Cove, built lavishly five years ago, after Secretariat.

"When the legs don't work, it's a different story," he observed.

"If the house can't be adapted we will have to move," said Gaetane Turcotte. "When you build a house, you do not plan for something like this."

On a beautiful Saturday, Turcotte sat in his den, in front of a massive, glass-covered trophy case which glittered brilliantly in the morning sun. His four young daughters watched cartoons on TV. In back of the television set was a photograph of Turcotte on Secretariat. Turcotte spoke hopefully of becoming a trainer.

"I go day-to-day," he said. "That's all I can do. You can't cry about what's happened. I'm going to walk. I'm going to be fine."

Place a bet on him. Make it a big one. Make it to win.

• *1978*

The boxer in room 602

H• e came back from X-ray into the waiting room on the fifth floor at New York Hospital and his wife, Miriam, pulled the white shawl tighter around his shoulders. The wheelchair seemed to swallow Willie Machado, who was a welterweight boxer until Friday night at Felt Forum, when another welterweight named Floyd Peavy hit him a right and then a left hook and knocked him out of the fight business and nearly out of this world.

Willie Machado was unconscious when he fell over backward and broke his neck against the lowest rope in the ring. Now it was Tuesday afternoon at New York Hospital. Willie Machado had come out of sedation Monday. They took an endotracheal tube out of his throat. They found out for sure he could move things. And it was a big thing in Room 602 at New York Hospital, a different sort of tale of the tape.

Miriam Machado wore a purple-and-white striped maternity jersey. She is eight months pregnant with the couple's second child. She said something softly to her husband in Spanish. Willie Machado shifted carefully in the wheelchair and his right hand came out from underneath the shawl and took his wife's hand. He was crying.

Loudly in English he said, "I thank God for my life." Willie Machado is one who lost the fight and won the fight. When the medical attendant, Charles, had come to his sixth-floor room with the wheelchair 20 minutes before, Machado, still wearing the huge cervical brace the doctors had put on him in the Felt Forum ring after Peavy concussed him, got out of bed himself and into the chair. The smart money did not have it working out this way Friday night. You could have bet on paralysis.

"I don't wake up until yesterday," Willie Machado said in the waiting room next to X-Ray L-5 at New York Hospital.

"You see them come in like he was," said Charles, "and you don't expect them to beat the game."

Willie Machado is 22 years old. He and Miriam came to Wallingford, Conn., outside Hartford, at the end of March from Ponce, Puerto Rico. They were living in the Wallingford home of Bob Kowalski, who is Machado's co-manager with a man named Earl Walsh. They run the Wallingford PAL Boxing Club. Kowalski had heard about Willie Machado from another of his fighters, Felix Cortez. Machado had done some fighting in Miami Beach, gotten discouraged with his management there, gone back to Ponce and his father's farm. Kowalski took the word of Felix Cortez that Machado could fight. He wired Machado money. Machado would come back to America to be a prizefighter.

"He figured it would take him four or five more fights," Kowalski was saying yesterday from Wallingford, after spending the weekend at New York Hospital waiting for Willie Machado to beat the game and wake up. "Then he was going to put a down payment on his house. Fighting was going to be the way that he didn't have to go back to Puerto Rico."

There was silence over the phone.

"He was a hell of a fighter," said Kowalski. "He could punch with either hand, he could move, he could come after you with combinations. Excellent fighter."

The record was 8-1 before Friday night. Willie Machado had seven knockouts. They were talking about him in Hartford as a comer. Harold Weston, the Garden matchmaker, heard. He made the fight with Floyd Peavy.

"They told me he was a puncher," Weston said yesterday. "They told me he was a fighter. And that's what he was doing until it happened."

Weston had the fight even going into the eighth. One judge had Machado ahead. Kowalski, of course, was seeing the fight through a manager's eyes.

"He was winning," said Kowalski.

Then came the right and the left. Machado was out before his neck hit the rope.

"I had just come back from a North American Boxing Federation convention," said Harold Weston. "They told us about necks hitting ropes. I was scared to death."

The doctors were in the ring before the referee had the chance to count, becoming the trauma team that was necessary to save Willie Machado. Dr. Edwin Campbell, the medical director of the New York Athletic Commission and a specialist in trauma. Dr. Barry Jordan of New York Hospital, a brilliant young neurosurgeon. Dr. Frank Folk from the NYAC. "You have to think broken neck right away," said Dr. Campbell.

The endotracheal tube was inserted into Machado's throat. Jordan immediately fitted the brace on Machado's neck. They didn't know it at the time, but there had been a fracture of the third cervical vertebra. "If you don't immobilize him immediately," said Dr. Campbell, "complete paralysis can result and the chance of coma is heightened immeasurably. When this happens on the football field, a kid can become a quadriplegic before he gets to the hospital. That's why it was so crucial for Dr. Jordan to get the cervical collar on."

A stretcher was called for. Willie Machado was in the ambulance and on his way to New York Hospital about seven minutes after Peavy knocked him out. He never did lapse into coma. Miriam Machado was driven from Connecticut. A Machado brother flew up from Puerto Rico. Kowalski and Earl Walsh and Miriam Machado kept the weekend vigil. But Willie Machado was going to be all right. He would never fight again. At some point there will have to be a different line of work for the down payment on a Wallingford house. But he had been saved during those seven minutes in the ring by Ed Campbell's impromptu trauma team. Sometimes when they are carried out of the ring, they wake up whole.

Machado was kept under heavy sedation through Monday because of the extreme discomfort of the endotracheal tube. He will be in a neck brace for several months. But, in the words of Dr. Ed Campbell, "the chances of complete physical recovery are excellent."

In the waiting room next to X-Ray L-5, Charles came for Willie Machado. He would wheel him into an elevator and take him back to Room 602. It was almost time for lunch. Machado would feed himself. His wife eased herself out of the chair, tucking El Diario under her arm, walked alongside the wheelchair, still holding her husband's hand.

Willie Machado took a painful breath and said again, "I thank God."

They disappeared down the hall. In boxing, it is what passes for a happy ending.

• *1985*

QUARTERBACKS, AND SO FORTH

Football has never been anywhere near the top of my charts. I have no feel for the game. There is no clubhouse to work before the game. And after the game, the big people are so spent, physically and emotionally, the locker room lacks any real drama unless someone is hurt. There are very few sports I would rather watch on television. Football is one. Of course, I have always had this fondness for writing about quarterbacks...

•

Part 8

Theismann's act may have drawn curtain

WASHINGTON, D.C.

F.or 10 games the numbers had been something he must have wanted to wipe off the bottom of his shoes. Joe Theismann was ranked 13 out of 14 quarterbacks in the National Football Conference. Only someone named Archer—private eye Lew? golfer George?—was ranked behind him. Joe Theismann had 16 interceptions and just seven touchdown passes. Only Vince Ferragamo had a worse interception-to-TD pass ration, and Vince Ferragamo had just lost his starting job with the Buffalo Bills.

Not even three years from the day in Pasadena when Theismann and the Redskins had won the Super Bowl, they were saying Joe Theismann, at 36, was too old. They were saying he couldn't throw deep and he couldn't Gooden the ball over the middle; they said he had lost his heater, as fatal for a quarterback as for a baseball pitcher. The Redskins were 5-5, though they had the best rushing offense in pro football. Take away the 44 points the Skins scored against the Falcons a couple of weeks ago, and the once magical Theismann/Redskins offense was averaging 13 points a game.

They were pointing the fingers at Theismann. He was no longer the colorful, swashbuckling quarterback who could talk and talk and talk. He was suddenly an aging athlete on the skids who talked too much. And the people in RFK Stadium were spending a lot of time talking back to Theismann, with boos that sounded like some collective voice of doom.

"Overall I'm not playing well," Theismann had said.

"It's my worst season overall," said Joe Theismann.

That they agreed with in Washington, D.C. Theismann had been the spokesman in good times; now he became the easiest target. The fans did not want to hear about the injuries to his offensive line, to the Hogs of lore. They did not want to hear about how Charlie Brown had been traded away and how Raider rejects Calvin Muhammad and Malcolm Barnwell had not exactly made anyone in D.C. forget Charley Taylor. Or Charlie Brown. They saw Joe Theismann missing open men, and throwing bombs that died like frisbees and not winning them in the last two minutes like he used to.

He had heard the boos coming into a Giants game the Redskins had to win. And he heard this question asked a lot, louder and louder: "Is he through?"

But this was a Monday Night game the Redskins were playing last night against the Giants. This was the sort of situation that begged for Theismann's flair. He had something to prove again, the way he once had to prove that he was big enough for the NFL; the way he once had to prove that his quarterbacking skills were big as his mouth. He had things to prove and a national stage and 13 ABC cameras watching him.

You know Joe Theismann wanted to push up the lid of the coffin and throw some touchdown passes and beat the Giants and start yapping all over again.

The first time the Redskins had the ball last night he zipped a completion to Gary Clark on third down and then he hit Don Warren in the flat for a touchdown. Redskins 7, Giants 0. Theismann ran off the field with a familiar bounce to his step.

"What's been happening has nothing to do with age or my ability," he'd said before the game. He was going to show everybody. He was going to turn this Monday night game into a prime special all about himself.

But then it began to go wrong for Joe Theismann, and the Giants game became the season, and the Giants who rushed him began to turn him into a rag doll. Leonard Marshall got him on third down on the Redskins second possession.

On the third Redskins possession, Jerome Sally fell on Theismann the way a building would.

And then with 14:13 left in the first half and the score tied at 7-7 came the hit from which Theismann did not get up. It was the sort of hit that quarterbacks fear, the way jockeys fear the fall in traffic and hitters fear the fastball behind the ear. It is the sort of hit that ends a season, and maybe a career, if you are 36 the way Joe Theismann is.

It was supposed to be a trick play. Gadget play. Theismann handed the ball off to John Riggins. Receivers streaked down the right sideline and down the middle and fooled no one in the Giants secondary. Riggins pitched the ball back to Theismann. He looked down the field. Nothing. And now the world started to close in on him.

Theismann stepped up in the pocket. Harry Carson was there. Theismann, looking like the escape artist he has always been, wriggled away from Carson.

Taylor came then. Lawrence Taylor. LT. If the boos had sounded like doom, Taylor was doom.

Theismann tried to fold himself up into the fetal position, just take the hit. And it seemed he had done that. But his left leg moved and his right leg did not. On the replay you could see Theismann's right leg bend in this terrible way, all wrong, and then disappear underneath him and Lawrence Taylor.

Phil Simms: "On the sidelines all we could see was blood all over his leg."

Theismann did not get up. The doctors came out and the trainer and Taylor stayed there, because he knew it was bad. The stretcher came finally. It was very quiet in RFK Stadium. Theismann got on the stretcher and then the cheer came, and kept building, as the fans tried to drown out the boos of the first ten weeks of 1985. Theismann's teammates touched him on the shoulder as the stretcher went by like a part of some funeral procession.

The cheer kept coming, maybe the loudest cheer Theismann had heard since September. The people would not stop.

The stretcher disappeared into the runway, then the stretcher disappeared into an ambulance.

The cheer stopped finally, then went to meet another one as Jay Schroeder hit Art Monk for 41 yards on his first pass. Theismann was on his way to Arlington Hospital by then.

A little while later, the announcement came: compound fracture of the right leg (tibia and fibula) for Joe Theismann, who will be in a cast for three months.

The prime time special had been about him, but had been all wrong. Now a season was over.

Maybe a career was over for Theismann, as Jay Schroeder's began.

• *1985*

Time and tide end
Paterno's dream

NEW ORLEANS

T he NBC radio man wanted to ask one last question but
he was wasting his time, because Joe Paterno had no more
answers. He had been standing in front of microphones
and hot lights for more than an hour, patiently discussing
a dream of his that had died. His Penn State team had
lost the Sugar Bowl to Alabama. The national championship was gone. Paterno himself had been shot dead by
a tired old gunfighter named Bear Bryant. Paterno
wanted to leave.

"I gotta be goin' to the bus now fellas," he said,
breaking out of the last tangle of writers. He tightened
the knot of his tie, ran a comb through his thick black
hair, and headed for the bus. Alone. This is how it goes
in his business. On Sunday night "60 Minutes" calls you
the "most beloved college coach since Knute Rockne."
Monday you lose the big game and walk out of the stadium alone.

Paterno scurried quickly down a hall, hands thrust
into the pockets of tweed slacks. A photographer ran up
to him, pulled Paterno's right hand out of the pocket,
shook it. A drunken fan yelled "We still love ya, Joe." Paterno walked faster. He took the comb out again and ran
it through his hair.

At the garage entrance, huge doors had been rolled
up to show that freezing rain blew across the parking lot.
Paterno had no raincoat. The Southern Sightseeing

Tours bus was in the middle of the parking lot. He shook his head, pulled the collar of his jacket up, and ran through the rain to the bus. A few hours before, under the ceiling of the Superdome, he had run as hard onto the field, arms raised in triumph, cheered by thousands and watched by millions.

That seemed like a long time ago. He was still chasing a national championship then. The day had grown dark and cold in the hours since.

Penn State, ranked No. 1 in the country coming into the game, had lost 14-7. They lost because they could not score from the Alabama one-yard line with two successive plays in the fourth quarter. They lost because they had 12 men on the field for a bad Alabama punt that would have given them the ball on the 'Bama 20 later in the quarter. They also lost, did Paterno's Nittany Lions, because ol' Bear Bryant took his whole playbook and kept throwing it across the Superdome at Paterno.

Paterno was asked if it was his most disappointing loss.

"It might be the most disappointing because I feel so bad for the seniors," he said at his press conference. "Me? I'll be around awhile."

After all the years when he had undefeated teams that were treated as impostors by the pollsters. Paterno came here to New Orleans needing only to win a football game to be No. 1. That was the dream. Penn State could not win the game. The defense was gallant, but the offense played as if the title rode on every handoff, every block. Chuck Fusina had a dreadful day. It is also worth mentioning that Alabama whipped Penn State every single time it mattered.

"There were a lot of bing-bang plays, and they all went Alabama's way," said Paterno. "That's why you play the football game."

Alabama seemed more willing to win. They showed more wrinkles than there are in Bryant's wonderful visage. Bear used every stunt and blitz, every misdirection play, every formation. There were screen passes thrown back across the field, flea-flickers, spin plays, spins and laterals off simple dives. The Bear can sometimes be a fox.

He is 65 years old, and sometimes he looks so ghastly and tired as to be close to death. The walk gets slower all the time. There have been so many games for him like yesterday's, so many times when a national championship rode on whether Alabama won or lost. Yesterday they won, and Bryant will officially have a fifth title tomorrow. So it is important to know that he gunned down Paterno in their personal due. Bryant gave a clinic. The old man can still do it.

"He means an awful lot to them," Paterno said the other day, speaking of Bryant. "Nobody panics with him there. There's no delays of game, no indecisiveness. You don't have players running in and out." The words are slightly haunting now. Because on the critical 12-man play yesterday, when Woody Umphrey's horrible punt would've given State great field position, Paterno had players running into the game, and not enough of them running out.

"We screwed up," said Joe Paterno.

So he lost. Bryant won. A few minutes after the Penn State buses left, the Bear, looking pale and dazed, came trudging toward the garage entrance. He had his arm linked with an Alabama state trooper, and was dragging his feet as he moved. The sudden chill from outside slowed him more. Ahead of him, a Superdome employee carried the Sugar Bowl trophy.

They pulled a blue limo almost into the building so he would not get wet. The trooper helped him into the car for the ride across the street to the hotel. He'd showed them, the old man had. The reflexes were a little slower, but the eye was still sharp. He'd won the gunfight. The car pulled away into the rainy night.

• 1979

Ghosts of 1963 spur Giants in Bear hunt

T• hey do not necessarily know the details of it all, the way the Maras do, or the fans, or the old Giants themselves. They do not know how cold it was at Wrigley Field in '63, or how much Del Shofner's ribs hurt, or how nobody knew for sure whether Y.A. Tittle would play the second half against the Bears on his bum leg until they strapped it with tape in the locker room and he said he would. The players who are Giants now and are going to Chicago to face the Bears in a big game probably do not know that Sam Huff left after '63 and Dick Modzelewski left, too, and the Giants went 2-10-2 the next season, and as storied a sports era as New York had ever known was over.

"I even lost my wedding ring in that cage they called a locker room at Wrigley," former Giant safety Dick Lynch said yesterday about the 1963 NFL Championship Game, which the Bears won, 14-10. "I lost the game that day, the championship, my teammates, and even my wedding ring. We didn't know it, but that was it, pal. It was over."

The new Giants do not know the this and that of these things. There is no memory of names like Lynch and Huff and Modzelewski, Katcavage and Robustelli and the late Jimmy Patton, Tittle and Gifford and Joe Morrison, who had 18 carries for 61 yards on Dec. 29, 1963, the Sunday when the Giants stopped being *The Giants*.

Most of the new Giants are under 30; their memories don't reach back to '63.

But, with a franchise where the past is more important than it is anywhere else in sports, where time never dulled old passions no matter what happened on the field, history seems to reach out to new generations of players, whether they much like it or not. Maybe the Giants of '85 don't know exactly why the Giants of '63, or '58, or '56 owned New York the way they did—they *still* own New York—but they know that the ownership is a fact, even if the football team is really the Jersey Giants now.

"You catch on to Giants tradition very quickly around here," said Chris Godfrey. "And if you're like me, it comes to mean a lot to you. I've gotten to the point where I get charged up when I see some of those black-and-white clips of the old Giants. You know, those glory day things. I get charged being caught up in the history of things."

Godfrey, a bright and soft-spoken big person from Michigan, is one of the offensive linemen whom Phil Simms has honored for their part in the Giant road to Soldier Field. The offensive linemen have helped Joe Morris have one of those Walter Payton-Marcus Allen-Eric Dickerson seasons carrying the football.

Godfrey did not know the history of Giants vs. Bears the other day when Giant history was his topic, did not know about all the championship games, or even the last one in '63. But Giant history has never been an exact science anyway; it has been an enduring and romantic idea.

"It is so easy to catch on," said Godfrey. "It's just all around you, the stuff from the past."

Stuff from the past. Lynch, now the radio analyst for the Giants on WNEW and a seller of government bonds ("Reagan paper," he calls it) for the Discount Corporation of New York, remembers all of it. Lynch's glory days, and those of his mates, ended Dec. 29, 1963 at Wrigley.

"They could have sold 100,000 tickets to that game if Papa (George) Halas would have moved it to Soldier Field," Lynch said. "But he kept it at Wrigley and had them push the bleachers right up close to the field, so the Bears fans could give it to us up close all day long. And they did."

Lynch helped force an interception off Bears quarterback Billy Wade. Tittle hit Frank Gifford in the first quarter, Giants 7, Bears 0.

Lynch: "Then YAT's (Tittle's) interceptions started to kill us."

Linebacker Larry Morris, the player of the game, picked off a Tittle pass and went 61 yards before being caught. Wade ran it in a couple of plays later. It was 7-7.

The Giants had a chance to score another touchdown, but Doug Atkins and Ed O'Bradovich made big plays near the goal and Don Chandler kicked a chip shot from 13 yards to make it 10-7, Giants.

The game is a jumble of memories for Lynch after that. Morris rolling over on Tittle's knee. Glynn Griffing, the kid quarterback—Lynch said, "Griffing wasn't really a football player; I think he might have been on scholarship to become one"—replacing Tittle briefly. Shofner not being able to reach up for a sure touchdown pass in the end zone because of ruined ribs. Lynch and others helping the battered Tittle up wooden steps to the Wrigley locker room at the half.

Lynch: "YAT just said, 'I'll play.' He was never much of a complainer, YAT."

The Giants defense, the most famous Giant defense of them all, made its last loud roar, holding the Bears to 222 yards total offense, only 94 rushing. But O'Bradovich intercepted Tittle deep in Giant territory and Wade ran it in again. Bears 14, Giants 10.

Lynch: "Their defense had been holding the world to 10 points. So they did it with us, too. We never let their offense get past the 50 on its own, but the intercepts killed us. I think Sunday's game might be a lot like that one. Lots of defense, mistakes killing somebody. It's one of the reasons I'm getting a sense of—what do you call it?—deja vu this week."

There is a lot of it going around this week. It is the Bears and the Giants again, in what seems like the true championship of the NFC. It has been a long time since the Giants were *The Giants*—since Dec. 29, 1963, as a matter of fact. Now they've got the chance to be big guys again. Even the kids like Chris Godfrey must understand that it figures the Bears are in the way.

• *1986*

Ten years after his super day, Namath still steals the scene

MIAMI

Ten years later, in the saloons and in the fancy restaurants, on the beach and in the hospitality suites, it is still Joe Namath's scene, still his game. As long as they play Super Bowls in Miami, they will talk about Joe Namath, and remember what he did here. They will talk about the broads and the Johnny Walker Red. They will remember the poolside press conference at the Galt Ocean Mile.

Mostly, they will remember how Joe Namath came to Miami a 17-point underdog, said he was going to beat the Baltimore Colts, said it loud, and beat them. Ten years ago, Namath turned this thing called the Super Bowl into a big game.

At the same time, he turned it into a lavish, private party, which he catered with his mouth and paid for with his brilliant skills. No one will ever again seize the moment as Namath did that January week in 1969, when he grabbed the public by the front of the shirt and didn't let go until late on a memorable Sunday afternoon. Namath made the world pay attention to him, made this his scene. Thomas Henderson tried mightily to do the same this year. No one will ever do it as well as Joe Willie Namath, from Beaver Falls, Pa. Like Hollywood Henderson, they can only try.

In a Super Bowl, in Miami, no one will ever fill Namath's white shoes. And maybe it does not matter where the game is played.

"I had a grand time," Namath said the other morning, the words still covered in that curious Pennsylvania-Alabama drawl. "A grand time," he repeated.

It was a grand party, and is all history now, part of the Namath folklore. If you are discussing Namath and Miami and 1969, legend is not too strong a word. He will always have Super Bowl III: the Jets 16, the Colts 7. The way people in Miami talk about Namath still, you would think he was quarterbacking one of the teams in Super Bowl XIII today.

They remember the argument and near-fight with Colts lineman Lou Michaels in a Lauderdale joint called Fagio's. Namath finally shut Michaels up by betting him $500 on the game, even, no points, no nothing. Michaels paid Namath the $500 after the game that Sunday. Mostly, people remember how Namath got up in front of 500 people at a Miami Springs Village banquet and said, "We'll win. I guarantee it." The Jets won, almost as big as Namath did.

"Anybody can make a guarantee," said Ray Abruzzese Thursday morning, standing in the unfinished middle of what will soon be a new Bachelors 3 on North Federal Highway in Fort Lauderdale. Abruzzese has pretty much traveled the whole road with Namath, from Alabama on. Abruzzese was one of the original owners of Manhattan's Bachelors 3, back in the days when Namath was young and owned the city.

"The guarantee was nuthin', " said Abruzzese. "It was winning the game. Joe won the game."

While Abruzzese watched the last minute construction inside Bachelors 3, Joe Namath stood in the back parking lot, surrounded by cement mixers and fork lifts and bags of cement as he took in the morning sun. He and Abruzzese and Bobby Van, the three original partners in Bachelors 3, are opening the new place. Van and Abruzzese watched nails being pounded. Namath was getting ready to play golf.

Namath has lost weight, and in tennis shorts and a golf shirt, the visible hide looked lean and extremely dark. There has been a lot of golf lately, as many as 45 holes a day, and no drinking. In January of 1969, Namath drank up most of the available Johnny Walker Red from Miami Beach to Fort Lauderdale, but he has not had a drink in six months. The act has changed slightly in the last 10 years.

Namath was asked to discuss the person he calls "Joe Namath, the ath-a-lete." He was asked what he remembers about that January week, when he was in the eye of his own storm.

"I remember the greatest excitement of my sports career," he began. He paused, then went on, the images flooding him haphazardly.

"I remember the bus ride to the game," he said, "and feeling different than I had before any other game. So much had been made of this one game, even among ourselves. It was real quiet on the bus. Then I remember Curley Johnson (the Jets punter), yelling out, "A chicken ain't nuthin' but a bird." That was just his Texas way of saying that it was just another game, and that seemed to loosen everybody up. But the adrenalin was runnin' pretty good."

Namath then talked about how it was after the game. After he delivered on his famous promise. All he had done was make the Super Bowl a big deal, and the AFL a league, and himself a new sporting folk hero.

"I've never experienced a feeling like that before or since," Namath said. "I've never had a feeling inside my body like I did after that game. We had all achieved something great that we set out to do."

A smile moved across Namath's dark, crooked face.

"There were some bad times before that season, and a lot after," he said. "That year was the best time I ever had."

Namath then discussed this year's game, and how he likes Pittsburgh "up to five points." He talked about Terry Bradshaw and Roger Staubach, and pretty soon he was talking about blitzes and sounding like a quarterback, like it was 1969. He will not go to the Orange Bowl Sunday, but will watch the game on TV.

An old friend asked him how he had celebrated his 10th anniversary of Super Bowl III.

"Had a lady last night," Namath said with a grin. It is well-known that he was not alone the night before the Baltimore game. Nothing much had changed in 10 years.

"All night?" the friend asked.

Namath gave his friend a disgusted look that said his ladies don't stay an hour. "All night," he said.

"Any sleep?"

"None."

"So it was an anniversary," the friend said, and Namath laughed. Then he slouched across the noisy, busy parking lot, the stoop shoulders still making him unmistakable. He was going to play golf.

As he neared his car, two young girls from the supermarket next door, dressed in blue-and-gold uniforms went running after him, carrying notebooks and pens. They were out of breath and giggling when they reached Joe Namath. You have to wonder whether they will run so hard after Hollywood Henderson in 10 years, in Miami.

• *1979*

Payton finally gets his due

W

alter Payton has gotten here four yards at a time, five maybe. He has never been one of the wonder boys. He was not O.J. when he started; he is not Marcus Allen or Eric Dickerson now. He has come to Super Bowl XX from cold Chicago Sundays and 4-10 seasons. He has bounced off tacklers here. He has straight-armed there. Four yards. Five yards. Two-yard gains that looked like 20-yarders. Payton always kept going, moving toward the front, knowing that is where he belonged.

"I am not a world-class sprinter," he said yesterday. "When I'm running, I try to get as many yards as I can. The object of the game is to get as close to the goal line as possible."

He is close to the goal line now. Payton, who has gained more yards carrying a football than anyone in history, is in a Super Bowl that his team, the Bears, is supposed to win. And suddenly, he is an overnight sensation. It is as if he has been renovated, like the Statue of Liberty. He is routinely called the most complete back pro football has ever seen, the best all-around *player* of them all. People hear that and nod and say, "Of course."

And, of course, Walter Payton has not changed at all. That is why he cocks an eye and smiles wryly at the American celebration of Walter Payton. He wants to know where everyone was on the cold Sundays, in the 4-

10 seasons. He does nothing differently. He is no overnight sensation. It is as if he has been some football Willie Nelson, singing all those years in all those honky tonks with the voice of an angel and suddenly being recognized as a "star" late in the game.

O.J. got hurt and stopped running. Dickerson has played three seasons and is already an immortal. Allen is supposed to be the total back. Well, if Allen keeps being total into the 1990s, then you can call him Payton, who just has kept running. Four yards. Five. Get up and do it again. Missed just one Sunday in his career. He could always do it all.

"Running backs come and running backs go," he says. "There's always a new kid for this season or that season. I've never gotten the attention others have gotten. But I'm Old Man River. I keep rolling along."

He has 14,860 yards rushing, career. He had 1,551, this season. He has caught the most passes of any Bear in history. He has blocked like someone fighting to be the 45th man on the team. When he has thrown passes, he has completed a lot of them for touchdowns. He missed the one game his rookie year and not one since. He has played on more bad teams than good and still been everything in Chicago.

There was a regular-season game earlier this season when Payton broke four tackles to get to the line of scrimmage. No gain. Dan Hampton turned to Steve McMichael on the sideline and said, "That's the greatest run I've ever seen." It has never been the open field for Payton.

He came from Jackson State, not USC. He never had southern California, never New York. There were the losing seasons. He did not play on a team that won a playoff game until he had broken the all-time rushing record. He isn't a sprinter, as he says. He doesn't have the long, lean lines of the others. There is no flash to the man. To this day, Payton is a reluctant interview, distrustful of reporters. He wants to know where we all were when he needed us.

There is anger in the man known as Sweetness, bitterness he denies but cannot hide. Sunday after Sunday, he was everything in Chicago. All he ever heard about was the others. People want Payton to clap his hands and gush now, shout "Hallelujah!" He will not do it.

"I've had better years than this one," he said yesterday, "and they were overlooked. The team has been successful this season and so success has finally come to me. It is discouraging and heartening at the same time. But I want to look around now and say to everybody,

'What about 1978? What about '80? What about 1977? Where were you all then?' I played my best this season, but I wasn't *at* my best. I played at a high level, but not at my peak. I played hard, but I've played better."

He was asked about the irony of him, Payton, the man with a rushing record it took 11 seasons to build, being treated like Lana Turner on a drugstore seat at Schwab's.

Walter Payton turned to the man who asked the question and stared and then quietly said, "How would you feel?"

Someone wanted to know if Payton is ready to carry the ball 30 times Sunday if Jim McMahon can't pass the ball. He smiled. There were all the cold Sundays when Payton carried 30 times because Bears quarterbacks couldn't throw the ball.

"I'll carry it 50 times if I have to," said Payton. "Sixty. Whatever."

They kept asking him about the past and Payton did not want to talk about the past. The past was stopping way short of Super Bowls. The past was hearing about Gale Sayers in Chicago or Simpson every-where. The past was four yards and five yards and Payton getting up and thinking, "For what?"

"I had to take negatives and turn them into positives," said Walter Payton five days before Super Bowl XX. Before a Super Bowl, at last.

Bounce off a tackle here. Straight arm there. Move to the front of the parade, after 11 long seasons. The wonder boys come and go. Nothing stopped Walter Payton.

• 1986

Strock a super shadow

on Strock stood near the goalpost at the Oakland Alameda County Coliseum in a place the morning sun had not found yet and only his eyes, which were the same color as his aquamarine Dolphins windbreaker, told you that he had already heard all the questions. The eyes offered you weary smiles and cool acceptance.

Once Strock stood and watched Bob Griese quarterback the Dolphins, and answered the questions about Griese. Now he does the same thing with Dan Marino. He was young when he played behind Griese. His day would come. It worked out differently. Marino came instead. Now Strock is 34 years old. The eyes said that Strock knows now that there are no guarantees about anything in sports. Not everybody gets to be great.

So Strock's day never came, not really. At Super Bowl XIX, he is a 6-5, 34-year-old casualty policy for Marino. So he stood on the football field in the early morning with hands in the windbreaker pockets and talked mostly about the kid, Marino, who in two seasons has started more games and thrown more touchdown passes for the Miami Dolphins than Don Strock, Virginia Tech, class of '73, ever will.

"I've answered a hell of a lot of questions about him," said Don Strock with absence of malice.

In two seasons, Marino has had everything. In 11, Strock has had a job. He has been a relief pitcher. He has been an insurance policy.

209

An Englishman thrust a microphone in his face and in a we'll-fight-them-on-the-beaches voice asked: "What sort of MAN is Dan Marino?" Another writer wanted to know if Strock envied Marino. Strock said, "Not when we got to the hotel last night." He meant the mob scene that follows Marino now wherever he goes. Someone else wanted to know if Strock expects to play against the 49ers Sunday.

Strock laughed with the eyes and said, "Maybe I'll get to fall on the ball the last play." Then he said, "I told coach (Don) Shula on his television show one time that I wanted to play more, but the problem is that Dan won't stop throwing touchdown passes."

There have been moments for Strock, of course. There has been the reputation in Miami as being the Gossage of the NFL, the Sutter, the Quisenberry. Across the years, there have been some crackling fourth quarters for Strock, some fine comebacks. There was the January day in the playoff when he came off the bench for David Woodley with the Dolphins down 24-0, and threw for 403 yards and four touchdowns before the Dolphins lost 41-38 in overtime. He calls it "a fond memory." But he has never been the one. Never Griese. Never Marino. He was never even Woodley. When Woodley was such a failure against the Redskins in Super Bowl XVII, Shula had chances to give Strock the call and didn't; when Strock finally got into the game, it was much too late for the Dolphins to catch the Redskins.

The timing has always been wrong. It has always been said that Strock could start On A Lot Of Other Teams. Maybe he will never know. With the Dolphins now, he is as much quarterback coach for Marino as backup quarterback. He stands on the sidelines in windbreaker and cap and talks over strategy and looks for keys from the defense and helps call the plays. Someone wanted to know if it is difficult for him to keep his spirits up.

"I'm paid an awful lot of money to keep my spirits up," he said.

There have been occasions when he became a free agent, occasions when he held out for an awful lot of money, occasions when he listened intently to offers from the late WFL and the USFL. He always came back to Shula and the Dolphins. He took the security. Maybe he just settled. Maybe being relief pitcher, backup man, watcher, insurance policy, part-time coach, was finally enough. He talks about his fond memories. He talks about having been to three Super Bowls when others who have played as long have never even seen the playoffs.

His latest contract will be up in two weeks, on Feb. 1. Strock says he does not know what he will do then.

"My wife and I will sit down after the season and have a long talk," he said.

Somehow the conversation moved to Strock's golf game. He was asked if he can at least beat Marino in golf. Strock laughed finally. "I hammer him every time out," he said.

He was still with the small group of reporters near the goalposts at the Oakland Coliseum. He was still in the morning shadows. Across the field, Marino had to stand up in the first row of bleachers to accommodate the 100 or so reporters hanging on his every 23-year-old word. It was no accident, of course, that Marino stood in brilliant sunshine. It follows him right now. Strock? He has always been half the field away.

• 1985

Jurgensen golden arm made Sundays Sonny

O nce, in a bar late at night, he smiled and summed up his career this way: "It was always second-and-nine," Sonny Jurgensen said. This was at the Masters golf tournament, at a seedy place called the Ro-zel Lounge, and his business was television then instead of football, but the conversation had gotten around to quarterbacks, as it often does with Sonny Jurgensen, because he was the man with the golden arm. Three men at the table talked about Unitas and they talked about Starr, and they talked about Tittle and Van Brocklin. Jurgensen would drag on his big cigar and sip his beer, and keep smiling and listen. And finally someone asked Jurgensen who was the best quarterback he ever saw.

"I was," Sonny Jurgensen said. It was past the hour when men tell each other the truth in bars, and that is how the conversation ended. Maybe you disagree with him. But Sonny Jurgensen had earned his vote.

He carried the golden arm across 18 seasons in the National Football League, and used it to light up so many dim, losing Sundays in Philadelphia and Washington. He always was facing second-and-nine, or third-and-10, and trying to bleed another first down out of a bad football team, trying to start one more drive, trying to keep the Eagles or the Redskins in a game. The belly was always hanging over the belt, and you always had the feeling that Jurgensen's Saturday nights were every bit as interest-

212

ing as his Sunday afternoons. But there was always the arm, and win or lose, Jurgensen would make cold Sundays blaze, if only for a little while, before his team lost again.

And there was always this sadness about him completing all the extraordinary passes and falling short, about Sonny Jurgensen never playing for a team that deserved the genius he brought to throwing a football.

On Saturday afternoon in Canton, Ohio, there will be another induction into the pro football Hall of Fame, and then a football game between the Falcons and the Browns. Willie Davis, the old Packer, will enter the Hall of Fame, and Jim Ringo, and an oldtime player named Red Badgro. George Blanda will also be inducted, because he was so brilliant at kicking field goals at an advanced age. Blanda was also a quarterback, and will be the 15th quarterback so honored by the Hall. Sonny Jurgensen was a quarterback, yes he was, and he was eligible for the Hall this time, because his last season with the Redskins was 1974. Jurgensen will not be in Canton Saturday, which is a crime.

There are two current and outrageous injustices where this football Hall of Fame is concerned. Paul Hornung is not yet a member. Neither is the great Christian Adolph Jurgensen. Someone ought to do something about this someday soon. Only if they ever saw Hornung beat a team five different ways. Only if they ever saw Jurgensen throw from the pocket, with the world hanging all over him.

He was blitzed and cheated by the fates, was Jurgensen, in Philadelphia and Washington. He succeeded Norm Van Brocklin for the Eagles after the Eagles had been champions, then saw the Eagles fall apart. He was traded to Washington in 1964 and saw his prime devoured by worse teams in Washington, like it was a piece of tenderloin. There was the one bright season of promise under the late Vince Lombardi, but then George Allen came to Washington and fell in love with Billy Kilmer. It was not going to work out for Jurgensen. And still he left his mark. He will not be forgotten by any fan who ever sat in Franklin Field or RFK Stadium and saw Jurgensen offer a little hope when there should have been no hope at all.

There were 2,433 completions in 4,262 attempts across the years. That is a 57% completion average. That is a monster. He threw 255 touchdown passes, and piled up 32,224 yards. He had 25,300-yard games. He is third in career touchdown passes behind Fran Tarkenton and Unitas. Between 1966 and 1968, there were 23 consecutive games in which he threw at least one touchdown pass. Only three men who played their entire careers in the NFL —Tarkenton, Unitas, Tittle—threw for more yards. They played on good teams, Jurgensen did not. Jurgensen never did taste the champagne.

But he kept on throwing with the golden arm. He kept completing third-down passes on all those Sundays when it was Sonny Jurgensen against the world. If there is no place for him in the Hall of Fame, they should tear it down and put up a Taco Bell in its place.

• *1980*

In Minnesota, the ice man still throweth

T arkenton was too old for this. The snow was piled high all around Metropolitan Stadium and the field was frozen and the snow was still falling, and the Vikings should have been out of the game long ago. The numbers were all wrong. Francis Tarkenton, who is 38, had already thrown the ball 50 times. Now he was down by six points and there were 90 yards to go. This was probably his last game in Bloomington. In 1961, in his first game there, he had thrown four touchdown passes to beat the Bears. He was 21 then. Seventeen years later, a fourth touchdown pass would beat the Eagles.

Another bitter Sunday in the snow. Another lost game for Fran Tarkenton to win. He was too old for this. But the Vikings needed Tarkenton to save them again. Nothing had changed.

"It was Russian Roulette time again," Tarkenton would say later. "The Russian Roulette offense. And the old special excitement."

There were seven minutes left. The Eagles led, 27-21. If the Vikings did not win, they would not make the playoffs. The ball was wet. Good footing was a memory. Tarkenton, as always, liked his chances.

"I loved them," he said. "The football game was just sitting there for us to take. We had a chance to earn our stripes again."

"The man was laughing it up in the huddle," said

Ahmad Rashad, who'd already caught one of Tarkenton's three touchdown passes. "He's that good. A situation like that is his lifeblood. He was ready to stick it down their throats."

"We are going down the field now and score," said Tarkenton in the huddle. Nobody doubted, or spoke.

He passed to Bob Tucker, his old Giants teammate, over the middle. Rickey Young got nothing up the middle. It was third-and-one at the Viking 19, 5:50 left. Chuck Foreman got the first down. Only 79 yards to go now. The Vikings knew Green Bay had won.

Rashad dropped a pass, Foreman got two yards. There was 4:58 left. Tarkenton faced third-and-eight. He dropped back, got plenty of time, and gunned the ball to a wide-open Sammy White crossing from left to right over the middle. Tarkenton's arm is supposed to have lost its snap. Tell the Eagles. First down at the 45-yard line. There was still a long way to go. But Tarkenton had begun to stick it down the Eagles' throats. The snow was heavier.

"He comes up with the play, doesn't he?" Eagles' coach Dick Vermeil would say later.

"I feel like I played three games instead of one," Tarkenton said yesterday morning. "I may need an arm transplant."

Foreman gained three yards, then slipped catching a screen pass and picked up just one. Another third down. Here Bill Bergey, the Eagles' middle linebacker, got called for a personal foul. The Vikings had first down on the Eagles' 37. Tarkenton had a break. He was still playing Russian Roulette. The trigger had been pulled. He had gone past another cylinder.

Three plays later, he would survive again. He had thrown an incompletion on first down. Foreman slipped again on second. A bomb to White was incomplete. It was fourth-and-10. The game was a play away from the two minute warning. The Vikings were a play away from oblivion. Tarkenton gave his instructions to Tucker, White, Rashad. Rashad swears Tarkenton grinned.

Tarkenton dropped back. Only he found good footing on the ice. He looked down the field through the snow. He saw white jerseys, the Eagles. Then Francis Tarkenton scrambled. He scrambled out of the pocket, to the left. He had to make something up. Now. Once again, for all the 17 years, the Vikings had to play his improvisational theatre, the best football has seen. He was too old for this.

"Give the offensive line credit," said Tarkenton. "They gave me time to look, and Bob time to get behind the linebackers."

Tucker, of course, had seen this before. "When I saw Francis start to scramble," he said, "I just started looking for a dead area." He found it, near the left sideline, at the 10. Tarkenton found him. The Vikings were alive. First-and-goal. Two-minute warning.

And it was over. The Vikings had no business being here, maybe no business being alive in this season. But they would beat the Eagles. A holding penalty that moved the ball back to the 20 was a minor annoyance. Rashad had told Tarkenton back in the first quarter that he could beat Herm Edwards on a hitch-and-go. Tarkenton had filed the information, but had not used the pattern. He used it now.

He drilled the ball between Edwards and safety John Sciarra. Rashad went up and got it, then fell into the end zone. It was Tarkenton's 30th completion of the game, his 304th of the season (an NFL record) on his 500th attempt. It was his 21st touchdown pass of the season. Rick Danmeier kicked the extra point. The Vikings won. If they can beat Detroit and Oakland on the road, they will be in the playoffs and maybe — just maybe — Tarkenton gets a last shot at the Super Bowl.

He deserves a shot. Tarkenton has had an extraordinary season for a 38-year-old man. Week after week, with no running attack, he has carried the Vikings. He broke a leg last season and was supposed to be finished. The Vikings lost to Tampa Bay at home earlier in the season and he was booed. He was supposed to be dead against the Eagles Sunday. Francis Tarkenton beats the odds. The last two minutes are his home.

"I have contributed more to this football team," Tarkenton said, "than any other I've played on." That is saying something.

He has come down to the last two games of what is probably his last regular season. He needs two wins. Even if he does not get them, his genius is told in the record books. And in Metropolitan Stadium, they will remember him as he was on Sunday when he was too old, ignoring the snow and the cold and the Eagles, saving the Vikings. It is going to be hard to convince those fans that Tarkenton is not the greatest quarterback there has ever been, Super Bowl or not.

• *1978*

A Few From
Magazines

Magazine writing is fun. The stories generally get you out of town, and jumping on an airplane is still part of the romance of the whole game. And the stories give you the chance to occasionally meet someone quite special, like Jim Abbott. The McEnroe piece, which was an Esquire cover, is the product of knowing McEnroe for 10 years, going all the way back to the Wimbledon of 1977. I jumped at the chance to do the Bobby Thomson-Ralph Branca story for the *Daily News* Sunday magazine, just so I could say I talked to the most famous home run of them all. Elmore Leonard? He's my favorite novelist, and I just took the assignment so I could meet him.

Part 9

Advantage, Mr. McEnroe?

"W atch this," John McEnroe says.

It is 9:30 in the morning at the McEnroe condominium at Turnberry Isle, one of those instant prestige addresses north of Miami where you don't have to worry much about bumping into the Golden Girls. McEnroe is in the baby's room with Estella, the nanny, and Tatum O'Neal, wife and mother.

Estella has just finished changing Kevin Jack McEnroe, nine months old. The boy already looks like his mama, the kid she was in *Paper Moon*. McEnroe says, "I think the only thing he's got from me so far is his hairline."

He takes Kevin out of Estella's arms and gives him to Tatum. "Anyway, watch this."

Tatum, already pregnant with the next one, smiles, takes the boy, and steps back. Kevin McEnroe shrieks and tries to leap into his father's arms.

"You're not a mommy's boy at all, are you, Kevin?" McEnroe says, grabbing the boy and holding him over his head. "You're a daddy's boy all the way, aren't you?"

McEnroe hands the baby back to Estella and heads upstairs, which looks like a lot of places where he has stashed his life over the last ten years. There are boots and discarded jeans over there, and a pile of rackets on the couch, and an electric guitar, and *The Miami Herald* opened to a story about the rock group Genesis, and a battered Chicago Bears cap. Next to the front door is a big black equipment bag, filled with sneakers and sweats and more rackets.

Tatum O'Neal apologizes for the mess. "He still never takes his bag away from the door. I think it's a pretty old habit. But he's not going to make any more quick exits. The boy's in love."

McEnroe is sorting through rackets. He is dressed in white shorts and a Lakers T-shirt and some new Nikes with flaps over the top. As usual, he looks like everything is on backward.

He is getting ready to practice with Jimmy Connors, who is playing in a tournament over in Key Biscayne. The two of them once nearly came to blows during a changeover at Wimbledon. That day Connors told McEnroe, "Next time, I'll let my son play you, you're about the same age." McEnroe said of Connors last July, "I don't think I could ever be that phony."

Now it's like they starred together in *Platoon*. Everybody gets older, even Jimbo and Johnny Mac. McEnroe, who can do everything to a tennis ball except make it recite the Pledge of Allegiance, at twenty-eight has become what Connors eventually became after his fall from number one: guy fighting to fool everybody and get back to the top.

And he would very much like to do that this year. Or next.

"Don't want to keep Jimbo waiting," McEnroe says, and kisses his wife on the cheek.

"Oh, honey," he calls to Tatum as he goes out the door, "you think maybe you could whip me up some pancakes when I get back?"

He came along in 1977, an eighteen-year-old, a nobody, with a headband and a bad temper and a left-handed tennis game so big it filled up that first Wimbledon until Connors finally stopped him in the semifinals. They couldn't even pronounce his name that year, but he spit and sassed his way out of the qualifying rounds and then won five matches in the main draw.

"Mc-EN-roe," the umpires kept calling him, "*Please* play, Mr. Mc-EN-roe."

Ten years and $10 million in prize money later, he's an American icon. You misbehave now in sports, you're acting like McEnroe. Who do you think you are, *McEnroe*? Ilie Nastase was bad. Jimmy Connors —believe me—has always been much, much worse out there than people think. But McEnroe, especially to the casual fan, just walked in and retired the trophy. And he's had some run. Reggie Jackson became an elder statesman after he left the Yankees, like he was running for Cosby or something. Ali got old. Jim McMahon was a flash-in-the-pan, one big bang.

Always there was John McEnroe. It figured he would end up in Malibu, and at Lakers games with Jack Nicholson. Even marrying a movie star made sense. John McEnroe *invented* the Brat Pack. He was the first one, way back in 1977, when Sean Penn was collecting baseball cards, or burning them, whatever he did. Nastase had come before, and so had Connors, but McEnroe was different, going where no man had gone before. It was tennis in a leather jacket. Nobody as good had ever been as bad.

Right away, he was better than everybody except Bjorn Borg. At Wimbledon in 1980, they played the most famous tennis match ever, five sets, 8-6 in the fifth, the whole thing elevated into legend by that 18-16, twenty-two minute, fourth-set tie breaker, during which McEnroe fought off five championship points.

Borg won the match, extending his streak of Wimbledon titles to five. But McEnroe came back to Wimbledon the next year and beat Borg in the final. Two months later, he beat Borg again, in the final of the U.S. Open; this time, McEnroe messed the Swede up. At twenty-two, McEnroe was number one, and Borg didn't want to play anymore. Borg skipped the postmatch press conference, got into a courtesy car, drove away, and never really came back.

McEnroe had lost his worthiest adversary. Tennis had lost its greatest rivalry. It was like Frazier bailing out on Ali.

After Borg left, McEnroe stayed number one in 1982 and 1983 and 1984. He may have missed the Swede and pined away, but he kept going. Rackets were broken, matches were interrupted, suspensions were earned, fines were paid, there was an ongoing war with Wimbledon and the British press and still photographers the world over. He once threw sawdust at a U.S. Open fan. He berated a female reporter in Canada to a fare-thee-well.

He has never exactly been thrilled by that shotgun mike CBS keeps near the court at the U.S. Open.

If you were in the one-hundredth row of the stands at one of his matches and you crossed your legs and scratched your nose, it sent him into a tailspin. "Don't you know I see *everything?*" he snapped once to a friend at the U.S. Open, explaining why he got so distracted by some obnoxious fans during one of his matches.

This ump was an incompetent fool. That one—or was it the same one?—was the pits of the world. He basically got away with all of it.

Borg was gone. He was the only game in town. McEnroe was a Beastie Boy swinging a Dunlop, getting bigger and bigger, making one fortune after another.

Then in 1986, it all came apart. When that happens, especially in tennis, it happens fast. If you don't believe it, ask Borg. I think he turned thirty the other day.

McEnroe was embarrassed in a first-round match at the Nabisco Masters tournament by someone named Brad Gilbert. McEnroe either looked washed up or just old that night, depending on how you were rooting. The next week, he announced he was taking a sabbatical. It was a beauty. Tatum had the baby. They got married. They went to his house in Malibu. In no particular order.

McEnroe came back last August, getting to the final of a tournament in Stratton Mountain, Vermont, where he faced Boris Becker. McEnroe had match points, was undone by a bad call on one of them, yelled some at the German kid, lost. But it was luminous tennis. Borg-McEnroe comparisons were irresistible; tennis needed a new rivalry and the fans and the writers take anything in the neighborhood.

McEnroe says, "Me and Becker could be something, but he's not Borg, okay?" Then he mocks the little boogie Becker does after a winning shot, pumping his arms, wiggling his knees Charleston-style. "It's not like *that* makes you an interesting person, if you know what I mean," he says.

The Stratton match had filled him with the old bravado. Even though he lost, he wasn't intimidated by Becker's two straight Wimbledons. "It looked like coming back was going to be easier than I'd thought," he says.

It wasn't. He lost in the first round of the Open to Paul Annacone, the greatest player in the history of Southampton, New York. While on sabbatical McEnroe had promised better behavior and he was true to his word, but it was like some pilot light had gone off, and his game with it. McEnroe lacked power, his volleys had lost their teeth. He was a step slow all day long. McEnroe appeared burned out, just as he had against Brad Gilbert in January. He played like a Smurf on the court where he'd won four singles titles. All of a sudden, at twenty-seven, he looked like a former number one trying to hang on.

Then McEnroe and doubles partner Peter Fleming were defaulted for showing up late to the National Tennis Center after getting stuck in traffic. So his whole Open lasted the couple of hours it had taken

Annacone to dispatch him. McEnroe, who treasured his Open championships the most because he'd been raised ten minutes away in Douglaston, Queens, had been run out of the tournament as if he were a scalper.

"If I ever get to be number one again," McEnroe says, "it will be because of the moment when they told me to get lost from the Open."

We are in a Philadelphia hotel room, in town for the Ebel U.S. Pro Indoor Championships, his first tournament of the new year. McEnroe, ranked fifteenth in the world, has won his second-round match over Mel Purcell. He lies on his belly in front of the television set, remote-control in his hand, white sweat pants pulled down to his knees, ice pack attached to bare buttocks.

It was McEnroe who brought up the subject of number one.

"You want to be number one in the world again?"

McEnroe says, "I'd like to be, but I don't have to be. It's not like I'm going to bag it if I don't make it back to number one *this* year. I'm not like all those jerks out there who think my biological clock is ticking or something. I just want to get back into the top five, and see what I need from there. But"—he shifts slightly on the floor—"like I said, if I do get back to number one, it'll be because of what happened at the Open. I mean, I sat in the house for a week after that. I was *steaming.* I just kept saying, 'Can you *believe* this shit?' All those guys who wanted to get even with me all those years were starting to get even. Tiriac was right."

Tiriac is Ion Tiriac, the bearish Romanian coach who made champions out of Nastase and Guillermo Vilas and now plays Colonel Tom to Becker's Elvis. McEnroe is referring to a comment Tiriac made at the Open last year, before McEnroe lost to Annacone, before the default.

Tiriac was standing outside the trainer's room, waiting for Becker to change. McEnroe happened to be there, looking skittish, a New York Islanders cap on his head, telling well-wishers, "I got a feeling it's going to get worse before it gets better."

Tiriac said to whoever cared to listen: "You know what is going to be the toughest thing for him now? He is going to start getting the Nastase treatment. All those years when Nastase was the best player, they have to put up with all his bullshit. But they all wait. Then comes the day when Nastase isn't Nastase anymore. And all the ones who wait are ready. Doesn't matter who they are. Umpires, linesmen, officials, other players. Is all the same. They say to him, Fuck *you* now.

You piss on us all these years? Okay, now we piss on you. McEnroe is going to get the Nastase treatment, wait and see please."

Couple of days later came the default. McEnroe knew what everybody else knew: if he were still number one, they would have waited until Christmas for him to show up for a first-round doubles match.

McEnroe uses the remote control on the television set, switching from the Joan Rivers show to a Philadelphia Flyers hockey game.

"I've never been defaulted out of a match in my life." he says. "No one knew what to say to me for a week. Well, I knew what to say: Screw it, I'm going back to being John McEnroe."

By the end of '86, John McEnroe had won three tournaments, beaten Lendl once, and been fined and suspended.

Tatum O'Neal says, "So this girlfriend of mine says, 'John McEnroe's coming up to the party later, do you want to meet him?' I thought, 'Why not?' "

Her husband is practicing with Connors. She is sitting on the sofa, wearing a white WORLD TEAM CUP, DÜSSELDORF T-shirt over a long white linen skirt. She looks younger than twenty-three, fair and freckled, softer and sweeter than she is in photographs. She is about three months pregnant. Estella has put Kevin down for the rest of the morning. A powerboat cruises past outside the dining-room window. Tatum O'Neal—Ryan's daughter, Griffin's sister, Farrah's whatever—sips coffee.

"John hates caffeine," she says. "I love caffeine."

The party was in early October 1984, at a record producer's home in Los Angeles. McEnroe does show up, as advertised. He is with Vitas Gerulaitis. John and Tatum are introduced.

"The next thing I know, he comes over and sits down right next to me. I mean *right next to me.* I thought, 'Oh my God.' " They chat. They hit it off, she thinks. There is another party the next day, at the home of Alana Stewart. She was married to George Hamilton and Rod Stewart. John and Tatum chat a little more. They discover they are both going to be in New York later in the month.

"He calls me up in New York. It's like October 27 or 28. He says, 'You want to see my new apartment?' Sure. And John took me to this place on Central Park—this quadruplex—and I promise you, I couldn't believe my eyes. I said, 'How old are you? Twenty-six? Twenty-seven? And this place is *yours?*' It just kept going up and up and up. I was overwhelmed. I'd seen nice places before in my life. But this was the nicest place I'd ever seen.

"There is also some chemistry going on. I can feel it. But about 11:00, I left. Then I had to go back to Los Angeles. Then I went to Las Vegas, where my dad was making a movie. John was off playing a tournament in Stockholm, and he misbehaved. One morning my father shoved the newspaper in my face with the stories about John and said, 'Look at this! How can you *like* this guy?' Uh, thanks, Dad."

I say, "Things different now between John and your dad?"

Tatum O'Neal smiles brilliantly and delivers the line like the kid who won the Oscar.

"Oh yes," she says brightly. "They're much, *much* worse."

McEnroe used to tell his friends he'd never marry an actress, he'd never move to L.A., and he'd never have a kid before he was thirty. But you can't stop love. "I know he wasn't marrying Farrah at her peak, or Madonna," Tatum says. "I'm not the paparazzi queen of the moment, okay? John McEnroe didn't marry the 'It' girl of the year. But I know what it's like to be inside the bubble and be young. Maybe he wanted someone a little more like him."

It isn't Joe and Marilyn, myth on myth. Nothing is ever going to be. It isn't even Sean and Madonna, but no doubt John and Tatum take the silver medal as the paparazzi pair skaters of the moment.

McEnroe says, "Let me put it this way: being with Tatum took me to a whole new plane. Until I met her, I'd never been in the *National Enquirer.*"

They spent most of their time in Malibu. The photographers hid in garages across the street or camped on the sidewalk. McEnroe would go to the grocery store, and he would be followed. He'd be shooting a Frisbee around with Ahmad Rashad, the NBC Sports commentator, on the beach, and they would discover a photographer from a British tabloid had screwed himself into the sand. When McEnroe took the sabbatical, there was a day when a Brit journalist— a lot of them think investigative reporting is remembering the limerick from the men's-room wall—rang the doorbell and said to Tatum, Excuse me, ma'am, isn't your husband in rehab at such-and-such?

McEnroe denies that he was in rehab anyplace, though rumors were very much in the air while he was away. Somebody knew somebody who had been with McEnroe at this hospital—we got that sort of call at the paper where I work. Another guy called up and talked about this treatment program in New Jersey or that one in L.A.

McEnroe says, "It's a lie. Anybody who knows me knows that I'm honest. I'm the worst liar in the world. I don't do that stuff. I wasn't in rehab. But all of a sudden that was the story on me. Even people I thought were friends didn't believe me when I denied it.

"I was going to Lakers games all the time. I was at concerts. I was in the public eye. But it made a good story, so no one wanted to check anything."

As it was, the thing he needed was rehab from tennis.

"At the end of 1985," McEnroe says, "I wasn't playing well to begin with, and then it seemed like all this stuff with Tatum and me just kept piling up. The combination did it to me. I knew I had to dig myself out of this hole I'd gotten myself into." At the Australian Open in December of '85, there came the day when McEnroe suddenly found his hands around the throat of a reporter. Only a warning from a bellhop kept the picture out of newspapers the world over. He lost to the immortal Slobodan Zivojinovic at the Australian Open—"first match I ever felt like I tanked in my life"—and then lost to Gilbert in New York a month later, and beat it.

In their Turnberry living room—they also own an estate in Cove Neck, Long Island—Tatum O'Neal says, "I think John is coming to the realization that it's just not a big deal anymore with the photographers. It's happened to Frank Sinatra his whole career. It happens to everyone in these businesses if they're any good." She giggles. "Well, not Lendl. The point is, after all these years, I'm used to it. It's my life, *our* life, and after a while you just say to yourself, 'My life is more important than all that.' One night we were out with Sean Penn and I started talking to Sean about it, because of all the problems he's had. And John just gave me this look. Like, 'Couldn't we be talking about something more important with Sean?' "

She says they forged their relationship during his six months away from tennis. Kevin was born in May. They were married in August on Long Island. Tatum was Ryan's daughter and now she was McEnroe's wife.

McEnroe: "Let's face it, it stinks being married to a professional athlete."

It was as if more tumult had been added to the tumultuous life of Tatum O'Neal. Her parents, Ryan O'Neal and former actress Joanna Moore, were divorced when she was a child. Her brother Griffin has had well-publicized drug problems and was cited last year for criminal negligence in the boating death of director Francis Ford Coppola's son. Ryan O'Neal has sired a child out of wedlock with actress Farrah Fawcett, who was Farrah Fawcett-Majors when she was married to the Six Million Dollar Man.

McEnroe: "It's a credit to Tatum how well she's turned out, considering."

Tatum herself says, "I look at the upbringing John's had and the family situation he came out of—how *normal* it all is—and I think how lucky he is."

She disappears into the kitchen and comes back with more coffee. She goes to the door and gives a listen for Kevin. Then she sits down and primly rearranges her skirt as she crosses her legs on the coffee table.

"I didn't realize how much support he was going to need from me," she says. "It took me a long time to adjust to that. Sometimes I find myself saying, 'Look, John, I don't know *how* to be a wife.' But I chose. I chose *John*. And eventually, I think I can be everything I want to be—support system, actress, wife, mother.

"I've learned patience. I let a lot of things go by. I wasn't used to that. I've got a hell of an Irish temper. You know, let's get everything out in the open and deal with it right now. We have some beautiful fights. He gets so angry with me, and he finally says, 'You know who you are? The female John McEnroe! And you know what else? You've got all his worst qualities.' "

John McEnroe says, "Are you kidding? When I was eighteen years old and starting out, I would have been thrilled to have the career I've had. You know, three Wimbledons, four U.S. Opens, the Davis Cup."

That was then, this is now.

"I felt he was going to be the greatest player of all time," says Bud Collins, *Boston Globe* columnist and NBC broadcaster. "He had everything. Genius. Artistry. And that serve. I thought he'd go past Roy Emerson and have the most grand-slam singles titles ever [Emerson had twelve]. Then he couldn't handle it, I guess. Plus, he was never in shape to begin with. I still love watching the kid play. I can see him winning another Wimbledon, or Open, maybe even the French if he ever works at it. But I honestly don't feel he's been true to his talent."

In what was supposed to be his prime, McEnroe didn't push himself. But then again he never did. Tennis always came so easily to him. From the time he was a kid at the Port Washington Tennis Academy on Long Island, he got special treatment from his coaches; even the late Harry Hopman, the legendary Aussie taskmaster, was soft on Junior.

If he did not abuse his talent, perhaps he took it for granted. Other players, such as Lendl, were torturing themselves on Nautilus machines and retaining conditioning coaches. McEnroe played his guitar and acted like a rock star. When he found out that Lendl was on the Robert Haas Eat-to-Win Diet, McEnroe joked, "I'm on the Haagen-Dazs diet." While Tiriac had Becker running up mountains in Germany, McEnroe was running around the country on his "Tennis Over America" tour, making big bucks in meaningless exhibition matches.

McEnroe, blessed with the skills of a champion, has always had the disposition of an artist: just put up the net and let's do it.

And when he was young, McEnroe did it to Borg, he did it to them all. Punch them out with the serve, get to the net in an eyeblink, then drop one of those volleys on the other side, the ball dying like a pillow hitting a mattress. In the long rallies, he would hit one ball with the top spin, slice the next one, hit the next flat, start the whole program over again.

"A nick here, a nick there," Arthur Ashe says, "and pretty soon you're bleeding to death."

One night he was talking about Becker's serve, the best he's ever seen. "Did Tiriac teach it to him?" McEnroe spits out some club sandwich and continues, "You're born with something like that. Becker just understands things that champions are supposed to understand."

McEnroe always hated practice. Instead he played doubles with Fleming to hone his game, smooth out the rough patches. He jokes about his work habits. That night in Philly, he put ice to his fanny, ice to his shoulder, he attached this elastic thing to his ankles and edged slowly across the room, he did sit-ups, he did curls. At one point during our conversation I said, "How old are you now?" and McEnroe said, "Twenty-eight. Which means twenty-eight years of not being in shape."

Last summer, on the verge of the comeback from the sabbatical, McEnroe decided to change all that. He cooled his longtime coaching relationship (if not his friendship) with Tony Palafox and hired a combination Zen master and drill instructor named Paul Cohen. There was yoga in the morning, brutal workouts in the afternoon. He ended up with perfect muscle tone but no upper-body power. Now he's dumped Cohen and gone back to Palafox, who is more like a graduate assistant than a teacher. He lets McEnroe be McEnroe.

"I made some mistakes in the last couple years." McEnroe says, "and they set me back." McEnroe believes that the biggest mistake he ever made was in not winning the 1984 French Open final when he had it in his grasp.

"You know," he says, "if I'd won that French, it might have changed the way everybody looks at my career."

No American male had won the French Open on the red clay of Roland Garros Stadium in twenty-nine years. In 1984, the final was against Lendl. McEnroe led two sets to none. Then he led two sets to one.

"Two sets to one, 4-3 in games, 40-30 on my serve," he will say whenever the subject comes up, like he's reciting a grocery list. "Five points from the match."

Lendl broke McEnroe's serve, eventually broke his back. The heat got to McEnroe, Lendl got to McEnroe, photographers got to McEnroe, he tried to whack an NBC hand-held camera. Lendl won the fourth set, the fifth set, the title. McEnroe didn't have the French, Lendl wasn't a choker anymore. McEnroe would win the U.S. Open later that year. It was his last grand-slam championship. He was twenty-five years old.

"I choked that French Open," he says.

For years, Lendl chased McEnroe. Now McEnroe chases him. It is not a buddy movie.

"The guy hasn't been good for tennis," McEnroe says. "He's been so selfish. And he's certainly not the kind of guy who brings out the best in others. He's hurt the popularity of the game so much. Borg was different. Borg gave this feeling to people. Borg became this huge celebrity without saying a *thing*. It's hard to say nothing and turn out as big as he did."

It was the best tennis show of all. There had never been quite the collision of excellence that Borg and McEnroe brought to their battles in the late '70s and early '80s. It was McEnroe's fire, Borg's ice. Net versus baseline. Righty, lefty. McEnroe would hit a big hook serve, take Borg into the flower boxes, and Borg would somehow punch a two-fisted backhand down the line for a winner. Borg would hit what was a sure passing shot against anyone else in the world, and McEnroe would dive and spit back a winning volley.

"The only way you could win a point," McEnroe said after the Wimbledon final in 1980, "was to hit a winner.

"Borg's a legend. I'm not kidding you, I still miss Borg. It took me a long time to get over his leaving like that. All of a sudden, he just bagged it, like, poof, he was gone. I thought, 'Wait a minute, we were just getting started, this was just getting interesting.' It affected me for a whole year. Then by the time I got my act together, there was Lendl and Jimbo ready to pounce. See, Borg never considered one thing: that I could screw up."

Between the Philadelphia tournament and the vacation at Turnberry, McEnroe had some wisdom teeth pulled, lost a match to Johan Kriek in Memphis, and played an exhibition match with Bjorn Borg in Toronto. Over the last few years, they've done this several times, like some rock 'n' roll revival. In Toronto, McEnroe asked Borg what he thought he, Mac, should do.

" 'Retire,' " McEnroe says, laughing.

"I gotta believe I can do it again," he says. "I think it took guts to walk away the way I did. Nobody ever did that. I think that's going to pay some dividends along the way somewhere. I'm not going to panic if I lose some matches. Everybody panics so fast. I'm going to be around for a while."

Courtesy car in Philadelphia. Tony Palafox is in the front seat of the van. In the back, McEnroe is talking excitedly about the Giants winning the Super Bowl, asking questions about all the Mets' offseason problems, announcing that all New Yorkers had to begin rooting for the New York Rangers, give New York a triple. McEnroe may be a Lakers fan, but he is still happiest at Madison Square Garden and Shea Stadium, drinking beers with his old Douglaston pals, watching the teams he grew up with.

He is asked what the biggest public misconception about him is.

He says, "That I'm not a nice person. Because I am. I'm just not nice 100 percent of the time. But I'll tell you this: I make a lot more people happy than not."

You know all the bad parts. What you don't know: McEnroe is smart, funny, honest, an intensely loyal friend. When rich young American players couldn't be bothered, he played Davis Cup, made it mean something again in the United States. Of course, this doesn't justify anything. Just balances out the scales, maybe more than you thought. He's no punk.

"Nobody ever talks about South Africa," says his father. "Chris Evert, Miss Perfect, took the money and went down there. Jack Nicklaus went down there and played golf. They offered John $1 million just to go down to Sun City and *lose* one match and go home. Then they offered him $5 million for five years if he'd come down. And my son stood up and said no. People can think what they want about him. But principles are high up on his list of priorities. My wife and I are thrilled at the way he's turned out."

John McEnroe Sr. is a balding, ruddy-faced Irishman every bit as tough as his kid. You want to mix it up with Junior, you have to get by the old man first. He grew up on Seventy-ninth Street and Third Avenue in Manhattan, when, as he likes to say, "Third Avenue was still Third Avenue, not some fashionable part of the Upper East Side." He came out of Fordham Law and was a successful memeber of Paul, Weiss, Rifkind, Wharton and Garrison, prestigious New York law firm, before his kid ever sneered at his first Wimbledon umpire. Ultimately, you want to set up anything important, business-wise, with John McEnroe Jr., you deal with John McEnroe Sr. And his presence in the stands has become a tennis fixture: the camera eventually finds him, squinting underneath a floppy white hat or some network's baseball cap, trying to be cool and Big Daddy—like while his son is doing something terribly embarrassing in a big match.

"He wasn't a fighter as a kid," the father says. "The only fistfight I can ever remember was when he was defending his brother Mark against this kid who was three years bigger than Mark at the time. And that time, I told him he did the right thing, defending his brother." There is still some Third Avenue there; it almost comes out "brudder."

The father laughs.

"Of course, he was always a hooter and howler on the tennis court," he says. "Except when he was first starting out. The kids were calling their own lines then, so he had nobody to argue with. So John spent a lot of time yelling at himself. But that was John. Playing Ping-Pong with his brothers, he tried to beat you. Pickup basketball with his friends, same thing. John *always* wanted to win."

Kay McEnroe, the mother, says, "The signs were always there. Even if he didn't get the best mark in Latin, in grammar school, he'd be *furious*. One time he got 94 and his friend got 98, and there was just no speaking to him."

Kay McEnroe is a tall, attractive, silver-haired woman who looks more like an ex-Vogue model than an ex-nurse whom her husband met a long time ago, while she was working at Lenox Hill Hospital. She is a lady, polite to the point of courtly, extremely close to her son, quite different from the rough-and-tumble of both father and son. She is also the quiet steel of the McEnroe family, even if she's not out in front running interference. To this day, when there is some sort of nontennis problem, John likes to run it by his mother.

"With John, I know I'll hear about it," she says. "My other boys [Patrick and Mark], they're more quiet. John's always been different. I expect I'll be mother to him for quite a while. He's always been very complicated, and I don't think that will ever change. But of the three boys, he's the one who never misses my birthday or Mother's Day."

The son's tennis always made the mother nervous, at whatever level it was being played. So did the sound and the fury when the ball the son thought was out was called in.

Kay McEnroe says, "My first reaction is that I'd like him to be quiet. The moment it happens, I think, 'Oh my God.' First and foremost, he's my child. And I don't want anything to pain my children, whatever the circumstances. So I'm thinking 'John, don't do that, it will only upset you.' " She giggles. "One time, oh, a long time ago, I said, 'Honey, don't worry, the next one will go your way.' And John looked me right in the eye and said, 'Mother, that's bullshit.' "

The father sighs when you bring up "pits of the world" and so forth.

"It goes back to what I said about principles," he says. "John always thinks he's right."

A lot of what has happened to John McEnroe Jr. he did to himself. He never knew when to fold his hand. But he has come to understand—he says—that it doesn't matter anymore whether or not he was right about every single line call that took place since Wimbledon of '77.

McEnroe on McEnroe: "The way I'm thinking now is this— 'What satisfaction is there in making someone feel bad, even if you're right?' Also, I don't want to go down in history as being Nasty Jr., or whatever. When you get to the stage where I am now—husband, father, twenty-eight years old—the whole thing just gets to sound like sour grapes.

"I don't know. After a while, when I'd get the bad call, what happened next was almost like an addiction. I mean, I'd feel my feet moving toward the chair before I'd even think about going over there. And so now I'm stuck with the rep, I understand that. I might only do something once or twice a match, but that's all people want to remember. The thing I hate is that people think it's an act. It's not an act. It was never an act. It's just something that became part of me that I'm trying to recover from because there are more important things to get on with."

Once John McEnroe Sr. and his wife were the ones who had to sit and watch when the fireworks came. Now it is Tatum who must sit there with the stiff upper lip, smiling bravely.

"I just think, 'John, get back into the game.' " Tatum says. " 'Forget about that point, get on to the next one.' He's come to know how proud I am of him when he *doesn't* do those things."

Tatum O'Neal, Kevin's mom, shrugs her shoulders, like she's trying to shake off the whole subject.

She says, "Mostly I think all that crap is a waste of time."

Addiction or just plain crap, take your pick. Bad behavior apparently doesn't go away just because John McEnroe says it will. In April, he lost to Miroslav Mecir in the finals of the WCT Finals in Dallas. Early in the match, McEnroe snarled at the chair umpire, "You're going to be hearing from me all day, and there's nothing you can do about it."

In the third set he threatened to walk out of the match. Later, after yet another call that seemed to cause him physical pain, McEnroe screamed, "It's a goddamn conspiracy." Good intentions are very nice, but it may be that if you are born round, you don't die square.

Tatum O'Neal says, "Watch it, honey, hot plate." She sets the plate of hot pancakes down on the coffee table in front of her husband. As McEnroe attacks his lunch with fury—at that first Wimbledon in '77, one writer described his "eating the traditional strawberries and cream without benefit of the traditional spoon"—he talks about something interesting that happened during his six months off.

They missed him.

The crowds missed him. So did the nabobs of the sport who sometimes thought of him as acid rain. Suddenly, there were no heroes out there, anti or otherwise. Lendl, on the court, has the personality of an IBM home computer. (What's the matter?" McEnroe asks sarcastically. "Do you like a robot being number one?") Becker, for all his screaming youth, really does have a personality that ends with scraped knees. Connors hasn't won a tournament of any kind since the first Reagan administration; all of his competitive qualities are still admirable, but he's an opening act now. By the middle of April, Tim Mayotte would be the only American to have won a Grand Prix tournament anywhere on the planet in 1987.

Tim Mayotte?

Borg and McEnroe played twenty-two minutes of tie breaker once at Wimbledon that were more gripping than anything that has happened in tennis the last couple of years.

So all of a sudden they missed Junior. Without him, the game lay in state. And wasn't nobody coming along. It's like parents who spend all those years telling the kids to keep the noise down, then go crazy with the quiet when they go off to college. All the ones who scorned McEnroe suddenly were dying of heartbreak when he went away.

He says, "I'm losing this match to [Johan] Kriek in Memphis a few weeks ago and, like, they *love* me. I'm thinking, 'Why couldn't it be like this eight or nine years ago?' "

A few minutes before he came back from practice for some of Tatum's flapjacks, she was saying, "Right now he's in good shape. He understands it's going to take some time to get into *great* shape. And when he gets into great shape, he knows he'll be able to play the way he wants to play. But God, people are so negative. Ever since he's come back, he's had to take so much crap from so-called friends and contemporaries and people in the press about how that clock is supposedly running on his career."

John walks in as she's speaking, tosses his blue headband and racket on the floor, flops on the couch, unlaces his sneakers, picks up the electric guitar and begins a loud, off-key version of "This Land Is Your Land." After a few bars, Tatum disappears into the kitchen, laughing and covering her ears. McEnroe says, "Listen, it's not too late to change my attitude, or my approach, or whatever. I've watched Connors use the crowd, and he's really good at it. I think I can get a big part of the crowd rooting for me. I think they understand that whatever they thought they knew about me, the bottom line is that I'm good for the game. I'm not a robot. It's like this: people either like or don't like what they think they know about you."

He strums a big chord, theatrically, on the guitar.

"I'm happier off the court than I've ever been in my life," he says. "For all the bad stuff that happened last year, it was a *great* year, because it was a family year. Now this year is for me, to start seeing if I can do it."

A month before, in Philadelphia, I'd asked McEnroe what he thought he'd be doing when he reached forty. He got up and paced the room. He has always been nervous energy, standing up, sitting down, patting his hair, flailing at imaginary ground strokes, shooting imaginary jump shots, like the room is Borg and it's jerking him around.

"The things I'd really like to do aren't realistic," he says. "I'd like to be in a rock 'n' roll band. Or the eleventh man on an NBA team. Or an NBA coach. I used to want to be the twelfth man on an NBA team, but I've upgraded my goals. Hell, I want to get into some games, get some minutes. Or maybe make a movie with Jack [Nicholson, fellow Lakers fan]. If Jack called and said, 'John, I've got to have you in my next movie,' that would be nice. It's also not going to happen."

For now, John McEnroe has to prove that at twenty-eight, he is not an old man in a young man's game. Things happened to him. Borg went away for good. Maybe number one wasn't all McEnroe thought it was going to be. Neither was being famous. He squandered too much of his genius in big-money exhibitions. He made way too much noise about small matters.

A few years ago, when he was still number one, McEnroe was asked what it would take for him to get the crowds on his side. "I'll have to get married, have a kid, and start losing," he said. He was referring to Connors, who was booed off the court at Forest Hills after losing the '77 Open final to Vilas, but who somehow turned it around and became the people's choice, at least in this country.

The remark is mentioned to John McEnroe, who is married, has a kid and, at least for now, is losing more that he ever has (in February, March, and April, McEnroe played four finals, lost four finals).

"I know," McEnroe says. "I know. Weird how things work out, huh?"

He shouts to the kitchen.

"Honey," John McEnroe says, "we got any more of that Aunt Jemima?"

• *1987*

St. Elmore's Fire

Here he is at Tiger Stadium in Detroit on a September baseball night hanging on to summer. He is getting ready to watch Jack Morris, the Tiger ace, go for win number nineteen against the Toronto Blue Jays. Elmore Leonard looks just like what a drunk mistakenly called him once in his drinking days, back at this joint called Stan's in Fort Lauderdale: little Princeton s.o.b. Tweed jacket, high forehead, soft voice, round tortoiseshell glasses, corduroy slacks. Not anything like a tough-guy novelist who works the street the way Updike works the suburbs.

"You know who you look just like?" says an usher.

He's stopped next to Leonard's seat on the aisle. The usher is from the Bismarck Food Service, wearing a blue Bismarck jersey, carrying a Bismarck bucket filled with soft drinks. Name tag says MARK, IRVING. He is fifty maybe.

Leonard says, "Who?" Then he does what he does about every ten minutes, which is light up a True green and smoke it down to his wrist.

"Elmore Leonard the writer." It is one thought to Irving Mark of Bismarck, no commas.

"Well, I am."

"No kidding?" Mark puts down the bucket.

"No kidding."

"I just bought your book. *Glitz.* The one in Atlantic City with the cop and the hooker and the crazy guy and so forth. Five bucks."

"Well, thank you."

"You write about Cass Corridor sometimes, don't you?" It is a seedy downtown Detroit place, near Wayne State University. It is an Elmore Leonard place.

"Yes I do. Couple of books."

Mark says, "I grew up in Cass Corridor."

The stands are filling up. There are probably thirsty people somewhere behind Leonard's seat between home plate and the first-base dugout. Irving Mark is still talking.

"No kidding. Elmore Leonard the writer. I recognized you from your picture on *Glitz*. They call you Dutch, right? For Dutch Leonard the old knuckleball pitcher?"

"I think my friends liked it better than El-more," says Elmore "Dutch" Leonard.

"Well, I gotta go right now," Mark says. "But let me tell you something in case I forget. You just keep doing what you're doing and you're going to be a very good seller. I know you're the 'in' thing but don't pay any attention to that, all right? Keep doing what you're doing, like I said."

Elmore Leonard, who finally got on the bestseller list with *Glitz* and who will be on it twice this year—*Bandits* now, *Touch* in the fall—watches Irving Mark move up the aisle. Later, he will say that he would have to write the scene from his own point of view, being floored as he was that he was recognized by an usher at the ball park. But for now he plays the scene out the way Jack Delaney would play it in *Bandits* or Vincent Mora in Glitz or Stick in *Stick*: deadpan, a little irony, cool. You have to be cool to write cool.

Leonard says, "Hey. Five bucks, and it had my picture on it. It just occurred to me he bought the book *secondhand*."

The best Elmore Leonard character might be Elmore Leonard. Check it out: Twenty years ago, he's packed it in as a full-time novelist. His big writing numbers in the early '60s are these classics—soon to undergo the wonders of colorization—from Encyclopaedia Britannica Films: *Settlement of the Mississippi Valley, Boy of Spain, Frontier Boy,* and the ever-popular *Julius Caesar*. Thousand bucks a movie, seventeen informative minutes in length. Leonard knocks these babies off when he isn't free-lancing ad copy for Hurst gear shifters. Hurst shifters? You bet. He says that if you had a hot rod in Detroit in 1963, you had to have a Hurst shifter or you were nowhere. Which is where Leonard was: western novelist at a time when the market was all dried up, little more than halfway through his first marriage, and an alcoholic who thought you weren't an alcoholic unless you ended up in a skid-row gutter.

"The years 1961 to 1966 were the low point, definitely," he says. "I had probably resigned myself to writing again sometime, but never full time."

Now, at the age of sixty-one, Elmore Leonard is an overnight sensation.

He reads another review where somebody asks the question, "Where has Elmore Leonard been?" And says, "Where have *I* been? Most of the time, it's where has *he* been. Like, I've been hiding?"

He hasn't been hiding. Even if he had been, Leonard couldn't hide anymore if he wanted to. It's not just ushers at the ball park. It's the Hollywood money men. It's the reading public, all those people lined up at their Waldenbooks. After *LaBrava*, the book before *Glitz*, there was a headline in *The New York Times*, and it was a little ahead of the game maybe, but it said it all in dry old *Times*-ese: WRITER DISCOVERED AFTER 23 NOVELS. *LaBrava* ended up selling four hundred thousand in paperback; *Glitz* hit the list; all of a sudden Leonard was on the cover of *Newsweek*.

"Sometimes," says Joan Leonard, his wife, "the good guys win."

The good guy is one of the big guys now. Arbor House is paying Leonard $3 million for *Freaky Deaky*, the one in the typewriter now, and the one after it. Of Leonard's twenty-five novels, twenty have been sold to Hollywood. Somewhere out there, someone is having a meeting right now about some Elmore Leonard property. The sun never sets on the Dutch Empire.

Funny thing is, he's been doing it pretty much the same way for thirty-five years, if you go back to when he sold his first western story to *Argosy*: "I am happy to report that your novelette, *Apache Agent*, is one which we like very much," wrote an editor named John Bender. "And, by all means, let us see some more fiction." The hard, lean writing—if he's a boxer, he's Tony Zale—was there from the start, in the five westerns he wrote until the middle '60s, and then after that, when he made the movie into crime fiction. Check it out: the work has been there. He's been on the shelves. Yeah, sure, "Writer discovered."

Dutch Leonard says, "I don't know. It's like there have always been a lot of Liberaces on the list—there *are* a lot of Liberaces on the list—and I've always been Herbie Hancock. No, not Herbie Hancock, people always really knew about Herbie Hancock. Where's Marian McPartland? She doing okay? Maybe I'm Marian McPartland."

So Leonard's this elegant jazz man who has been working lounges all these years and suddenly somebody decided he should have been working the big rooms all along.

It all comes out of the study in the brick house on the corner of Fairfax and Pine in Birmingham, about ten miles north of Detroit. The study is a quiet and cozy room in a quiet and coy house. Leonard has written the last eight books in this room, lived in the house since he and Joan were married in it in 1979. Why change anything? On the bookshelves across from the antique desk is a lot of '60s research material, because *Freaky Deaky* is about some '60s revolutionaries, and a scam in the '80s, and a cop who's getting off the bomb squad because his girlfriend is afraid he's going to lose his hands, and. . .

Leonard will make it work, don't worry. No problem. *Bandits* is about and ex-hotel thief named Jack Delaney who's working for his brother-in-law at a funeral parlor, an ex-nun named Sister Lucy who worked in a leper hospital in Nicaragua, an ex-cop, a contra colonel, and $3 million that is going to move around some. It is set in New Orleans. In the study I say to Leonard, "Oh, another ex-thief, ex-nun of the lepers, contra colonel in New Orleans novel, more of that hackneyed material."

Leonard laughs and lights up a True green. "It's like all of them," he says. "None of it relates until I sit down and start to write, and then it all fits together, like a what's-his-name cube."

Joan Leonard, a pretty blonde, pokes her head around from the kitchen. She has come in from shopping.

"Any word on *LaBrava?*" Al Pacino is interested in the script Leonard wrote.

"Now Pacino wants to talk to me."

Joan says, "Cold feet?"

"I don't know."

Joan says, "Can he *read?*" and disappears back into the kitchen.

Leonard goes back to talking about his writing. This he likes to do. And he likes to *read* his writing aloud. Spend any time with him and he will give you a little shot of his work. The opening of *Freaky Deaky*. A description of Lynn Marie Faulkner's apartment, with her Waylon Jennings poster and velour couch, from *Touch*. Leonard becomes an actor running lines on you, taking on attitudes and inflections, all that. He doesn't want you to miss anything.

He says, "Listen, I know I'm different. I know my stuff has a different sound to it. But I never really thought it was *big* enough. I'm not plotty enough. I'm not very good at story really. I can keep them turning pages, but I'm not strong on narration. I'm always afraid I'm going to sound like I'm *writing* the words. So over the years I've found out what I can do and what I can't. I'm weak on images, for example, so I go with my strong suit. What interests me is dialogue. I compensate is what I do. You could say my style is the absence of style."

Who needs style when you have an ear like Dutch Leonard's? That ear takes us to the streets of Detroit, Miami, Atlantic City, New Orleans, where grifters and con men and dreamers and the most wonderfully badass dudes any Princeton-looking s.o.b. out of the Encyclopaedia Britannica Films office *ever* drew are talking about some kind of score. Leonard has hung with cops, ridden in squad cars, sat in the courtrooms and precinct houses, seen busts up close. His college classmate, Bill Marshall, is a South Florida private eye. But Leonard says, "All that stuff is minor."

I say, "Then how do you get it right?"

He says, "There's just always been this sound that interests me. It's the sound of savvy people, or people who *think* they're savvy and talk that way. To me, they're so much more interesting than educated people. I'm not all that interested in the way *educated* people think. I mean, my main characters are smart and they've got this attitude, you know. I don't know. I guess I'm still a kid on the corner of Woodward Avenue listening to my friends, who were all blue-collar kids. I was an enlisted man in the Navy (World War II, Seabees). I hung around with enlisted men. I *listened* to enlisted men, not on purpose, just listening like you would. I spent a lot of time in my life *with* these sorts of people."

Elmore Leonard was born in New Orleans in 1925 and moved to Detroit with his parents in 1934. Catholic education: University of Detroit High School. He picked up his nickname then: Dutch, after the old Washington Senators knuckleballer. He was small, 130 pounds, but he loved sports, baseball most of all. He says, "I had the desire. I read books on how to play first base. How do you do it?" When the war came, he joined the Navy, ended up in the South Pacific. Got married and joined an ad agency, Campbell-Ewald, in 1949. The marriage, which finally ended in divorce in 1977, would produce five children. The ad agency? Day job. Dutch Leonard, who had been listening real good his whole life, on Woodward Avenue and on Navy ships, was going to write. He would come out of the box writing west-erns.

"A genre has a form," he says. "That's great when you're starting."

He would get up at dawn, before the kids, and make himself sit down and write a couple of paragraphs before he even put the water on for the coffee. *Apache Agent* was the first sale. Over the next ten years, he sold thirty stories to magazines and five western novels and even made a couple of movie sales, beginning the relationship that has evolved to where Hollywood now has got his house surrounded. The first movie—*3:10 to Yuma*—starred Glenn Ford and came from a 1953 story that had appeared in *Dime Western*. *The Tall T*, from a Leonard novelette, starred Randolph Scott and Richard Boone. And it was all going great until there were about six thousand westerns a week on television in the late '50s, and nobody wanted to read about or see cowboys anymore. "I worked my ass off," Leonard says. But by 1961, after ten years, he figured that maybe he had fired his last gun. The final novel of the first western run was *Hombre*.

So he wrote his films and free-lanced his ad stuff and then, in 1965, he got a call from his New York literary agent, the late Margue-rite Harper, who told him that the movie rights to *Hombre* had finally been sold for $10,000. Leonard says, "It was a lift." It was some juice. He went back to fiction. He kept the Hurst shifters account for a while—think about the hole there'd be on the bookshelves right now if it hadn't been for Hurst shifters—and started writing a novel. Work-ing title, *Mother, This Is Jack Ryan.* It would end up being called *The Big Bounce.*

"We were living month to month on Hurst money, and I was writing *The Big Bounce*," he says. "I considered that making my run."

He finished *The Big Bounce*. Marguerite Harper took ill as she was reading it and sent the manuscript to H. N. Swanson. The legendary H. N. Swanson, the literary agent whose Hollywood clients included Hemingway and Faulkner and, Swanson's words, "a fellow named John O'Hara, plus Fitzgerald." Swanson, who is eighty-eight years old now and still out there working, still full of vinegar, read the book and called Dutch Leonard.

Swanson: "Did you write this book?"

Leonard: "Of course I did. My name's on it, isn't it? Yeah, I wrote the book."

Swanson: "Kiddo, I'm going to make you rich."

Over the next three months, *The Big Bounce* was rejected by eighty-four publishers and film producers. Another nice Leonard twist: *Bounce* finally came out as a Fawcett (paperback) Gold Medal original and got sold to the movies for $50,000 and made into a dreadful movie with Ryan O'Neal and Leigh Taylor-Young.

Leonard: "Fifty thousand bucks was about what I was going to have to borrow, quick." He was back in business. Since then, of course, he has sold everything that comes off the desk in the study in Birmingham to Hollywood.

Swanson: "I don't think any author, anybody you can name, can match his record. In a crowded field, he stands out. It took him more time than usual, of course."

More time than usual. You could say that. Leonard says he was always optimistic, thought he was doing okay, but that's now. He wrote a few more paperback originals, two of them westerns, then sold *The Moonshine War* to Doubleday in hardcover. Hollywood would either buy, or option. Swanson, known as Swanie, was out there doing his part. But the people weren't buying the books. The book money was nothing special.

"I learned early that if a publisher doesn't sell your book," Leonard says, "people aren't going to buy your book." If the low point for him professionally was the early and middle '60s, the low point emotionally was the late '60s, early '70s. Leonard was running, but not getting any closer to daylight. He was borrowing from friends, meanest sport in America—paying it back when movie or book money would come in, but not getting over having had to borrow it in the first place, because you never do.

Leonard kept turning out a book a year. And he kept drinking. A small audience knew how good he was at both.

The Saab makes its way slowly through Bloomfield Hills, the tiny Detroit suburb next to Birmingham. Leonard talks about the private schools we pass and the expensive homes set back in the woods. No big deal. Little tour of the area.

I ask him where he thinks he'd be right now—writing-wise, life-wise—if he hadn't finally stopped drinking in 1977. And Leonard says, "I'd probably be dead." But Leonard held on, didn't lose his job, didn't end up in the gutter, but he was a drunk. When he drank, he got drunk. It's just like Jack Ryan says in *No. 89*, he was powerless over it once he got started. By 1974 his first marriage was all but over. He had moved out of the house, into a Birmingham apartment. That was the year he went to his first meeting of Alcoholics Anonymous.

Leonard says, "I went to my first meeting and I felt at home right away. I'm like everybody else. I *did* think you had to end up on skid row if you were an alcoholic. Nothing tragic had happened to me. I didn't have blackouts. But a friend told me he thought I had a problem. Thought I should try AA. The first meeting, I admitted to myself I was an alcoholic. But it still took a while for me to accept. It took me three years to catch on to what the program is all about." He had his last drink in January 1977.

Leonard's first-person account of his alcoholism is in Dennis Wholey's book *The Courage to Change*. He tells of being diagnosed in 1970 as having acute gastritis, and how the doctor tells him that gastritis is something you only find in "bums." But how a month later he was drinking as much as ever. He tells about how, at the end, he began drinking before noon. It is hard to see him now as the loud, I'm-hilarious-aren't-I? drunk he says he was, but it goes that way a lot with recovering alcoholics. They go through life hearing people say, "Not *you*. You never had a problem. Really?" When you are Dutch Leonard, who writes like a dream and looks like Princeton, a lot of people just don't believe it. Recovering alcoholics, in the telling of their stories for friends, often have to act as prosecutor. Yeah, I was a drunk, and I can prove it to you beyond a shadow of a doubt.

Nine A.M., January 24, 1977, he had his last drink. Scotch and ginger ale, as he recalls. And slowly, from there, Dutch Leonard started to get to the good parts.

In the late '70s, he left Doubleday for Arbor House, run then by Donald Fine. "He decided to sell me as me," Leonard says. "Up until then, they kept trying to make me out to be the second coming of some dead mystery writer. Chandler, or Hammett. I barely *read* those guys."

Leonard was nowhere near the best-seller list, but each book was selling a little more than the one before. The paperback money was getting fatter. Hollywood was still buying them up. And the reviews were getting better and better. John D. MacDonald, author of the Travis McGee series and another man who did his time in paperbacks, wrote that Leonard was "astonishingly good."

In 1984 Leonard's career just upshifted, as if he were using one of those Hurst shifters on himself. Burt Reynolds made *Stick*; it would end up being a shockingly bad movie ("Lots of machine guns," Leonard says. "And scorpions. Burt couldn't understand why I didn't like it. He went on CBS with Phyllis George and said, 'I thought he

[Leonard] was a beautiful guy. Then he turned on me.' "). But it got some attention. *LaBrava* won the Edgar award in 1984; the paperback rights went for $360,000—his first big score with the publishers. The paperback rights for *Glitz*, after it made the list, went for $500,000. The paperback rights for *Bandits* were part of a cool million-dollar deal. One afternoon in the study in Birmingham, the phone rings; it is Swanson's office. Arbor House wants to buy the next two Leonard novels for $3 million. They talk some, Leonard uh- huh's a lot, says "if you're comfortable, I'm comfortable," hangs up the phone.

"I'm going to keep writing a book a year," he says, butting out a True green. "I've *been* doing that for a long time. But I'm not going to lock myself up for that many books. I've been busting my butt all these years to be independent."

I say, "Why did it finally happen to you?"

He shrugs and says, "I don't know. If *LaBrava* had come after *Glitz*, it would've been *LaBrava* that made the list. Or if *Stick* was the last one, it would've been *Stick*. The popularity is unrelated to the work. Maybe it was the Edgar plus the reviews and some word of mouth, I don't know. But all of a sudden, people were picking them up and saying, 'Hey, this is pretty good.' "

It is a Tuesday night and the Tigers aren't on television. When Joan Leonard puts the set on, Bruce Willis and Cybill Shepherd are yelling at each other on *Moonlighting*. There is a funny scene in *Bandits* where Jack Delaney breaks into a hotel room and gets spooked because Willis and Shepherd are screaming at each other on a television set in the next room. Leonard never uses their names, or the name of the show, but if you've ever seen *Moonlighting*, you know he is having some fun with what is supposed to be state-of-the art TV dialogue. It's like the umpire saying to Jim Bunning one time when Ted Williams was at the plate: "Mr. Williams will let you know when it's a strike." Mr. Leonard will let you know when the dialogue is right.

On the set, Bruce Willis goes into the bathroom and shuts the door. Leonard looks up from a magazine and says, "That's the most he's shut up in two seasons." Gets up and turns off *Moonlighting*.

We have come from dinner at a restaurant called Sebastian's in nearby Troy. Elmore and Joan Leonard have told stories about his five kids and her two, and about how they used to call her the Cookie Lady at his AA meetings (she'd show up with a plate of cookies, leave them, come back later, and pick up her future second husband).

Leonard also talked about how he has never had a continuing

character (true, Stick showed up in two books, Jack Ryan in two), because when Hollywood buys a book, it buys the character. Leonard
laughs and tells you it's always the same character, with a different
name and a different job. Stick is an ex-con. *Mr. Majestyk?* Hero's a
melon picker. Vincent Mora's a cop in *Glitz*. Bryan Hurd in *Split Images* and Raymond Cruz in *City Primeval* are cops. They all have been
beat on by life, they all can drop a cool, wise-guy line on you, they are
all tough, don't try to push them around.

But again: maybe the best character of all is Leonard himself.
Maybe the best scam he ever invented was about himself, hitting it so
big that he gets the movie people in Hollywood and the publishers in
New York coming and going, getting them to pay now for the work he
was doing all along. The whole scam is in one book—*Touch*.

Leonard wrote it in 1978. It is about, his words, "mystical things
happening to ordinary people." There is a young man named Juvenal,
who has been blessed with the stigmata, a condition that exhibits itself in a person's bleeding from the same wounds Jesus Christ had on
the cross, and subsequently being able to heal the sick. And there is
little Lynn Marie Faulkner and a rotten talk-show host and a right-
wing crazy Catholic and...

It might be Leonard's best book. Bantam owned it for eight years.
Didn't publish it. Didn't know what to do with it. Cut to 1985. *Glitz*
hits the list. Leonard is the literary Lana Turner. Bantam calls and
says, "We must publish *Juvenal* [original title]." Leonard thinks *ha-ha-
ha* and tells Bantam that the rights have reverted to him, which they
have.

Swanson says to Bantam, "You didn't do your homework." Offers
them the book back for a ridiculously high figure. Bantam demurs.
Arbor House, which is where he wanted to go anyway, buys the ten-
year-old book for more that $300,000.

And now he's sold it to the producers of *Gallipoli*. It's going to be a
movie.

Beat them at their own game. Dutch Leonard smiles again as he
reads to you from the introduction to *Touch*:

"I just wanted to explain that it's been sitting around for ten years
because publishers didn't know how to sell it, not because I didn't
know how to write it."

• *1987*

The Kid Who Wins
One-Handed

I t is three-quarters of a mile from Room 111, Rumsey Hall at the University of Michigan, to the baseball field at Ray Fisher Stadium, and as Jim Abbott walks across the sprawling campus, he has plenty of time to think and fret, as any freshman pitcher would. He thinks freshman thoughts. He has freshman doubts. He wonders if a high school fastball is good enough for college hitters.

"I feel the pressure," he says. "After all that's happened to me in my life, I don't want to get lost in the shuffle now. I don't want to be just another high school pitcher who got lost in college."

Jim Abbott, 18, is not just another lefthanded high school phenom, no matter what happens when the varsity baseball season begins for real this month in Ann Arbor. Jim Abbott was born without a right hand.

As he heads across campus each day, he smiles nervously as he readies himself for practice. He has come too far to fail. He smiles because he is eager.

"I'm battling against the odds again," Abbott says. "I've got to prove myself all over again, because I'm different. I'm back at the bottom, working my way up. But I'm going to make it."

In the 10 years of my job as a newspaper columnist, I have never been as touched by an athlete as I have by Jim Abbott, the one-handed kid from Flint, Mich., who has been different, at least so far in his young life, because he has been better, not because he is crippled.

248

"I'm just at another crossroads," he says, "with people staring at me."

His right arm ends at a narrow stub—a wrist that quit—with one small finger protruding. The right arm is about 10 inches shorter than the left. On the mound, Abbott starts with the stub stuck in the pocket of his glove, which has the pocket turned around, facing home plate. At the end of his follow-through, as a fastball already is being Federal Expressed to the plate, the good hand slides into the glove as easily as a knife going into soft butter.

When he must catch the ball, he takes it in the glove. Then, with deftness and economy, the glove is being turned around as it is tucked under his right arm, the ball comes out, and Abbott has it in his left hand, ready to throw again.

Ted Mahan, Abbott's Connie Mack League coach in Flint, says, "He used to drop the glove once in a while. I can't remember the last time he did *that*."

If Abbott could not make the switch, he could not pitch. He was outfitted with a hooklike prosthesis when he was 4. He threw out the hook when he was 5. He would play the hand he was dealt.

"I *hated* that [artificial] hand," Jim Abbott says now. "That's why I gave it up before I got to the second grade. It limited the things I could do. It didn't *help* me do anything. It was ugly, it drew attention to me, and I threw it out."

I say to him: "But you had to know having one hand was going to draw attention to you your whole life."

He says: "I planned to be different because I was a great baseball pitcher."

His boyhood seems artificial because he is out of some improbable storybook. Jim Abbott knew hurts. There were, briefly, nicknames like "Stub."

"He heard all the predictable mean things that 5- and 6-year-olds say," says his father, Mike Abbott. But the jokes and nicknames did not last long. Jim Abbott became the best in the neighborhood, in all the games. But mostly baseball. "He was going to show everybody," his father says.

The father, a 37-year-old account executive for Anheuser-Busch, watched the son over hundreds of boyhood hours throwing a ball against a brick wall. He would throw. Switch the glove. Catch. Put the glove under the arm. Take the ball out. Throw again. And again.

Jim started in a Flint Midget League when he was 12. There was a story about him in *The Flint Journal*. The road to deciding between a

University of Michigan baseball scholarship and a Toronto Blue Jays bonus contract as a high school senior had begun.

"The only thing that would have been a handicap for me," Jim Abbott said one day last summer, sitting on his stoop, pounding his fist into a new Rawlings glove, "is if anyone had ever been negative around me. If anyone at any point had said, 'You can't do this' or, 'How do you expect to do *that* with one hand?' I probably wouldn't be playing ball of any kind right now. But my mom and dad and my coaches and my teammates have always said, 'Just go do it.' So I've played. I love playing basketball. I love football. I'm going to miss playing football now that I'm out of high school. But I just kept getting better and better at baseball. And I've been successful at every level I've pitched."

"We told him a long time ago," says his mom, Kathy Abbott, 37, a Flint attorney, "that if he wanted to play, he had to be able to do what the other kids do."

"I'm not going to tell you there weren't nights when he came home crying," says Mike Abbott. "But there really weren't a lot. He has been blessed with a great heart."

Jim Abbott is 6 feet 4 and 200 pounds. With his shock of sandy hair and open, ingenuous face, he looks like he ought to be starring in one of those summer movies for teens. He shot up to his present size between his sophomore and junior years at Flint Central High. No more brick walls by then, of any kind. Most times when the ball came back to him, it came from his catcher, because the batters were swinging and missing so often. Abbott was throwing baseballs past high school teams in the spring, Connie Mack teams in the summer. The scouts, college and pro, began to hear about this one-handed kid ("Huh? One-handed pitcher? *Come on!*") who was lighting up the radar guns with a 90 mph fastball. The scouts came to watch. When they saw the left arm, they forgot about the missing right hand.

In his senior year at Flint Central, Abbott had a 10-3 record with a 0.76 earned run average. He struck out 148 batters in 73 innings. He gave up just 16 hits. That works out to two strikeouts an inning, a hit every four or five innings. When batting, he stuck the stub at the end of the bat, near the handle, and closed his big left hand around it.

Using this system, Jim Abbott only managed to hit .427 for Flint Central, with seven homers. He also played quarterback on the football team. Flint Central went 10-2. Against Midlands High, Abbott

threw four touchdown passes in the first half. There isn't a rule anywhere that says The Natural has to have two hands.

When I first heard about Jim Abbott, one-handed pitcher, I remember Monty Stratton, the one-legged pitcher for the White Sox,
and how hard it was for him to field bunts. I asked Jim about bunts,
first thing.

Jim: "One game when I was pitching in the ninth grade, they
bunted on me eight times in a row. I threw out the last seven. That
was enough of that."

Mike and Kathy Abbott married young. They were each 18 when
their first son was born without a right hand. Like him, they have
learned as they've gone. They have helped him turn the abnormal
into the normal, a potential negative into an inspiring and uplifting
positive. Jim Abbott would be a more complete baseball player with
two hands. I find it impossible to believe he could be a more complete
person.

"We think," says Mike Abbott, "that if the baseball thing went
up in smoke tomorrow, Jimmy would be adjusted enough to go live his
life without baseball."

Once, quite seriously, I asked Jim Abbott what he *can't* do.

Quite seriously, he replied: "I can't button the darn buttons on
my left cuff."

"Who does it?"

"My mom, usually. My roommate in college."

"After watching him pitch, I didn't think of the right hand at all
—*at all*," says Don Welke, one of the scouts who helped make the Toronto Blue Jays' farm system into one of the best in baseball. "For me,
he was just another outstanding prospect."

The Blue Jays felt that Abbott's impairment might discourage
other teams, so they waited until the 36th round of last year's amateur
draft before taking him. Some saw it as a publicity stunt—as a back-
handed compliment, if you will. The Blue Jays were, and are, serious
about Jim Abbott's future.

"His drafting wasn't for publicity," says Don Welke, who urged the
team to take Abbott. "We look down the road and see him as a major
leaguer. He has a major league arm, a major league heart."

Jim Abbott, however, had that major league heart set on Michigan.

"A couple of years ago," he says, "to play college ball at any level
was a dream I never thought could come true. I remember on my first

visit to Ann Arbor, I looked at the campus and thought how pretty things were and how neat it would be for someone to go there. Then I stopped short and said to myself, 'You can have this. It's you they want. You can play college baseball here.' I think I can have both my dreams. I can play college ball and have pro ball still waiting for me down the road."

A week before he left for college, I asked Jim if he was afraid about the future. "I am," he said. "But I really think they're just normal fears for a guy going off to college. You're talking about my hand, right? I had to stop being afraid a long time ago. What fear there's been, I've used to get better."

We were sitting in front of the Abbott house. He was showing me his new glove. "You know," he said, "I hear a lot about how inspirational I am. But I don't see myself as being inspirational. Whether you're rich or poor or one-handed or whatever, your own childhood just seems natural, because it's the only one you know. I've met kids with one hand lately, or one arm—8-year-olds, in that range—and they tell me I've helped them by example, and I do feel great about that. But I don't think *I'm* that great. If I can inspire kids in any way, I'd just hope they could get the same enjoyment out of sports I've had."

And now, on this afternoon, it was time for a game of catch. Jim Abbott walked about 30 yards away and began tossing the ball to me. It began to make bigger and bigger popping noises in my glove as the kid got loose. After about five minutes, I promise I did not notice the shortened right arm, or the glove switch, any of it. I just made sure to watch the ball. I wanted to be sure I was quick enough with my glove so that a baseball thrown by Jim Abbott did not hit me between the eyes.

I thought: I'm like the hitters. I feel overmatched. But I wanted to remember this game of catch, because I began to feel strongly that it would be important someday that I knew Jim Abbott when.

I have used the word hero a lot in writing about sports, carried away by the moment. Jim Abbott is a hero. He is like most true heroes. He doesn't make a big deal out of what he does. He just gets on with things. He plays the hand dealt him, at the University of Michigan now. Without bitterness and without complaint, he has become a champion, no matter what happens in Ann Arbor this spring.

• 1986

Distant Replay

*Alvin Dark started the inning off with a single, between Ro-
binson and Hodges. No problem. Newcombe was on the
mound. The score was still 4-1, Dodgers. Three outs to go . . .*

I • t is a dance they have danced many times.
It is a careful waltz, arms extended, all by the numbers, stiff and formal. They are pleasant but wary, polite
but not warm. They were joined for one unforgettable
moment 35 years ago, and have been feeling each other
out ever since, seeing how it goes every time, one man always taking the measure of the other, easing into the familiar moves.

The subject of the most famous home run in baseball
history is not discussed between them. Neither man
brings it up unless asked. With each other, it is simply
not done. The talk is generally small. Nobody steps on
anybody's toes.

"Where'd you park?" Ralph Branca asks.

Bobby Thomson smiles.

"The guard took a look at my company car," Thomson says, "and sent me over to the back parking lot."

It is an August afternoon at Westchester Country
Club. Bobby Thomson has driven from New Jersey to
have his picture taken with Ralph Branca. After the pictures, the two men will have lunch, and then Branca and
his wife will drive to Saratoga and Thomson will go back
to New Jersey. It is a social occasion, but not too social.

"You go get the car," Branca says, "and come up and
take my spot and I'll go park around the corner and I'll
meet you back at the front door."

Thomson says, "Fine." He starts to walk off to his car. "How you been?" he calls back to Branca.

"Great. You?"

"Fine." There is still a hop to Thomson's step as he walks up the driveway toward grass tennis courts. Not the joyous bounce around the bases from Oct. 3, 1951. But there is still a light jock's step. Branca, who has a bad knee, moves a little slower.

Branca says, "Winkie all right?" He means Thomson's wife.

"Playing the club championship this afternoon."

The cars are moved, Thomson takes some lilac-colored golf clothes out of the trunk, the two men get into an elevator—most famous home run of them all, crammed into a space five feet by five— go upstairs to a suite in the clubhouse. Branca changes, too. They go out by the 18th fairway to have the pictures taken. Thomson is given a New York Giants cap, Branca a Brooklyn Dodgers cap. In the eyes of the world, one is a Giant, one is a Dodger, forever.

Thomson takes off his glasses. "I look dopey with the glasses and the cap," he says.

The two men take their places.

The photographer smiles and says, "Interrelate, guys. More interrelating."

The two men look at each other and grin. The grins are like clouds parting suddenly. That is all they have done, really, since the Polo Grounds, on that October afternoon in '51. They do not see each other so much, usually at dinners or baseball-card shows or at the odd golf tournament. But they are linked forever, like it or not. No two names in the history of baseball, perhaps sports, interrelate more.

Thomson and Branca. Branca and Thomson. The shot heard 'round the world. In the third game of the National League play-offs, Branca threw an 0-1 fastball to Thomson and Thomson hit a 3-run homer to left at the Polo Grounds. And the Giants won the pennant. The Giants won the pennant!

Thomson hopped around the bases and through the madness and was carried into legend. Branca slowly walked to center field, where the clubhouses were, and to his own sort of legend.

The dance had begun. The subject of the home run, even though unspoken, is always there. It is never 35 years away, never.

The photographer chatters on.

Thomson and Branca put their arms around each other's shoulders.

"This enough interrelating for you?" Thomson asks.

Don Mueller, known as Mandrake, followed Dark's single with a single of his own. Branca was warming up in the bullpen. But Monte Irvin popped out to Hodges. One out. The Dodgers had blown that 13 1/2-game lead to the Giants, but now they were two outs from the pennant. . .

"I've been saying the same thing over and over for years," Bobby Thomson says. "All it meant to me at the time was that we beat the Dodgers."

This is a couple of weeks before the picture-taking in Westchester. Thomson is sitting at a back table at Rusty's restaurant on Third Avenue. At the next table is Thomson's oldest daughter, Nancy, and her two children. After lunch, they will go to the Museum of Natural History. Thomson wears a blue blazer and a red golf shirt underneath, and there isn't a soul in Rusty's restaurant who knows that the silver-haired grandfather with the silver-framed glasses is the most famous home run of them all.

The waiter comes by and Thomson orders an omelette and a bottle of beer.

"Where was I?"

"You said you thought it was a big deal because it beat the Dodgers."

"Oh, yes. You see, I still can't get over what a privilege, what good fortune it was to play at that time. Forget the homers or anything. First place, last place, it didn't matter. It was a different ballgame when we played the Dodgers."

"But it couldn't have taken you long to figure it was more than just beating the Dodgers."

"The first moment my thinking went beyond that was when I got home," he says. "We were living on Staten Island at the time. And my brother Jim said, 'Do you realize what you've done?' I laughed and said, 'Don't ask me such a silly question, I was there.' But Jim wouldn't let me go. He said, 'No, no, Bob. Don't you see that something like what you did might never happen again?' "

To this day, Bobby Thomson, like Ralph Branca, talks about the home run as being "one of" the most famous in baseball history. He talks of Bill Mazeroski's bottom-of-the-9th home run off Ralph Terry to win the 1960 World Series for the Pirates. He talks of Bucky Dent off Mike Torrez in the 1978 Yankees-Red Sox playoff game, and Chris Chambliss' bottom-of-the-9th, 5th-game pennant winner off the Royals' Mark Littell in '76. They were all memorable in their way, dramatic, pieces of the lore of the game.

And somehow, none has replaced Thomson taking Branca deep. It was the Giants vs. the Dodgers. It was the Giants' comeback from 13½ back. It was the bottom of the 9th, it was New York, defeat to victory in a swing of a bat. It was everything. It remains a trivia buffet:

"Who was on third?"

"Clint Hartung. He ran for Mueller."

"What future NBA champion was in the Dodgers dugout?"

"Bill Sharman."

And on and on. Shot heard 'round the world. Still.

Bobby Thomson is 61 years old. He is a national-accounts sales representative for Westvaco Corp., a major paper company. He has been with the company since 1960, when he retired from baseball.

"Did it change your life, the home run?" he is asked at Rusty's.

"It changed it in terms of people knowing Bobby Thomson's name," he says. "And getting me invited out, and having lunch and talking to you. But my LIFE? No, it didn't change my life. When baseball was finished, I had to go from there. If I hadn't hit the home run, I would've still had the same family and I would have had to go out and get a job once I was through with ball."

He says that it was during the winter of 1951 that he began to realize the dimensions of the home run, the size and scope of it. It is one of those life events if you were around in 1951, and over the age of five. You ask people where they were when Thomson hit it out, they tell you.

"I wish I carried a tape recorder around with me that winter," Thomson says. "Everybody had a story. I remember a shoe salesman telling me he was helping a woman and he was listening to the game on the radio, and he just threw one of the shoes across the room and the heel stuck in the wall."

Thomson's lunch comes. He claps his hands together. "Now look at this," he says to his grandchildren. "Will you look at the size of this omelette." The one who hit the most famous home run of them all is a regular guy. Apparently, he was always a regular guy. He was the regular guy who twice took Ralph Branca deep the first week of October 1951.

Twice. It is part of the trivia buffet. The Giants won the first game of the playoff series 3-1. The Giants only needed what Thomson gave them in the fourth. Two-run homer off Branca.

"Not many people remember that one," he says. "I also hit one

the last game of the regular season. I guess you could say I was on a bit
of a home-run tear."

Newcombe would never get another out in 1951. Neither would the Dodg-
ers. Whitey Lockman doubled to left-center. Dark scored, Mueller went to
third. Mueller twisted his left ankle, finally left the field on a stretcher. Har-
tung, the former phenom, ran for him. Manager Charlie Dressen had Branca
and Clem Labine in the bullpen. Branca had started Game 1, Labine had
shut the Giants out the day before. Dressen took the ball from Newcombe
and signaled for Branca...

The one who threw the ball prefers to discuss the Before of his career,
even the After, which was not exactly a day at the beach. And other
famous home runs in baseball history. And just about everything except Bobby Thomson and all the business of Oct. 3, 1951.

Branca was 26 years old that day and threw one fastball, and it
was all it took to mark him for life. The time since has been more
than half Branca's life.

"Thirty-five years I've had to live with this," Branca had said on
the phone a few days before, when the interview was being set up.
"Guys kill people and get out of prison after seven."

Now it is the glorious afternoon, the interrelating for the photographer over. The lunch terrace overlooks the practice putting green at
Westchester. Thomson is on another part of the terrace, having lunch
with Ann Branca, whose father was on the board of the Brooklyn
Dodgers. The baseball thread runs through the family. Ralph and
Ann Branca's daughter Mary is married to Bobby Valentine, manager
of the Texas Rangers.

I ask Branca the same question Thomson was asked: "Did it
change your life?"

"It only changed me, as far as I'm concerned, in what happened
to me the next spring," he says. This is his story; he sticks to it. "I hurt
my back the next spring, and I was so eager to prove to people that I
could come back after that home-run pitch that I didn't stop, and I
ended up with a sore arm. The sore arm impacted on my career a hell
of a lot more than that home-run pitch, I'll tell you that."

At the age of 21, Branca won 21 games for the Dodgers, with a
2.67 earned-run average. Twenty-one at 21. "Dwight Gooden does it
and everyone goes crazy," Ralph Branca says. "How come no one talks
about me doing it?"

If he hadn't pitched the way he did down the stretch for the fal-
tering Dodgers in '51, not only would the Dodgers have blown the

13½ game lead, the Giants would have won the pennant in the regular season. And Dressen must have thought a lot of Branca: He chose him to start the playoff series, and finish it.

But Thomson took Branca over the left-field wall. Then came the sore arm the next spring. Branca could perhaps have recovered from one. But not both. He pitched 16 games for the Dodgers that 1952 season, won four, then he drifted to the Tigers, and out of baseball. He was finished at 30.

"You know what bothers me more than anything?" he says. "It bothers me that nobody seems to know how good I was."

He stares out at the putting green, moves some chef's salad around, takes a sip of a diet soft drink, looks at you with the sad eyes. The conversation, even as it circles around the Thomson homer, seems to exhaust him.

"I pitched effectively for the Brooklyn Dodgers at the age of 19," he says. "When I was 20, I pitched important games down the stretch. I had two shutouts in 1946. I started the first playoff game in National League history."

He tells you more. About getting into Branch Rickey's doghouse because he once sent back a contract calling for $600 a month. About getting into Charlie Dressen's doghouse another time because he refused to pitch batting practice, because he thought you could pick up bad habits. About trying to hook on with the Yankees before calling it a day in the big leagues.

Branca looks at you and what he really says is, Listen to me, I was more than one lousy fastball.

At the age of 60, he is a salesman for the White Plains-based National Pension Service. Branca has been with the company for 11 years. He is a fine golfer; during lunch he is happiest talking about the components of his golf swing. His two daughters and their husbands both live close to Westchester Country Club. He and Ann have horses at Saratoga.

I say to him, "You're nice to talk about this, because you must be awfully sick of it."

"I take it as it comes," he says. "If I feel like getting into it, I do. If I don't, I don't. You find out a lot about people by who brings it up and who doesn't."

He is asked what he remembers best about the day.

"The parking lot," he says. "I remember going out to the parking lot. Ann was in the car with a friend of ours, Father Paul Rowley from

Fordham. And I said to Father Rowley, 'Why me? Why did this have to happen to me?' And Father Rowley said 'God gave you this cross to bear because you are strong enough to bear it.' "

Then Branca looks up, and tries to work his face into a smile.

"What I basically remember is that Bobby Thomson was better than me that day, and hit a home run."

I tell him that Thomson said he was mostly elated on Oct. 3, 1951, because he beat the Dodgers.

"Yes," Branca says. "I felt bad because we lost the game and lost the pennant."

There is a long delay while Mueller is attended to. He is carried off the field on a stretcher finally, Hartung replaces him. Lockman is on second, it is 4-2, it is Branca against Thomson.

On deck for the Giants is a kid named Willie Mays.

Bobby Thomson says, "I don't take credit for a lot of things that have happened to me in my life. But I had the ability to do what I did that day. I gave myself a chance. Do you see? I gave myself the chance to do something great. I was able to get totally determined. I *wanted* the damn ball. I was maybe too determined when I dug in, because I took a strike right down the middle.

"It's funny, I didn't pay that much attention to the pitching change. I was watching them work on Mueller. Then I noticed it was Ralph."

Thomson smiles—it's a warm thing. He goes on:

"So there I am, the count is 0-1, and I'm saying to myself, 'Wait and watch, you sonofabitch. Wait and watch. I'm so busy saying wait and watch that I take that first strike. Then, of course, I popped the next one."

He lives in Watchung, N.J. He does not go to many baseball games, maybe one a year at Shea Stadium, one in Philadelphia, with clients. But he is out in public a lot because he is a salesman, and so the home run is with him every day of his life, soon as he is introduced.

"Let's face it," he says. "It's nice to be remembered. But I don't think about it all that much. I'm too concerned with schedules and expense accounts and planes and such. It's not like I ever lived off it."

At Rusty's, Thomson sips some beer, smacks his lips, gets a little foam on them, makes it disappear with a sweep from the back of his hand.

"People are always telling me where they were when I hit the ball," he says. "You want to know where I was when Bucky Dent hit that home run off the Red Sox?

"I was driving to a business meeting outside Syracuse. I was on the Thruway, and I was listening to the game on the radio. And I pulled over to the side of the road, and just sat there, and I had a tremendous feeling all of a sudden for Bucky Dent, because I understood how his life had just changed. He was a little like me, you know. Unexpected hero."

As he finishes his lunch at Westchester, Ralph Branca looks across the room at Thomson. They will probably not see each other again in 1986. Next year, it will be the same thing as it has been for a very long time: they will be at card shows, at golf tournaments, at dinners. I think of something a friend has told me, a friend who has seen them at such events over the past several years.

"They're in the same place," the friend said, "but they're never really together."

I watch Branca's eyes set on Thomson and I say, "Nice man, isn't he?"

Branca says, "Yeah, good guy, Bobby. Humble guy. You gotta like him."

Branca threw a fastball, high and inside. Thomson tomahawked it to left, short left in Polo Grounds. The minute it was hit, Giants manager Leo Durocher threw up his arms in triumph. Dodgers leftfielder Andy Pafko went to the wall and watched it go, stunned. As Branca was stunned. Thomson began a trip around the bases that is described in the newspaper stories as "romping." And "cavorting."

Bedlam at the Polo Grounds. Shot heard 'round the world. Miracle of Coogan's Bluff.

In the radio booth, Russ Hodges kept repeating: "The Giants win the pen- nant!...
the Giants win the pen-nant!...
the Giants win the pen-nant!...
the Giants win the pen-nant!...
the Giants win the pen-nant!...
the Giants win the pen-nant!"

At the front door of the clubhouse at Westchester Country Club, Thomson and Branca shake hands. Thomson will get his car and drive back to Watchung. Branca will put his car back in place, and in a little while drive with his wife to Saratoga.

The dance has again been danced successfully. The choreography by now is second nature. No toes stepped on, no false moves. No mention of Oct. 3.

Bobby Thomson hangs his sports jacket in the back seat of the company car and says, "Let's face it. It's fun for me to talk about it. But not for him."

Nine times Russ Hodges yelled. . . the music that began the dance for Branca and Thomson:

". . . *the Giants win the pen-nant!*"

For two men, the echoes do not end.

• 1986

Al the Bad

A l Davis is walking up Rodeo Drive in Beverly Hills. As usual, he does not look anything like the smartest man in professional football. He looks like a touring golf pro from Las Vegas, white-on-white, a shark knifing upstream through all the glitter.

Davis is dressed in a white Los Angeles Raiders wind-breaker. Underneath the wind-breaker is a white velour sweater. There is a diamond ring on his pinkie that could have been lifted from Elizabeth Taylor's hope chest. There is a Raiders Super Bowl ring on his left ring finger, three terrifying diamonds, each set in a football-shaped crest against an onyx base. On his left wrist is a chunky silver bracelet featuring another onyx stone, with more diamonds spelling out AL.

It is a quiet Sunday morning on Rodeo. The window-shoppers all know who Al is. He is the Raiders. Maybe the Japanese tourists don't know him, but they get him in the cross hairs of their Minoltas anyway, sensing they should. In a town of stars, Al Davis is the most unusual, a guy out of P.S. 189 in Brooklyn with plenty of Fonz in him who built the most successful football machine there is and brought it to L.A. when just about everybody said he couldn't. Tell Al anything but no.

"Hey, Al, who's gonna play quarterback?"

"We're doing it this year, right, Mr. Davis?"

"Hey, Al. Just win, baby." It is the phrase Davis made

famous when the Raiders won their last Super Bowl a few years ago.

Al loves it. He waves. "Yeah, just win." he says.

He stops in front of Giorgio.

"They gotta do something about this little cologne thing," he says. His nose is nearly pressed to the window.

What?

"See that little cologne thing in the front? Spray thing? I have that. But goddamnit, it's still not right."

Davis is looking with his courtroom eyes at the little Giorgio cologne thing.

"Everything else in the window, all those other accessories, they're silver and black," he says. Silver and black are the Raiders colors. They're Al's colors too, except he often substitutes white for silver. "Except for the cologne thing, which as you can see is *gold* and black. I told Peter about it."

Peter?

"Peter. Guy who runs Giorgio. He says he'll get it done for me."

Al likes guys who can get it done. The Raiders didn't get it done last year. Al chewed on that failure the whole off-season. But then, Al still chews on games the Raiders lost in 1974. All of a sudden he'll turn to you and say, "Goddamnit, we had Pittsburgh 10-3 going into the fourth quarter, and we couldn't get it done."

For Al, the world is divided into the ones who get it done and the ones who don't.

The West German kid who landed his Cessna in Red Square the day before, he got it done.

"I'd like to talk to *that* guy," Al says. "Could be a Raider. He's a self-starter. I'd just like to meet him, see if he could bring some of that spirit to our organization. See if he could come in and kinda dominate in one area, or if he'd just become part of the rest of the group."

He crosses the street, walks past Van Cleef & Arpels, looks in the window at Battaglia, keeps going past Sotheby's. In front of Sotheby's, he passes two young black men, one wearing a FILADELPHIA T-shirt, the other carrying a camera.

The one in the FILADELPHIA T-shirt says, "Al Davis?"

Davis stops. He needs this the way the rest of us need oxygen. "Yes, sir." He smiles. He is having a very nice morning. Although he's on Rodeo Drive, it's like he's walking through a bunch of tailgaters on his way into the Coliseum for a Raiders game.

"Who's gonna play quarterback, Al?" It is a question he hears all the time. The Raiders had big quarterback problems last year. Jim Plunkett got old, Marc Wilson played older than Plunkett, which is older than water. Davis has been talking about going into this season with an unknown named Rusty Hilger.

Now he stretches his arms out wide, grabs all of Sunday morning.

"Hey," he says. "Whaddya need a quarterback for when you got me?"

There is no All-Star team for owners in professional sports. In fact, you'd let very few of them into the game. Ted Turner is a cartoon character, Cap'n Colorization. George Steinbrenner is a constant tantrum. Georgia Frontiere is hair spray. But Al is an original. His fellow football owners would like you to think he is Bugsy Siegel. They are jealous, most of them. They are rich kids, and Al keeps taking their lunch boxes.

Football might be business for everyone else. For Al, it is blood. He has taken on the other owners, his own league, the city of Oakland. Year in and year out, his team is the baddest. Every few years, it is the best. The Cowboys might be America's Team. The Raiders are Al's team.

"The mystique and the fear help our organization," he says. "If there is fear." He smiles a shark smile. "Which there should be."

Al's countersuit was already under way when the NFL sued to keep him from moving the Raiders to Los Angeles. Davis's suit named former Chargers owner Gene Klein as one of the principals. Davis says Klein "was one of the main guys trying to condemn my goddamn football team." Klein later suffered a heart attack. Klein said, Al Davis did this to me! He sued Davis. He got awarded $10 million by a San Diego jury. Home jury advantage. The judge in the same court reduced the award to $2 million. Al says, Keep watching as $2 million becomes nothing.

I say to Al, "But you gave a guy a $10-million heart attack?"

He says, "You mean with that Klein?"

"There have been other $10-million heart attacks?"

"He says that because he was named individually, he got that heart attack," Davis says. "First of all, my lawyers named him. It's ridiculous. And he deserved to be named."

Al has always had problems with the other owners. He thinks he has a reason.

"I guess they think that I think I'm better than them," he says. "Which I do."

Al probably could have run anything—a small country, a large police action. He chose the Raiders. Over the last twenty-five years, the Raiders have the best winning percentage in pro sports.

"A great man is someone who's not necessarily great in what they're doing," he says. It comes out *doin'*. A lot of Davis's speech is still President Street, Brooklyn. "They can inspire in others the will to be great. That more or less fits me. . . .I say: Don't let 'em tell you they're gonna do it. *Make* 'em do it."

I ask if back in Brooklyn, as a kid, he knew he would do something big in his life.

"Yeah, I thought I'd be good," he says. "It's a lousy thing to say, it's conceited and all, but I understood at a very early age how to run a team."

How early?

"P.S. 189. Every kid who went to that school knew what I was gonna do."

He came out of Erasmus Hall High School. He graduated from Syracuse University in 1950. For the next ten years, he knocked around as an assistant coach, college and pro.

Finally, in 1963, Al became coach and general manager of the Raiders. They were 1-13 the year before he showed up. Then thay were 10-4. Al was Coach of the Year. Sammy Glick was running. Assistant coach. Head coach. General manager. When the American Football League needed a merger with the National Football League, it made Al commissioner. That was April 1966. Eight weeks later, there was a merger. Pete Rozelle, the NFL commissioner, was no match for Davis.

"Ah, that was just a guerrilla war," Al Davis says. "The establishment gets impatient in a guerrilla war. They want it to be over. Then you've got 'em. Pete never knew how to fight in the street."

With the merger won, Al went back to the Raiders. He said he'd only come back for 10 percent of the team, and that his stake had to be more than that of any of the other partners, and he had to have the title "managing general partner." He still has the title. Over the years, he has built the 10 percent into 30 percent. They didn't win a Super Bowl until 1977, but in the last six years, they have won two more. The last one was in 1984. They were the Los Angeles Raiders by then. Al proved they could do it in Oakland, they could do it in Los Angeles, they could probably tour the Ice Capades and keep winning.

By moving to L.A., Al also proved the team was his baby, he'd rock it the way he wanted. "I've, ah, never been one of those guys who believed in 'my league, right or wrong,' " Al says.

It happened this way: Back in 1980, Al was trying to get a new and better deal with the city of Oakland. He hinted he might go to Los Angeles if he didn't get it.

"They tried to fuck me in Oakland," Al says. He is eating hash in the Hideaway restaurant at the Beverly Wilshire Hotel. "They tried to lock me into an inferior stadium. Rozelle was trying to show they could keep me in Oakland, that the Oakland people didn't have to give me a deal. They had me locked in there, boxed in there. This is a place [Oakland] the league was bragging about, how great the stadium was. Rozelle never stayed in Oakland in his life. He always stayed in San Francisco. If it's such a great place, let's see when it gets an expansion team."

Davis took the Raiders to Los Angeles. The city of Oakland had sued to take the Raiders away from Davis. Lost. The NFL sued, saying Davis was breaching his contract with the league, moving without a vote of the owners. Lost. Davis's countersuit won $35 million, plus lawyers' fees. Some of the $35 million might be offset by a court ruling won by the NFL last year. But Al is in L.A. Just win, baby.

"No one likes to be pushed around," Al says. "I'm not about to be pushed around by them."

He eats some hash, drains a glass of water.

"Remember John Foster Dulles?" he says. "I heard him one time on television. Of course, he was a one-man foreign-affairs deal. Anyway, they tried to pin him down one time on a certain philosophy about the nuclear bomb. He didn't use the word *pragmatic,* but he said that every day is a different situation, and you have to say 'I'd rather be right than be consistent.' I've always used that."

Davis often likes to give the impression he would rather debate politics with George Will than discuss the 3-4 defense with George Allen. He knows history, business, books, mergers, the law, street fighting, but what he knows mostly is football talent. Players whose careers are supposed to be over come to the Raiders and become stars again. Jim Plunkett was washed up. Al got him, won two Super Bowls with him. Did the same thing with Lyle Alzado. Al doesn't care about his own reputation, why should he care about anyone else's? He likes good football players. He traded for Green Bay wide receiver James Lofton when Lofton still had an unresolved court case charging him with a sexual offense. Al said, "We'll get it done with Lofton." Lofton was acquitted. He'll probably help the Raiders with their fourth Super Bowl.

Al says, "A great leader doesn't treat problems as special. He treats 'em as normal."

He assumes you know what great leader he's talking about. He smiles at the waitress.

"Yes, Mr. Davis?" she says.

"Carla, honey, be a good girl and bring me some ice water."

It comes out *wat-ah*.

Howard Cosell says, "The best thing, very best thing about Al Davis is the way he loves his wife."

Al Davis calls his wife Carol "Ca-ROW-lee." He met her in 1951. He was coaching at Adelphi. He says she was a "big time New Yawk girl."

In October 1979, on a Friday morning sometime between midnight and dawn, Al's not clear on the exact time, Carol Davis suffered a stroke.

"Heart attack, stroke," Al says. "Massive something. They had her on one of these respirator deals. The plugs were keeping her alive. Every so often her heart would stop, and they'd give her some, ah, voltage."

Every night, Al Davis would sit in the hospital room with his wife, hold her hand, talk to her for hours. He talked about the Raiders, about football in general, about their youth, and about their life together. He says now, "I, ah, talked about our dreams. I mighta made some promises, too."

On the tenth day, he told the doctors and nurses he could have sworn she'd opened her eyes. A doctor told him he was seeing what he wanted to see. "Fuck you," Davis remembers telling the doctor.

"I think at that point they were starting to talk about the plug, you understand what I'm saying?" Davis says.

On the fourteenth day, Davis was sitting in the waiting area outside his wife's room when he heard some yelling. Nurses came running in his direction. One of them said, "Mr. Davis, do you want to talk to your wife?"

Davis went into the room.

Carol Davis said, "What happened?"

He told her, "You were sick, baby."

We stroll by Bijan, a Rodeo Drive boutique where most customers have to make an appointment to shop. Not Al. When he goes into Bijan, the salespeople come running as if wolves are chasing them.

He nods in the direction of the store. "Cute place," he says.

I mention all the problems he's had over the years with the NFL and some of its owners and Pete Rozelle, and ask if he's Moby Dick to Rozelle's Captain Ahab.

Al says, "Nah, I'm more like Billy Budd. Billy was just a young kid, innocent like, who had some deviousness to him, you know? And he annoyed the goddamn whatchamacallit master-at-arms, Claggart, because all the shipmates liked Billy. They responded to Billy. He could lead them. They liked him, and they didn't like this Claggart guy, but he had the power in name, in naval law."

I say to Davis, "Billy Budd got hanged."

"Yeah," Al Davis says, "I've always kinda laughed at that, because I'm not that innocent. When it gets down to it, Billy Budd took the Gandhi approach. You know? Turn the cheek? Well, goddamnit, I've always wanted to win."

He makes one more pass by Giorgio, walking back toward the Beverly Wilshire, where he's parked his car. Al gives a hard look at the same accessories as before.

There is a Brooklyn slouch in his gaze. Here come the courtroom eyes again. An attitude, you understand? Even in the Pat Boone clothes, Davis looks the way Alzado used to as he got ready to separate the quarterback's head from the quarterback's shoulders.

And I'm thinking: If that guy Peter knows what's good for him, he'll get it done with the little cologne thing.

• *1987*

Shooting from the Lip III

Bonecrusher Smith fought Tyson like he wanted to be included in the Arthur Murray heavyweight unification series.

Have the New York Knicks reached the telethon stage yet?

I saw a picture of George Steinbrenner in the newspaper the other day and he was wearing a "Top Gun" cap. I also think he has a really neat new decoder ring.

Darryl Strawberry has 500 hits now, and if he keeps up his current pace, he's going to pass Pete Rose in 29 years.

It's sort of stopped being important to me how John Madden gets around the country.

I think I've got it now: Gary Hart can't be president for getting caught doing what JFK did the whole time he *was* president.

Reggie Jackson says his autobiography (written with M. Lupica) should have been "another Hemingway." It was news to me. Because here's every single thing Reggie knows about Hemingway: He thinks Mariel is cuter than Margaux.

If Dwight Gooden was really serious about renegotiating his contract, he must think the Mets give out bonus mileage on trips to rehab.

You sometimes get the idea the Yankees have eight players left in their entire farm system?

An AP story opened this way the other day: "Ben Hogan, formerly one of golf's top players, underwent an appendectomy yesterday. . . ." It was like saying, "Fred Astaire, one of the better dancers in 30s musicals. . . ."

I had a feeling Bobby Knight sending a letter of apology to Puerto Rico wasn't going to do the trick.

Forget about saying no to drugs. Can't we just say no to drug autobiographies?

John McEnroe blaming his problems on a court microphone is like Jim Bakker blaming his problems on the motel.

Why do sports columnists on television always have to wear hats?

Who do you suppose has talked to more dead people, Bob Woodward or Shirley MacLaine?

Actually, Woodward has talked to more, but MacLaine has *been* more dead people.

I thought *Fatal Attraction* was about Steinbrenner and Billy Martin.

If Ronald Reagan had public relations like the National Football League does, Robert Bork would be on the Supreme Court now.

While I was at Wimbledon, *The Sun* ran a story headlined, "Lendl's bizarre sex secrets." I knew the paper was bluffing, but I read the story anyway. In tennis, bizarre sex secrets can cover a lot of ground.

GOODBYES

Sometimes goodbyes are the easiest columns to write.

And the hardest.

They seem to touch people the most; mostly, they touch the writer most of all. I wish I never had to write the one about Dick Howser. Or about Bill Veeck. I met Veeck too late in his life; I would like to have a few more lunches with him at Miller's, in Chicago.

The one about McLain won some kind of award, I forget which one. The one about Victoria Crawford is my favorite. After it appeared, the Mets invited her and her family to a game, even took her around the clubhouse. She died not long afterward.

The one about Willie Mays is included because it was written the day Thurman Munson died. Willie said goodbye after a couple of editions.

Part 10

A life of daring and caring

I
●

t was always much more than a life. Michael Burke lived a novel. It was a beauty. It did not end until Thursday, about 11 a.m. New York time, when there came from Ireland the preposterous news that he was dead from cancer at the age of 68. Only then did Michael Burke run out of possibilities.

"He thought he was invulnerable," his friend Howard Cosell said yesterday. "He just assumed that he would live forever, always looking 49 years old."

Here is the only proper eulogy for Michael Burke today: He knew everybody. He did everything. There was something wonderfully American about that.

He was a football star and a war hero and a spy. He worked for the CIA and for CBS. He ran Ringling Bros. and Barnum & Bailey Circus and Madison Square Garden. He was president of the New York Yankees. Most of all, Michael Burke was a New Yorker. The real love affair of the piece was with New York. It was the only place big enough for all his big ideas.

Think about the sweep of Burke's 68 years. Think about the romance and variety of it all. There were ups and downs, and there was always someone shooting at Michael Burke, be it Jimmy Hoffa or wise-guy reporters, but Burke kept moving ahead with great style, enjoying himself thoroughly, writing this remarkable story as he went along. He never felt cheated for a day. See, every day was too rich with opportunity. He got after every one with wit and zest and grace.

I have a friend, Tony Kornheiser, who wrote once for a New York newspaper, and he used to call Burke all the time, whether he needed Burke's comments for a story or not. "I just like to listen to him talk," Kornheiser said. When Burke's marvelous autobiography, "Outrageous Good Fortune," was published in 1984, we all found out he wrote as he talked, which is the way he lived. It was done with flourish and flair. More than anything, I think, he wanted to be a poet.

Was he the best sports executive of all times? No, he was not. CBS bought the Yankees in 1964. Burke was named president in 1966. He inherited a ruined dynasty, an aging team in shambles. Things did not change for the Yankees until George Steinbrenner bought the team in 1973. Yankee fans blamed Burke for all of it. "Well," the Yankee fan tells you now, "I'd rather have Steinbrenner than Burke..." It is as though running a baseball team is the measure of a man somehow. Burke proved it wasn't so. A lot of bums win in baseball. Michael Burke was a gentleman.

"Maybe those fans forget," Cosell said, "that Burke probably did more than anyone to keep the Yankees in New York."

It was near the end of Burke's Yankee days. Sonny Werblin already had gone over to New Jersey to begin work for the Meadowlands complex. Werblin wanted the Yankees; the plan was for an all-purpose stadium to lure both the Yankees and the Giants across the Hudson. Burke said no. Yankee Stadium would be rebuilt. It ended up costing the city 10 fortunes, but the Yankees stayed in New York. It would have been easy for Burke to make the Mara play. He did not. The Yankees stayed. "I'll always be a Yankee," Burke used to say theatrically. There was a lot to what he said. He was always more a Yankee than the ones who sniped at him.

It was Burke who brought Grambling College's football team to Yankee Stadium in 1968 to play what he called the Urban Bowl. The Grambling-Morgan State game sold out the Stadium at a time when racial tensions ran high in New York City. Walking out of the park that day, a fan grabbed his hand and said, "You won one today, Mr. Burke." Burke, being Burke, said, "We all won one."

He went from the Yankees to the job as president of the Garden. Outrageous good fortune. The Rangers did not win the Stanley Cup during his Garden years, though they came close in 1979. The Knicks became a mediocre team. Money was spent foolishly. There was the folly of trying to sign George McGinnis, already under contract to the 76ers. They were not all Burke's mistakes. In the McGinnis situation, he took the rap for others.

But Burke brought the Masters tennis to the Garden. The Garden promoted Ali vs. Norton at Yankee Stadium. The Garden got into the concert business, particularly rock'n'roll, as it never had before. And Burke worked mightily to bring the 1980 Democratic Convention to New York. He was always more showman than sportsman, and what was so bad about that?

In 1948, Hollywood made a movie about his days in the OSS. It was called "Cloak and Dagger." Gary Cooper played Burke. In the '50s, Burke stood up to Jimmy Hoffa when Hoffa tried to bully the circus. Again: knew everybody, did everything.

He was William Paley's protege at CBS. Burke was born during World War I and won the Navy Cross and Silver Star during World War II and spoke out against Vietnam. Michael Burke got full value from his share of the 20th century. There was always another adventure on deck.

The last part of the adventure came in Ireland. He went home to County Galway in 1982, to ride horses, always in that funny Pittsburgh Pirates cap, and write his book. He would come through New York every so often; I knew I could find him at the Algonquin. The New York visits were always too short for him. There was never enough time for him to drink it all in.

He took sick in December. He began to suffer blackouts. In the hospital, they discovered a weak heart and a lump on his neck. They gave him a pacemaker. When the heart was strong enough, they operated on his neck. The tumor was malignant. Michael Burke, 68, started chemotherapy. It seemed to be working until a few weeks ago. The blackouts started again. His second wife, Timmy, went over from London. She was with him when he died.

They will bring Michael Burke home now. He is of County Galway, and Connecticut. He will be buried in Connecticut. But truly he was of New York. The love affair was with New York. Its style was Burke's kind of style, its passion was his kind of passion. There probably will be a memorial service at St. Patrick's. Michael Burke would have liked that. It will be the last New York room to be filled with all his big ideas.

• *1987*

His legacy is a big, unfillable void

CHICAGO

E verything got old on him, used-up, except the mind. Bill Veeck used to joke that he wasn't so much dying as running out of parts. Then he would bark out a laugh and drink from a glass of beer, and make you believe he would live forever.

"I'm legally blind," Bill Veeck said one day on the phone a couple of years ago, after another extended visit to another hospital. "I can only hear out of one ear. I've got a leg and a third, a lung and a quarter. I've given the world all the edge I'm going to give it."

The line went something like that. Bill Veeck, who died yesterday, would have remembered it exactly. He would have rummaged around in that marvelous old head and found the words, and produced them like coins from his pocket. He spent the last 40 years of this remarkable and magnificently American life walking around on a peg leg because not all of him came back from Guadalcanal. He spotted us all those parts and faculties. But the mind stayed sharp until he died of being Veeck for so long. The mind always kept him a couple of steps ahead of the game.

And so he died, at age 71. And there will be no more lunches at Miller's restaurant in Chicago on summer afternoons. No more of him at Comiskey's Bards Room. No more stories. No more of Veeck, one of the true giants the game of baseball has ever known, going after the phonies and the stuffed shirts who were always his sworn enemies in baseball. Dammit. Dammit all.

Maybe now some of the ones Veeck always terrorized can find a place for him somewhere in the Hall of Fame. They waited long enough; he can't even chuckle at the lateness of the honor. See, if there is no place for him still, the joint in Cooperstown is incomplete. The Hall needs Veeck's memory, his energy, his spirit, his wit, his clear and shining love of the game. His father ran the Cubs when he was a kid and from then on he was a goner.

"It was a lifetime of summer days and nights," he said the last time I saw him, last June at Miller's, before I went off to a Mets-Cubs game.

I was 13 or 14 when I first read his autobiography "Veeck as in Wreck," still the best sports book of them all. I knew nothing then of Veeck, or the old St. Louis Browns, or sending midget Eddie Gaedel up to bat, or the great run with the Indians, or the fireworks displays or the fan giveaways. But I knew from the first page that the man doing the talking in this book was different. He was a flinty maverick and loved trouble, but he loved baseball more, like a kid. Like me. The book made him a hero for me. He became a friend later. He goes out both ways.

There was this night in the Bellevue-Stratford in 1983. Veeck was writing about the Phillies-Orioles World Series for the Chicago Tribune. We had all gotten to Philadelphia from Baltimore that morning. There was a big Philadelphia reception that night, in honor of the World Series coming to town. I saw Veeck in the lobby, moving about on the peg, holding court.

He said, "If you're not going to that stupid party tonight, meet me downstairs in the bar at seven." I did. I don't remember how long we sat in that bar, drinking beer from tall glasses (he was a champ at this), watching sports scores come by on a screen like the Dow Jones average, him telling stories, me listening. He railed against the late Ford Frick still, the commissioner who was always such a problem for him. He spoke warmly of Hank Greenberg and old Cubs like Hack Wilson, and of Lou Boudreau. He made fun of Bowie Kuhn, and George Steinbrenner, and Jerry Reinsdorf and Eddie Einhorn, the two men to whom he had sold the White Sox after his second time around with the Sox.

"Abbott and Costello, but without the material," he said of Reinsdorf and Einhorn.

That night I asked: If he could ask one last thing from baseball, what would it be?

"I'd like to see Reggie have one more great day in the World Series," said Veeck. It figured that he would love the theatrics of Reggie Jackson, the swagger. When it came time to write the last page of Jackson's autobiography, we finished up with Veeck's quote. Reggie loved Bill Veeck's theatrics, *his* swagger.

At the end of that '83 World Series, Veeck sat next to me while I finished up a column at Veterans Stadium.

"What are you writing about?" he said.

"About Rose and Perez and Morgan, and how it was neat that they could take one last ride together with the Phillies, even though they lost."

Veeck said, "I've got a poem that fits." He grabbed a big piece of scratch paper and scrawled it out. It was from Robert Browning. The lines were about what a wise bird is the thrush, singing each song twice over so as not to forget the first fine, careless rapture of youth. It did fit. I used it. The original scrawl from W. Veeck is over the desk at home still.

I said, "When did you read that poem?" Veeck: "Around 1920, I think."

When I got home, I checked out the poem in Bartlett's. Veeck had two words wrong. I called him and told him. He was quite pleased.

"Memory is a wonderful thing, don't you think?" said Bill Veeck.

The last time I tapped his was that day in June, at Miller's. Veeck was in the process of forgiving the Cubs for selling bleacher seats as advanced tickets, and would return to Wrigley before the season was out, after a self-imposed—and extremely well-publicized—exile. He would take off his shirt and drink his beers and take in a few more Cubs games.

"There are very few things in this life you can do spontaneously anymore," he said, explaining his anger about the bleacher seats. "Going to the ballpark in the afternoon should be one of them."

He told new stories about the old Browns that day. He called Ed Williams stupid for hiring Earl Weaver and firing Joe Altobelli. He pounded his fist on the table over long-term contracts. He said to "Say hello to Roberto," meaning Robert Fischel, his old p.r. man, now a vice-president with the American League.

As I got up to go, he smiled and said, "Enjoy young Gooden. The lad reminds me of why I loved the damn game so much in the first place."

Monday I read that he had gone into the hospital because of a respiratory problem. I knew I was coming to Chicago Thursday. I decided I would wait to call him. Somebody called me instead yesterday morning. I thought of the last line from the "Wreck": "Look for me under the arc lights, boys. I'll be back."

There is so much more to say about Bill Veeck, who was merely so much of the history of baseball in this century.

The only eulogy the old man would have cared about came from the White Sox fan driving the cab yesterday at O'Hare Airport. "Mr. Veeck wasn't like other big shots," the cabbie said.

• 1986

We'll never again see the likes of Bobby Orr

We sat up in Section 99 in Boston Garden in those days. We would look down from Section 99 in that rotten shambles of an arena, with smoke so thick it could choke you, and there was Bobby Orr giving a command performance night after night, turning Bruins games into open-air concerts. He played these wild jazz riffs out there, crazy things, stretching for impossible notes all the time, hitting them so often you had to laugh.

There were 360-degree spins at full speed, invented on the fly. The slapshots which came out of this lovely, fluid motion and became murderous bullets for goalies. The rushes which made players on both teams stand spellbound. The blind passes. Some have said Bobby Orr revolutionized the game for defensemen. That is not quite right. Orr played a different game, in a high place.

Orr retired for the final time this week. The killer knees have stilled the extraordinary talent once and for all. He stayed away for two years after the sixth operation, and he began to hope that he could play. But when he came back with the Black Hawks this season, he could play reasonably well one of three nights. He was maybe 35 percent of what he was.

If you have even once played the game the way Bobby Orr did all the time, you could not settle for being human. He could not hit those glorious high notes anymore. He could not come close, and so he quit. Music has gone out of the sport, this time for good.

When he was young, before things started to go wrong inside the knees and the knees became monsters, when Bobby Orr would start up ice in Boston Garden, and this wonderful, frightening noise would begin to build in the old building, in that instant, hockey was perfect. Freeze the frame. Close up the NHL. Orr really did turn the whole thing into a song.

To say now that he was the greatest hockey player of all time, which he was, which he will be, does not even begin to describe what it was like in Boston Garden when he was young. You did not have to know anything about hockey to realize what you were seeing.

"He'd pick up the puck behind our net and he'd stop for just a moment," Phil Esposito was saying the other day. The image was only in memory, but Esposito became excited. He was smiling. It was as if Orr really were about to begin another unforgettable rush.

"First you'd hear this deep, low rumble from the crowd," Esposito continued. "Bobby'd start out. Now he was picking up speed, going over center ice—yeah, he *was* flying—and all of a sudden, the noise has become this . . . this giant roar. Jeezus, it was something."

We are lucky to have seen him for 10 years. It just happens this way sometimes, and the special ones are taken from us early. Maureen Connolly fell off a horse and Sandy Koufax had arthritis and Lew Hoad had a horrible back. Bobby Orr had six knee operations. Mickey Mantle and Joe Namath had knees and were able to play on. Orr is different. Orr is 30 years old.

From now on, wherever they put on pads and skates, they will talk about Orr in different tones from the great *mortals*, the Howes and Hulls and Richards. They will tell the stories and remember this play or that shot. They will recount the night in Oakland when he dropped his glove at center ice, left it there, picked up the puck, came roaring back, picked up the glove, did not lose stride. Did not.

They will remember the goal he scored to beat St. Louis and win the Stanley Cup in 1970, and how in the photographs the next day, Orr seemed to be flying as the puck went into the net. Maybe he was.

Before Orr joined the NHL, no defenseman had ever scored 20 goals or had more than 65 points. Orr scored 46 goals in 1974-75. In 1970-71, he scored 139 points. He was voted the game's best defenseman eight straight times. The first time he stepped onto the ice in

Boston Garden, as an 18-year-old in 1968, he was the youngest player out there, and the oldest. You could not take your eyes off him that night. The place looked like it had been built around him.

So they can tell me that Bobby Orr has retired all they want. He hasn't. He is 22 and I'm in Section 99 and he's just crossed the other team's blue line and the noise has built. Freeze the frame. Close up the NHL.

• *1978*

Sentimental trip for Willie Mays

H e took the "A" train yesterday, took it uptown, all the way to 155th and 8th, where it all began. Willie Mays took the "A" train to the place where a ballpark named the Polo Grounds once stood. Duke Ellington wrote a song about that train once, a long time ago, in 1950, when Willie Mays was young. Willie Mays was 19 that year. He came to New York the next summer. He began to play some music of his own. The game of baseball would never again look quite the same.

The original "A" train had to be brought from a museum in Brooklyn yesterday, and the Polo Grounds is gone, and Duke is gone, and Willie Mays goes into the Hall of Fame this weekend. But for this one day, none of that mattered. Willie Mays was going uptown one more time. You have to think the Duke could have supplied some light, airy jazz for that. Yeah. Willie Mays was going uptown.

Leo Durocher was waiting for him uptown, and so was Bobby Thomson, and Monte Irvin, and an old Southern fellow named Dusty Rhodes. And maybe Willie Mays was being inducted into the Hall of Fame early, up in Harlem, near Coogan's Bluff, at the bottom of the John T. Brush Stairway. There is a housing project called the Polo Ground Towers at 155th and 8th; there used to be a ballpark. Willie Mays performed magic in that ballpark. He was young there.

As the train took him to Polo Grounds Towers yesterday, chasing years away as it moved through the city, someone asked Mays if those early years in New York were his happiest in baseball. It was hot in the train. An oldstyle fan above Mays' head blew the hot air around. Willie Mays laughed at the question, and the laugh was like a cool breeze.

"I didn't have to come to New York to be happy playing baseball," he said in the high-pitched voice that has never changed. "I was happy in Birmingham. I was happy when I was 11 and 12 years old."

He never needed a train to take him to the ballpark. He lived two minutes away, on 155th and St. Nicholas Ave. On his way to the park, he walked down the long Brush Stairway; he walked back up on his way home. He played stickball on St. Nicholas, with the kids in the neighborhood. Mays said he was always surprised his stickball-playing got so much attention.

"Hell, it was the same game we used to play back in Birmingham," he said. " 'cept we called it 'Tennisball' back home. Played with a broomstick and a tennis ball in an empty lot. The only difference when I got to New York was you hit the ball on a bounce. We hit it out of the air in Birmingham."

The train was pulling into the 155th St. station.

"What am I thinking?" Mays said quietly. "I'm thinking this is the place where I got my first hit."

Someone yelled, "All off for Yankee Stadium!" Mays laughed his cackling laugh. "I missed my stop," he said. He never missed much else in that neighborhood. You could not hit a baseball over his head at the Polo Grounds. You could not throw a fastball past Willie Mays. That is what they say.

Mays moved out of the train and up the steps, trailed by an army of television cameras and reporters. At the top of the steps, a lot of kids were waiting for Willie Mays. They had been waiting in the midday heat for some time. Nearly 30 years ago, he played stickball with kids on these same streets. That legacy is as strong as any.

A young girl named Charlene, who had pigtails and braces and gave her age as 12, was asked how many home runs Willie Mays hit.

"Six-hundred and sixty," she said promptly, and flashed a tremendous grin.

Mays began walking through the project to an asphalt playground in the back called "Willie Mays Field." A ceremony was waiting for him on "Willie Mays Field." Mays is now a spokesman for the Colgate

Women's Games, a nationwide series of track and field events for young women. On the eve of his induction into the Hall of Fame, Colgate decided to honor Mays at Polo Grounds Towers. The speakers' stand, fittingly, was in what was the Polo Grounds outfield. It took Mays a long time to get to it. There were more kids, maybe 500 of them, waiting for him as soon as he walked onto the playground.

Mel Allen hosted the ceremony. He introduced old baseball writers, and politicians, and Willie Mays' wife, Mae. Irvin, who roomed with Mays that first summer, spoke, and so did Thompson, who moved to leftfield in the Polo Grounds to make room for Willie Mays when Mays came up to the Giants on May 25, 1951. Mays was 20. He was hitting .477 for Minneapolis at the time.

Then Durocher, an old man now, spoke.

"You had to be blind not to see there was a superstar standing in front of you the first time you saw Willie Mays," Durocher said. "There are guys making $800,000 a year now who couldn't shine his shoes. He's the greatest player I ever saw."

Willie Mays stood before the microphone then. People at Willie Mays Playground stood, and some kids in the back yelled "Say Hey!" The speech was brief; he says his speech in Cooperstown will be longer. Mays thanked Colgate and Durocher and his former teammates. He said he hoped he would live as long as Leo Durocher. He said that America does not embrace all athletes as it embraced him, and he is grateful for that.

The people cheered. Willie Mays walked across what was once his private domain: the outfield at the Polo Grounds. You could not hit a ball over his head there, not on a bet, not when he was young. Willie Mays walked briskly yesterday. It seemed as if he were heading for John T. Brush Stairway, toward a stickball game on St. Nicholas Avenue.

• 1979

This Mets' watcher is something special

M
•

rs. Victoria Crawford's fingers found the lime-colored drapes which billowed softly in the evening breeze. The drapes were a guide; she dragged her fingers down until they found the Sony portable radio on the coffee table beneath the window. She turned the radio on. She didn't have to bother with the station dial, because the Sony is always tuned to WMCA. That is the Mets station. A very special part of Victoria Crawford's day was beginning.

There was a station advertisement for Strauss Communications on the radio. Victoria Crawford, who is 69, carefully shuffled across the small living room to her favorite chair, a big gold chair with a plastic cover. She slowly lowered herself into it, draping her arms at her sides, over the arms of the chair. The chair faces the radio; it faces away from a television set, which is of no use to Mrs. Crawford, who has been blind since 1962, the year her favorite baseball team, the Mets, was born.

"I love this chair," Victoria Crawford said in a sweet, high-pitched voice. "I can't see that old television anyway, and here, I can catch the breeze and listen to my games."

On the radio, the "Meet the Mets" theme song was playing. Victoria Crawford leaned forward in her chair, tilting her head slightly in the direction of the radio. She clapped her hands together, and giggled.

"I like that theme," she said. "Here they come." Another night of baseball was beginning on the Sony radio, which sat in the middle of the table, next to a picture of a much-younger Victoria Crawford, wearing a red dress and smiling.

The apartment, which is part of the Frederick Douglass Housing Addition on Amsterdam Ave., between 102d and 103d, has three rooms: living room, kitchen, bedroom. It costs $82 a month; Mrs. Crawford pays with her Social Security; she is quick to point out she has never believed in welfare. Her husband has been dead for two years. She was blinded in an accident in January of 1962. Her main pleasure is listening to New York Mets games, which she has done religiously for 17 years, without ever seeing them.

There are three radios in the apartment, one for each room. There is a big old Juliette on the nightstand next to her double bed. There is an XAM band radio on top of a shelf in the kitchen. When Mrs. Crawford is moving around her apartment, she does not want to miss a pitch. She has probably listened to more Mets games than any living person. She is surely their greatest fan; the Mets are her best friend.

"Oh, I'm sure I'm not the greatest fan," she said. "I'd like to be known with the greatest fans, though, because I do enjoy these games very much." She was sitting upright in her favorite chair, like a judge, almost at attention. She adjusted her clear-lens glasses, which had slipped slightly down her nose.

On the radio, Steve Albert was going over the batting orders for the Mets and the Braves. The game was almost ready to begin. Victoria Crawford began tapping the fingers of her right hand on the arm of her chair.

"I can really visualize these games," she said. "It's almost as if I can see them hit the ball, make a bunt, get on base, get thrown out. The announcers are such a great help to me. Without the radio announcers announcing these games so well, I wouldn't be able to see these games."

She was asked if she missed Lindsey Nelson.

"That young Steve Albert is doing a fine job," she said. "But I do miss Lindsey Nelson. My, he could announce a game so clear! Why, I remember one time in 1968, he was describing a catch by Cleon Jones. You should have heard it. He said that Cleon had to climb the wall to catch that ball. Why, Lindsey said you could see Cleon's footprints on the wall!"

Craig Swan struck out Bob Horner to end the Braves first inning.

"(Wayne) Twitchell pitched well the other day," she said, "but Craig Swan's our best, no doubt about that. He's the stopper."

The room was pleasant and dark and cool, and every so often, disco music would catch the breeze and float up from the street below. To Victoria Crawford's left was a small table with a bowl of fresh fruit, a dish of walnuts, a jar with peppermint sticks. Over the couch, where a visitor sat, was a bright-colored oil painting. Her daughter Josey, who lives down the street, had taken her to a gallery and described a series of paintings. "Then I picked out the one I liked above all others," she said. The painting was lovely; the loveliest object in the room was the Sony radio.

Mazzilli was at the plate.

"Two balls," said Mrs. Crawford. "They're gonna walk him again. They really walked him the other night, didn't they?" Mazzilli had walked twice against the Reds Wednesday night.

Mazzilli singled in the Mets first run. Victoria Crawford leaned so far forward in her chair that she had to grab the arms for support. Her feet slipped slightly on the green rug in front of her. She squealed with delight, again tilting her head toward the radio.

"RBI!" she shouted. "How can they keep Mazzilli off the All-Star team?"

As a girl growing up in Selma, Alabama, she had loved playing baseball. When she could see, she was a Brooklyn Dodgers fan. She said she could never warm up to the Yankees "because I never thought they had enough colored players." When the Mets were born, she adopted them. For 17 years, their games have filled up small parts of her long days.

"Al Jackson was always one of my favorites," she said. "L'il Al, they called him. It seems like he used to strike everyone out. Oh, and I just loved Cleon Jones and Tommy Agee. They were from Mobile, Alabama, you know. Boy, could they play ball. Did you ever see them?"

She said she loves listening to West Coast games late at night. "One hour of the day isn't any different from any other," she said matter-of-factly. She said that John Stearns batting average was down, but she expected him to hit soon. She was asked about Ed Kranepool, who's been with the Mets as long as she has. "I don't think he has it anymore, but don't print that, because I wouldn't want to hurt his feelings." She smiled and patted her hair, still wet from a bath. She had not taken time to dry it because the game was starting.

Her schedule is the radio. She follows the standings through the radio. She said she never moves the dial from WMCA if she can help it. For 17 years, Victoria Crawford has used the radio to reach out and touch the Mets in her sweet way.

Friday night, in her favorite chair, she listened to the Mets beat the Braves, 2-1, leaning forward only when something would go well for her team. She wore an immaculate white blouse and pressed pink slacks and yellow bedroom slippers. She kept asking her visitor if he wanted something to drink; the visitor said that listening to the game with her was just fine.

"I'll tell you," Victoria Crawford said, "I'll be very happy when the Mets pick up their attendance. At one time, they had very high attendance, you know. You should have seen the crowds."

• *1979*

The day the music died in Boston

T
•

hey stood for a long time in Fenway Park when it was over, quietly at attention while the organist played marching music. The afternoon was gone, hope was gone, the season was gone, and the beautiful little park was again a tomb for its fans, as it has been in a lot of Octobers. On the field, a hated baseball team called the New York Yankees celebrated victory. The people kept staring at them dreamily. And no one moved. Maybe they thought that if they stayed the season would not be over.

There has always been a saying in Boston that while baseball isn't a matter of life and death, the Red Sox are. The Red Sox were dead. In the 163rd game of this special season, the Yankees had scored one more run. Rich Gossage had just thrown a fastball to Carl Yastrzemski in the bottom of the pennant race. Yastrzemski, a proud old hero who'd already knocked in two runs, popped that fastball up. There was not going to be one last series in Yankee Stadium, or Fenway Park, not one more swing of the bat for Yastrzemski or Jim Rice or anyone. The scoreboard said 5-4 Yankees. The Yankees were a run better. And no one wanted to leave Fenway.

The fans were paralyzed by all the ifs that must rule the last day of a pennant race like this one. If Lou Piniella had not made his great running catch off Fred Lynn with two on in the sixth. If the ball Piniella lost in the sun in the ninth, the one hit by Jerry Remy, didn't bounce right into Piniella's glove. If Bucky Dent had not turned into Bobby Thomson with his three-run homer. All those ifs. The organist kept playing the marching music.

"We're not the world champions for nothing," Lou Piniella would say in the winning clubhouse, when asked about all the little plays that enabled the Yankees to get a nose in front, like some kind of baseball Affirmed. "They played like world champions," Yastrzemski would say in the clubhouse at the other end of the runway.

The Yankees *had* played like world champions. Gossage held the Red Sox off in the end. A home run by Reginald Martinez Jackson provided the difference. The Yankees were going to Kansas City to begin a whole new passion play with their old friends, the Royals. They had done something quite difficult first. They had silenced Fenway Park.

The Red Sox' 14-game July lead was said, ancient history. The gallant comeback that brought them to this tiebreaker playoff game, a comeback from a 3¹/₂-game deficit with only two weeks left, was wasted. All the pre-game partying on Boylston Street and in Kenmore Square and on Yawkey Way had turned into a magnificent wake. The best pennant race that anyone is going to see for a very long time had been won by the Yankees, by Ron Guidry and Dent and Piniella and Gossage and Jackson.

"Three seasons ended today," Jackson said in the clubhouse. "There was the first half. That belonged to the Red Sox. The second half belonged to us. And today? Today was a season all in itself."

Jackson smiled. His 400-foot, Reggie Jackson-model October home run in the eighth had ultimately meant victory for his team. Reggie is so used to all of this. He was a lock to be a central figure in yesterday's drama. He is one of the great money players of his time. He knew what a fine victory his team earned, a victory that began in July, when Bob Lemon became manager of the Yankees.

"I'm glad we don't have to play them anymore," Jackson said.

No one could endure any more of this Yankee-Red Sox material. The three seasons that Jackson talked about ended with a game that was several games, a full three-act production.

There was the first game, the one that took place over the first six innings, the one that had ex-Yankee Mike Torrez handling his old team, staked to a two-run lead by a Yastrzemski home run off Guidry, and a Rice RBI single. Then there was another game in the Yankee seventh, Act II, which saw Dent stun Fenway with a three-run homer that dropped into the bottom of the screen at the top of Fenway's famed Green Monster. Dent used a bat borrowed from Mickey Rivers, one sent out by Rivers in the middle of his at-bat. Dent had become another of baseball's unlikely heroes. The Yankees would leave the seventh ahead 4-2. Torrez was gone.

"I never did see the ball hit the screen," Dent said. These unlikely heroes are notoriously short-sighted.

Then there was the final game, the last act. Jackson's home run off Bob Stanley in the eighth. Two Red Sox runs in the eighth. The Red Sox getting two men on in the ninth as their fans began to dream grand dreams. But Rice hit a shot to Piniella, which Piniella saw, and caught. Yastrzemski popped up. It had been a beautiful excruciating game to end a wonderful season-long battle.

The game began with Guidry against Torrez. It had a home run from Yastrzemski, a big man in so many big games in his 18 seasons. It had Jackson, of course. And it ended with Gossage facing Rice and Yastrzemski with the winning runs on the bases. The game had everything. The season had everything.

The Good Lord must love his baseball.

By the time it was over, and the people had begun their painful October procession out of Fenway Park—a terrible New England ritual—Yastrzemski, who is 39 years old now, was standing in front of his locker talking about "terrible knots in my stomach." Torrez talked about how "in my heart, I know I did my best." Carlton Fisk slowly peeled off his clothes and talked about all the ifs.

"If that ball doesn't bounce up and hit Piniella right in the damn chest . . .," Fisk said. He was talking about the ball Remy hit in the ninth. He had no answers. His voice trailed off. He turned to his locker and spit some tobacco into a paper cup.

"One run," Carlton Fisk said. "One run after 162 games, and they won and we lost, and what more can you say?"

"You don't bet on where they start," said Jackson. "You bet on where they finish."

They finished at Fenway Park on a diamond of an October afternoon. The Yankees went to Kansas City when it was over, the Red Sox and their fans went home. A lovely war ended at Fenway yesterday, a war decided by a run. The run made the ballpark quiet. It will stay quiet for a long time.

• *1978*

A part of the NBA died with Eddie

T. here were no millionaires when they started. There were no shattered backboards. There were just these men named Walter Brown and Ned Irish and Danny Biasone and Eddie Gottlieb, who had this crazy dream about a pro basketball league. They built the dream in empty arenas. They lost money. People laughed at them. But they kept breathing life into the pro game.

The games were played in the 69th Regiment Armory in New York, and the old Philadelphia Arena, and the Onondaga War Memorial Auditorium in Syracuse, and Boston Garden. Slowly, the sport grew, thanks to Brown and Irish, Biasone and Gottlieb, the truest believers. They ran hard, scheming and dreaming. They called it the Basketball Association of America, the forerunner of what was to become the NBA.

No one ran harder than little Eddie Gottlieb in Philly. He had sad eyes and pasty skin and wore a bow tie. They called him "The Mogul," even in the old days. He was coach and general manager of the Warriors when they won the first BAA title in 1947. He promoted the team on streetcorners and he sold the tickets and then he counted the cold house. He made up the league schedule. Even in the old days, they joked that Eddie Gottlieb carried the NBA around in his briefcase. They joked that if he got hit by a car and died, the NBA died with him.

Eddie Gottlieb finally died on Friday, in Temple University Hospital in Philadelphia. The league didn't go with him. But a big part of its rich history did. Something important is gone from the NBA. Eddie Gottlieb is gone. He was 81. He never married. He leaves no family. He is survived only by the National Basketball Association.

He never did retire from the NBA. Up until this season, Gottlieb still made up the NBA schedule, as he had for 30 years. Other sports had computers; the NBA had something much more valuable: Gottlieb. Only this season, at the age of 81, did Gottlieb reluctantly turn the schedule over to a computer. But Gottlieb still had final approval of the schedule. He still had the title of "consultant," and an office down the hall from Comm. Larry O'Brien's. He still was a member of the league's Rules and Competition Committee. He still wore the bowtie. He was, of course, an institution. He was "The Mogul."

"It keeps my brain going," Gottlieb said once, when asked why he kept working on pro basketball. "When you stop using this"—he pointed to his head—"then you really get old, and you're in trouble."

When the schedule was still his private property, you would walk into his little office and find the NBA season spread out on his desk. It would be July or August, and everyone in the NBA would be out of season except Eddie Gottlieb. The paper would be piled deep on the desk, yellow legal paper and graph paper and loose-leaf paper. Some of it would be scattered, and some would be in folders, some would have slipped to the floor. Gottlieb's skin would be the color of the yellow legal paper, and his eyes would look like black holes. But he was making a season, as always.

I asked him once if making the schedule was fun for him, a challenge.

"Fun?" Gottlieb snapped. "There is no fun attached to this, none whatsoever. At four o'clock this morning I was up working on this thing, and you ask me about fun? Ten hours I've been at this already today. Ten hours. Ten hours of this will make you crazy." Gottlieb smiled then. He was talking about his baby. When they took the paper away from him this season, they must have done so with guns.

Another time, I asked him how long he had been making schedules.

Another smile. "Since I was born," Eddie Gottlieb said. "Yeah, I guess I been at this a couple years past. Back in the old days, I was even in charge of semi-pro baseball in Philly. I was scheduling 200 baseball games a day. And I made up the schedule for the old Negro

National League. Hell, I handled all baseball and basketball games around Philly. At one time or another, I guess I've handled just about everything."

But Eddie Gottlieb loved basketball. Maybe no one ever loved basketball quite the way he did. He used to run something called the South Philadelphia Hebrew Basketball Association out of the Philadelphia's Broadwood Hotel.

"It was basketball, then dancing," he told me. "A very nice Saturday evening for yourself and a date."

When the NBA started in 1946, he was right there. First, he was coach and general manager of the Warriors. In 1952, he bought them for $15,000. Every year, he made the schedule. He sold the Warriors in 1962, and the team moved to San Francisco. Gottlieb moved with them. He was still making the schedule. In 1964, he retired from the Warriors. The league hired him as a consultant. In 1972, he was inducted into the Hall of Fame. One institution joined another.

Walter Brown is dead now. Danny Biasone, who merely saved the game by inventing the 24-second clock (and who should go into the Hall of Fame immediately), is retired in Syracuse. Ned Irish is in Florida. The NBA is a league in which the average salary is $160,000. You have to wonder if millionaires know these names.

The millionaires ought to know Eddie Gottlieb, mogul, died Friday. Never again will you find him behind the stacks of paper. He won't tell you anymore of his marvelous stories about the old days. The NBA is minus a treasure. He was 81. He is survived by a league.

• *1979*

McLain sentence: 23 years

"I don't know how you get to where I am today from where I was 17 years ago."

—Dennis McLain

TAMPA

T
he judge, Elizabeth A. Kovachevich, was late for lunch and unhappy about that. But it was time for the hard business of law in the second floor courtroom of the U.S. Courthouse, Federal Building, Downtown Postal Station, Tampa. It was 12:41 in the afternoon and a fat man who used to be Dennis McLain sat slumped in a folding chair in front of her bench. Elizabeth Kovachevich was going to send the last 30-game winner in baseball away for a long time.

Kovachevich took off her reading glasses and looked down at McLain, who in this same courtroom in March had been convicted of three counts of racketeering and conspiracy and extortion, and one count of possession of cocaine with intent to distribute. The sentencing had been continued once, last Friday. There would be no further delays. McLain was about to conclude perhaps the biggest fall a great and celebrated professional athlete has ever taken in this country. In 1968, Dennis Dale McLain had been 31-6 for the Tigers.

"Perhaps your greatest gullibility, Mr. McLain," the judge said, "is your failure to admit your own wrongdoing ... And I must tell you that with regard to the drugs, this court will deal with you harshly."

McLain barely moved, just slumped a little more into his own felony and disgrace, the rest of his life, as the sentences hit him like bullets. Concurrent eight-year sentences for the racketeering and conspiracy and extortion. The fourth count was for the cocaine. Kovachevich paused and gave McLain 15 years. It works out to 23 years, one-third of which McLain must serve before being eligible for parole. McLain had been right in his closing statement. It was such a long way from 1968, when he won 30.

"It seems so long ago," said Dennis McLain, who said later through his lawyer, Arnold Levine, that he would appeal. "It seems like it never happened."

As far as Elizabeth A. Kovachevich was concerned, and a prosecuting assistant U.S. attorney named Ernest Mueller and the state of Florida, it never had. In the second row of the visitors' benches, Mrs. Sharon Boudreau McLain, daughter of Lou Boudreau, began to cry into a white handkerchief. Her oldest daughter, Chrissie, age 19, put her head into her mother's shoulder and began to sob in harsh, painful gasps. Another daughter, Dale, given her father's middle name, reached behind her mother from the right and touched her sister's hair. This was no longer the family of the most celebrated pitcher of his day, a double Cy Young Award winner (in 1968 and 1969). This was about a 265-pound convicted felon in a gray sports jacket and cheap gray polyester slacks who was being sent off to do a lot of time by a judge who did not care about baseball, only the law.

He had always been a wise guy, Dennis McLain, even when his right arm was a credit card and he became part of baseball history. He had been suspended by then baseball commissioner Bowie Kuhn in 1970, for running an informal bookmaking operation out of the Tiger clubhouse, and for gambling. And over the years, he had graduated from all that, become a pathetic, overweight imitation of a hero. Now he was, in the parlance of the street, an official wise guy. Do the crime, do the time. Twenty-three years. No parole until the eighth.

Racketeering. Conspiracy. Loansharking. Possession of three kilos of coke with intent to sell. The last 30-game winner had hit a grand slam. He would go to prison with other bums convicted in the state's case, men with less famous names like Seymour Sher and Frank Cocchiaro and Larry Knott. The world had finally caught up with a righthander named McLain.

There was a moment in the second floor courtroom that was all irony and tragedy, when McLain had stood to address the judge, pulling himself out of the chair with a tremendous effort, like a man hefting a sack of laundry. His left hand was at his side, his right hand was behind him, on the hip. He leaned forward just slightly. It was as if Denny McLain were looking in for a sign.

"I'll pay for my conviction the rest of my life," he said in a hoarse, almost inaudible scrape of a voice. "I'll do that even if I appeal and am acquitted. I must live with my shame and my disgrace. Wherever I go, people will have unkind words about what I've done . . . I don't know how many errors and mistakes I've made in my lifetime, but I know now I've made enough for at least two people."

Even at the end, the last 30-game winner did not get it. McLain had made enough mistakes for an army. When the right arm had lost its magic and he had become just another hero from a game who belonged to the past, McLain had still thought he could throw high hard ones past the whole world.

"He was sheltered by the White Sox (in the minor leagues) and the Tigers," said Arnold Levine in his pre-sentencing plea. "He was put upon a pedestal. What did he know about the world? What did he know of life? He was no scholar. He happened to have a sensational arm, that's all it was. He received adulation from the public, and was protected by that public. He's a convicted felon and people still want his autograph."

McLain has been incarcerated in the Seminole County Jail in Sanford, Fla., since his conviction in March. He came to the U.S. Courthouse, Federal Building, from there yesterday. The sentencing was scheduled for 11:30 a.m. It did not officially come until 12:41 p.m. After that, there was one more statement from Levine, one more from Mueller. Elizabeth Kovachevich then asked Dennis McLain if there was anything else he wanted to say.

McLain rose again.

"I'm 41 years old," he began, then the words got away from him and spilled all over in front of Kovachevich's bench, and McLain began to cry. It was over. A marshall in a light-green summer sports jacket took him to a holding cell. Sharon McLain and her two daughters went to see him there.

Larry Knott was brought in then. The judge gave him 15 years. It took her about 15 minutes. It was time for her lunch. It had been a full morning's work for Elizabeth A. Kovachevich. She had hand-delivered 38 years of time to a couple of felons, one of whom was Dennis Dale McLain, who had a sensational right arm once, who was the last 30-game winner in baseball.

• *1985*

Ernie Davis rates more than an item

I
•
t was a minor football item in the newspaper on the day when Willie Mays made the baseball Hall of Fame, and it really didn't matter much unless you ever saw Ernie Davis carry a football on an autumn afternoon. Then it mattered. Because if you saw him 20 years ago, in Syracuse, N.Y., in a fat, old gray place called Archbold Stadium, then it is hard to think of him being a posthumous selection to the National Football Foundation Hall of Fame, as he was on Tuesday, in dead quiet. It is hard to think of Ernie Davis being dead since 1963.

Because if you were a kid back in the late '50s and early '60s, and your father was a Syracuse fan who took you to Archbold Stadium, Ernie Davis was all you ever wanted to be. And the announcement Tuesday that he'd finally made the Hall of Fame was bigger than a few paragraphs in a newspaper, even if it was the wrong sport on Willie May's day, and the wrong Hall of Fame, even if Ernie Davis had been dead a long time.

Davis went into the Hall along with three other posthumous selections: Dr. Joseph Donchess of Pittsburgh, Pug Rentner of Northwestern, Coach Babe Hollingberry of Washington State. Normally, the selection would be a great thing for one important reason. Normally, Syracuse would pick out a home game, and the plaque would be presented there, and Ernie Davis' name would live in Archbold Stadium for one more afternoon.

But next season, Syracuse must play all its games on the road while a new stadium is being built. On the day Davis made the Hall of Fame, Archbold Stadium was in the process of being torn down.

The afternoons remain. Davis wears No. 4. He is breaking Jim Brown's Syracuse records. The leukemia has not yet started to kill him. Looking back, Davis is a little bit of Earl Campbell, a touch of O.J. Simpson. Davis looks like he is going to be the greatest running back of all.

Brown put Syracuse on the football map, but his real greatness came in the pros. Larry Csonka and Floyd Little would each gain more yards than Brown or Davis. In Syracuse, they speak differently about Ernie Davis, and the autumn afternoons of 1959, 1960 and 1961. Maybe because they were the only ones he would have.

He was the first black to win the Heisman Trophy. He did that in 1961. He led Syracuse to the national championship in 1959, as a sophomore, and then Davis beat Texas in the Orange Bowl. He scored 35 touchdowns at Syracuse in his career, gained 2386 yards, averaged 6.6 yards a carry. He was 6-2 and 215 pounds, and on a football field, Davis could do everything. No, that is not quite right. On a football field, Davis could do anything.

Davis ran coach Ben Schwartzwalder's famed scissors play off tackle. He ran up the middle, and over people, and he ran outside. He threw the option pass for touchdowns. In his last college game, in the 1961 Liberty Bowl against Miami, Syracuse fell behind 14-0. What happened after that is best described by Ben Schwartzwalder:

"Ernie took over. He carried three of every four times, taking tacklers with him, and gained 140 yards, and we finally won, 15-14. Ten guys stood around and watched him." The 10 guys played for Syracuse, and they were doing the only sensible thing. When Ernie Davis carried the football, you watched him, gladly. You could not take your eyes off him.

The Redskins made him the NFL's No. 1 draft pick in 1962, then traded him to the Browns for Bobby Mitchell in one of the league's most famous trades. Davis and Jim Brown were going to play the same backfield. The thought was staggering. It was, of course, going to be the greatest backfield of all time. Until Ernie Davis got sick, in the summer of 1962.

He was in Evanston, Ill., practicing for the annual College All-Star game. He had a bad reaction to a tooth being pulled. It was called a "blood disorder" at first. Then the mumps. Then mononucleosis. Ernie Davis had leukemia, had had it since April. He would never play another game. He was going to die.

"I was never in pain and I never felt sick," Davis wrote in the Saturday Evening Post a few months before he died, thinking the leukemia had gone into remission. "That was the hardest part. I would lie there (in the hospital) feeling good and strong, as if I should be able to do what I wanted to do, which was play football for the Cleveland Browns, but I couldn't leave. Nobody knows much about leukemia. It's supposed to be cancer of the blood. All I know is that it hasn't made me feel sick."

Davis thought he had beaten leukemia that winter of 1963, even played basketball with the Browns basketball team, and looked hopefully toward playing football in 1963. The leukemia reappeared in the spring. It finally killed Ernie Davis on May 18, 1963. He was 23 years old.

So he never played pro football in the same backfield with Jim Brown. So the afternoons at Syracuse were the last he had, and Archbold Stadium is gone. So he has been dead a long time. Ernie Davis was special, very special. Maybe he would have been the best.

And it seemed that on the day he made the Hall of Fame, he deserved more than a box in the newspaper. If you saw him in Syracuse, you felt you owed Ernie Davis more than that.

• *1980*

A full baseball life graced by dignity

I
•
t is a great life. They let you hold onto one of the best parts of youth, the part about baseball games on summer days and nights. If it breaks right, you get celebrity and big money and the kind of clear-cut triumph games can bring. If you have the proper skills, you are part of the big-time parade of big-time sports.

And those of us who are a part of it too, getting paid to watch the games, look for the good guys, the ones we think deserve such a life, the ones who make enough winning and losing—but not too much.

We look for dignity. We look for modesty. We look for the ones who understand how lucky they are. We look for gentlemen.

Dick Howser was such a gentleman. He died yesterday.

He was Rookie of the Year once with the Kansas City A's, as a shortstop. He coached some third base for the Yankees. He managed a couple of teams, won a world championship at the age of 49. He got cancer at 50, died at 51. He was a quiet little bulldog of a man. He tried not to make a big deal out of anything, but he kept walking through his own baseball generation with a grace God either blesses you with, or doesn't.

When he was so rudely let go by George Steinbrenner of the Yankees, after a Yankee team that Howser managed won 103 regular-season games, he did not whine.

He did not complain. Dick Howser thought there was a way you were supposed to act in life. When he was struck down by a malignant brain tumor—glioma is the word—Howser did not whine. He did not complain. There was a way you were supposed to act in death, too.

"We'll get this thing done," Dick Howser kept saying. He always talked about getting it done. When his Kansas City Royals were down 1-3 in games to the Blue Jays in the 1985 American League Championship Series, Howser said the Royals could still get it done. And they did. And the Royals came back from 1-3 down in the World Series against the Cardinals.

When I found out last summer how sick Dick Howser was, I kept thinking about him in those seconds after the last out was made in the seventh game of the '85 Series. I thought about how happy he looked, running toward the celebration around Bret Saberhagen, tucking his Royals cap away so as not to lose it, looking smaller than everybody else, like he always did.

I thought about cancer hitting him nine months after a moment like that.

After the first surgery last year, the one in which the doctors determined the tumor was malignant, I wrote a column about Howser. I considered him my friend. I wanted to get down in a column how lucky I thought it was to come across a gentleman such as Howser in the line of duty.

The column eventually found Howser. He wrote back. I have written of his letter before. Not to make a show of it, or our friendship, or the fact that Howser found time to reply. Just because it showed a lot of Howser in a little bit of space: sneaky wit, toughness, faith in God. This is the letter:

Dear Mike,

   I want to thank you for the "Howser" article. As usual, it was very accurate. I have the faith, the doctors and the support. I'm pleased with the way things are going. Once again, thank you for your friendship. Keep the faith.

   Sincerely,

   Dick Howser

   P.S. God loves you.

He had been a Christian before his illness. After the illness, his faith deepened, and so did Dick Howser's peace about the whole thing. He fought all the way, of course. He tried an experimental surgery in California. He even tried to come back and manage the Royals this spring. It was a symbolic gesture on the part of John

Schuerholz, the Royals GM. I think Schuerholz, another of the gentlemen of sports, and the rest of the Royals gave Dick Howser something to shoot for over the winter.

He could not do it. The cancer had taken too much of him. He was too frail. He gave it up after the first weekend. He went home. We all knew he was going home to die.

A couple of weeks ago, there was a news story about Howser being rushed to St. Luke's Hospital in Kansas City, and then there was nothing until yesterday, when the news moved over the wire that Howser had died at 2:45 in the afternoon.

I have written before: Howser was no more heroic than anyone else who fights disease. He just happened to be one I knew. And I know that from now on, I will have a little bit of a frame of reference. Again, when you have grace like Howser's, you just instinctively know there is a way to do it.

He was a little bit more than a name they will find someday with other Rookies of the Year, or in the long list of Yankee managers, or managers who had a 1-0 record in the World Series. He was strong, he understood the long season as well as any manager in the game, he earned the respect of everybody who ever played for him. He stood up to Steinbrenner when it was necessary. He shrugged off the second-guessers, he could handle pitchers. He kept it all in perspective.

And he loved Florida, and golf, and old Florida State pals, and Nancy Howser. He made a lot of friends. He stuffed an awful lot of good baseball memories into 51 years.

He liked the life.

And, by God, he got that World Series finally in 1985. It doesn't change anything, and it doesn't make him a better man, or a better Christian, and he would have been the same fine manager if the Royals had lost that last game.

So today, I'm not going to remember the shrunken man under the floppy golf hat calling it quits this spring in Fort Myers.

I will remember Dick Howser making that rush toward Bret Saberhagen the October before last, smiling like a kid, grabbing the most shining moment of a most worthy baseball life.

He was where he belonged.

Front of the parade.

• *1986*